Scottish Traveller Tales

Scottish Traveller Tales

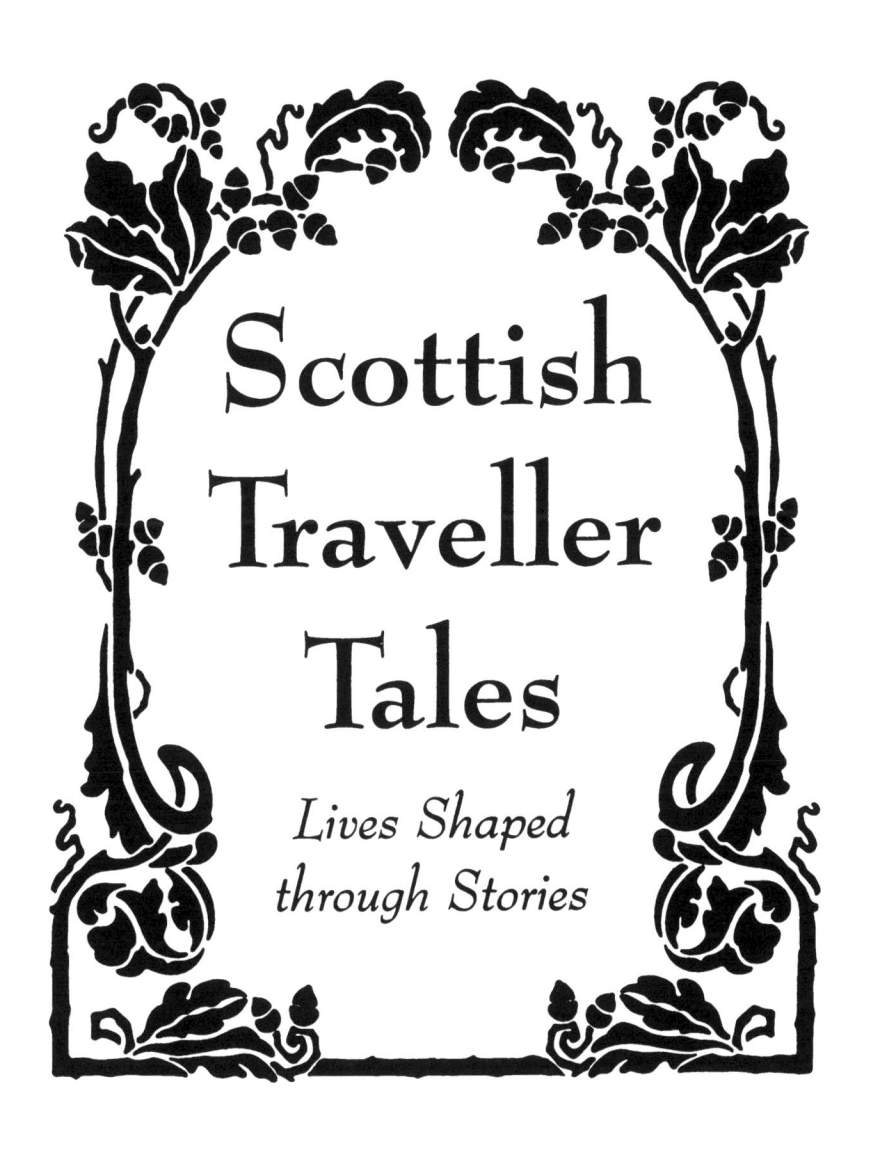

Lives Shaped through Stories

Donald Braid

University Press of Mississippi / Jackson

www.upress.state.ms.us

Photographs by Donald Braid unless otherwise noted

Copyright © 2002 by University Press of Mississippi
All rights reserved
Manufactured in the United States of America

Print-on-Demand Edition
∞
Library of Congress Cataloging-in-Publication Data available

ISBN 13: 978-1-934110-98-0   ISBN 10: 1-934110-98-1

British Library Cataloging-in-Publication Data available

For Sue and Ezri

Contents

Acknowledgments ix
Note on Transcriptions xi

Introduction:
"*Let's Have a Cup of Tea and I'll Tell You a Story*" 3

1. "That's Not a Crack; That's a Story":
An Overview of Traveller Storytelling Traditions 51

2. "It Could Have Happened":
Storytelling, Identity, and Worldview 104

3. "I Never Met My Grandfather, But I Heard Stories about Him":
Storytelling and Community 144

4. "You'll Have to Change Your Ways":
The Negotiation of Identity in Storytelling Performance 202

5. "Did It Happen or Did It Not?":
Creativity, Worldview, and Narrative Knowing 250

Conclusion: *Lives and Stories—Stories and Lives* 283

Notes 293
Works Cited 301
Index 311

Acknowledgments

Although I bear responsibility for the ideas and interpretations I present in this book, this work would not exist if not for the support and inspiration of many individuals whose names do not appear on the title page.

First and foremost, I thank the Travelling People who have shared their lives, songs, and stories with me. Some Travellers have become friends. Others were gracious enough to endure my questions and give me insight into their lives and stories. This book is as much theirs as mine.

Thanks are also due to my teachers at the Folklore Institute at Indiana University, and especially to Richard Bauman, Mary Ellen Brown, Henry Glassie, and John H. McDowell, for their guidance, support, and critical feedback. In addition, I am grateful for the financial support I received from several sources at Indiana University: Research and the University Graduate School, the College of Arts and Sciences, and the Folklore Institute.

A number of individuals at the School of Scottish Studies at the University of Edinburgh provided assistance. It was Hamish Henderson's suggestion that first sent me to visit Duncan Williamson. Alan Bruford, Joan McKenzie, and Rhona Talbot allowed me access to the school's archive and assisted me in my research there. Peter Cooke and Linda Williamson not only gave me access to their research but also gave me their permission to use Duncan Williamson's performance of "Cinderella" in chapter 3 and Betsy Whyte's performance of "The Black Laird and the Cattleman" in chapter 5. Additionally, I thank the School of Scottish Studies for granting permission to publish these stories in this volume.

Many others helped in important ways. Thomas Burton from ETSU shared part of our stay in Scotland and was a supportive voice as I pursued my research. Thomas Acton pointed me to sources and introduced me to others working with Gypsies and Travellers throughout Europe. Jim and Linda Whiteford rented us a cottage on their farm and, with our neighbors Duncan and Ethel, supplied us with a bed, carpets, furniture, dishes, and even a washing machine. Ted and Christine Poletyllo, Jock Lundy, and Kate MacGregor, among others, are remembered for their songs and stories during ceilidhs. Kirsten Peterson reminded us to explore the Scottish landscape.

My editors at the University Press of Mississippi, Craig Gill and Anne Stascavage and Virginia Schulman, have been both thorough and kind. I thank them for their help in shaping the manuscript.

I thank Laurel Sercombe for her careful work on the musical transcriptions. Seth Berrier entered the transcriptions into the computer to produce the illustrations for the book.

I owe a debt to Margaret Brabant not only for her encouragement in the writing process but also for her clear thinking and willingness to engage in discussions about substantive aspects of this work.

Ezri, my daughter, provided both joy and distraction as she played in my lap while I worked on the manuscript. I am grateful her arms were not long enough to reach the delete key.

Finally, I thank Sue Grizzell, my wife, for sharing in and encouraging my research in Scotland, for being a voice of reason and readability, and for putting up with the long hours I spent in the study during the writing process.

Note on Transcriptions

Much of the data in this book comes from audio recordings made during field research. It is therefore important at the outset to clarify both the numbering system I use to indicate the sources of specific texts and the system of notation I use in rendering oral performance on the printed page. Citations beginning with "SA" reference recordings that are lodged in the archives at the School of Scottish Studies at the University of Edinburgh. The citation SA76.201, for example, indicates tape number 201 from the year 1976. Citations beginning with "TS" reference recordings that I made during my own field research. The citation TS85005, for example, indicates my recording number 5 from 1985. At this time, my field recordings have not been archived.

Throughout this work I present the words of my consultants as accurately as possible. Yet this task is fraught with complications since spoken language rarely conforms to the expected norms of the written page. Add to this the fact that most Travellers speak in a dialect that combines English, Scots, and Traveller cant (their own secret language—and *cant* is the term they call it by), and the problems of representation multiply. Because my goal is to make this work accessible to as wide an audience as possible, I use predominantly English spellings. Where words differ significantly in sound or meaning from English, I use Scots or Traveller cant spellings and gloss the meaning in footnotes (my reference for the Scots language is Robinson 1985). In some cases, I use variant spellings to indicate local pronunciations. In making these choices, I in no way intend to introduce an "eye dialect" or to communicate negative social information about my consultants (see Preston 1982).

The notational system I use in transcriptions is designed to reveal specific features of the form and style of performance that are relevant to understanding the stories as oral literature (see Bauman 1986, x). In order to reveal formal patterning of the stories while preserving a sense of the rhythms of oral performance, I break the stories into lines that are based partly on the pauses in delivery (see Tedlock 1972) and partly on syntactical structures (see D. Hymes 1981; V. Hymes 1987). Blank lines mark the boundaries between verses. Sequences that build on a single idea are transcribed as a series of lines with increasing left indentation. Lines that serve as metanarrative commentary have been indented to further clarify the formal patterning.

I use the symbol "/" to indicate transitions in speech that mark, for example, change of character but that do not interrupt the flow of delivery, or that result when one speaker is cut off by another. A hyphen (-) is used to mark very brief pauses within a single line. An em dash (—) marks uncompleted thoughts in the sequence of narration. Bold face type and capitalization are used to indicate loudness or stress.

Words enclosed in parentheses with a question mark [(xxx?)] represent my best guess at transcribing words or passages I found difficult to hear. Where I could not understand the spoken words at all, I mark the utterances with [(?)]. Comments in square brackets ([ ]) are my notes about nonverbal aspects of the performance, such as audience response, gesture, or elements of context. These words were not spoken by the narrator.

In interview transcriptions and story transcriptions, I have edited the speaker's words in minor ways to clarify meaning. This has primarily involved deleting confusing false starts or stuttering. To improve readability I have also edited out back-channel comments (such as "mhmm" and "yeah") where they do not contribute significantly to meaning. In cases where I have omitted segments of speech, I mark these deletions with ellipses (. . .).

Although I set general guidelines for the kind of transcriptions I wanted, the musical transcriptions presented in this book are the work of Laurel Sercombe. With regard to the choices she made in capturing the music of Duncan Williamson and Jimmy Williamson, Laurel writes:

For Duncan's three songs, my aim was descriptive transcription; that is, I tried to notate exactly what Duncan did in the particular verses/refrains I transcribed. Each verse/refrain is slightly or quite different from every other, and all must be heard to fully appreciate Duncan's interpretive artistry. The incomplete versions presented here suggest his overall approach to melodic material, but they do not adequately demonstrate the nuances that make Duncan's performances so beautiful and affecting. Although I have transcribed most of the ornaments, the subtle rhythmic variations just don't come across on paper.

For Jimmy's first two songs, the transcriptions include my guessing at his intent in a couple of places, so they are not so completely descriptive. The use of guitar and a steady meter (mostly) suggested to me that dropped beats in a couple of places were not intentional. The exception is the second line of "Slow Going Easy," where he shifts to a quicker tempo to reflect the point that "life is much faster now . . ."; I indicated "rush" at this point and "a tempo" where he returns to the original, slower tempo. In the transcription of "The Good Old Days," I return to a descriptive approach, in order to demonstrate how the structure of Jimmy's text dictates the shifting, almost free meter of the song as he performs it.

Scottish Traveller Tales

Introduction

"Let's Have a Cup of Tea and I'll Tell You a Story"

A single experience can transform an entire life. For me, one such experience was my discovery of the world of oral storytelling. Another was my encounter with Scottish Traveller storyteller Duncan Williamson. Before any of this happened, I had been happily living my life with a bachelor's degree in physics, first supervising physics-teaching labs for the University of Illinois, then working as an engineering technician in a research group in physical chemistry at the University of Washington in Seattle. I loved science and technology, and I was good at coaxing data about physical processes from reluctant equipment in the research lab. The arts intrigued me, but I never dreamed of becoming a scholar and writing about the world of human experience.

One day, some friends in Seattle took me to hear a performance by storyteller Ken Feit.[1] I was enthralled by the way he used words, voice, gesture, and facial expression to engage me in a moral, intellectual, and imaginative dialog. Intrigued by storytelling, I sought out other storytellers and started telling stories myself. I read folktale collections and explored works on folklore theory. I became active in the Seattle Storytellers' Guild, a nonprofit organization devoted to educating the public about the art of storytelling. What excited me most, however, were my interactions with traditional storytellers, tellers who had grown up in communities where storytelling was a natural part of daily life. I got to know storytellers such as Ron Evans (Chippewa Cree and Assiniboin), Ephat Mujuru (Shona, a Zimbabwean people), Ray Hicks (the mountains of South Carolina), Vi Hilbert (Upper Skagit, a Lushootseed-speaking people in Washington State), and Joe Heaney (Irish). I understood that storytelling is alive in their communities. It is a form of education as well as entertainment. It provides a powerful medium for understanding and transforming the world of lived experience. Perhaps because of these layers of connection between their stories and lives, tellers such as Ron Evans and Ephat Mujuru conveyed a depth of engagement that I did not feel with many storytellers on the concert stage.

Then, in September 1985, I traveled to Scotland, the country where my parents were born and where my relatives still live. I was interested in mountains and ancient monuments like the stone circles and archaeological sites that are found throughout Scotland. Given my growing interest in storytelling, this trip also seemed like the perfect opportunity to explore traditional storytelling in Scottish culture. I visited bookstores and bought collections of Scottish stories. I followed my father's suggestion that the School of Scottish Studies at the University of Edinburgh would be a key center for research on Scottish storytelling and made the long walk to the school. When at last I stood on the landing before the school, I was dismayed to find the door locked. As I turned to leave, I thought, "Wait a minute. How often am I going to get a chance to come back here? I may as well knock!" After a few minutes, Angela West, the school's administrative secretary, answered the door. I explained that I was a storyteller from America and was very interested in the work the school was doing with Scottish storytelling. She apologized profusely, saying that it was between semesters and there really was no one there to see me. During our conversation, however, a man was winding his way up the stairwell that formed the school's entrance hallway. His voice boomed down, "Why don't you send him up to me, then?" I raced up the steps after him.

This man was Hamish Henderson, a Fellow at the school and one of the fieldworkers who in the 1950s had "discovered" the richness of Scottish Traveller storytelling and ballad-singing traditions.[2] When we reached his office in the attic, we were both a little out of breath. "There is no need to talk right away," he said, and handed me a red booklet published by the Central Regional Council Traveller Project. The booklet contained a story transcribed from an oral telling by Traveller Duncan Williamson. The name seemed familiar, so I reached into my backpack and pulled out the book I had bought half an hour before, *Fireside Tales of the Traveller Children*. It was a book of stories told by Duncan Williamson. As we talked, Hamish said that if I was really interested in Scottish storytelling, I should visit Duncan. He said Duncan lived in Kincraigie farm cottage near the town of Strathmiglo, in Fife. He had no telephone. When I asked if I should write to Duncan before I visited, Hamish said, "No, just show up at the door."

The next afternoon I sat in the back of a bus bouncing along the back roads of Fife, heading for Strathmiglo. I was reading Duncan's book—figuring it would be nice to be familiar with his stories before I met him. Because of a miscommunication, I had missed an earlier bus and was a little grumpy at getting such a late start. But the stories were wonderful, and soon my grumpiness was gone. I looked out the bus window and saw a sign that said "Strathmiglo." "How many stops in town?" I asked the bus driver. "Two," he said. Since I had no idea where I was going, I got off at the first stop. I stood for a moment wondering how in the world I was going to find a farm cottage that was *near* Strathmiglo. Then I realized I only had a few pages of Duncan's book left to read. I took the easy way out. I sat on my backpack at the bus stop and read on. A red van pulled up across the street, and I thought it odd that the driver did not get out. "Perhaps he came to meet the bus and doesn't realize it has come and gone," I thought. I read on. A couple of pages later, I realized that the driver of the van was staring at me. I thought about what I must look like perched on my pack. I wondered how long it had been since my last shower. I read on. Finally, I finished the book and stood to stuff it in my pack. As I did so, I heard the van door open. I turned and saw a man running across the street toward me. He held out his hand and said, "What did you think of my book? I'm Duncan Williamson!" When I told him I had come looking for him, Duncan was amazed. He said he had been sure I was reading his book only when he saw the cover as I put the book away. He had come into town to pick up his children, Tommy and Betsy, from the school behind the bus stop, but he loaded me into the van as well and we all drove to Kincraigie farm cottage. There I met Linda Williamson, Duncan's second wife. Linda was an American woman who had come to the School of Scottish Studies to write her Ph.D. dissertation on Traveller ballad singing.[3] She met, fell in love with, and married Dun-

Kincragie farm cottage, 1985

can, whose first wife had died several years earlier. Linda was now working on recording, transcribing, and publishing Duncan's vast repertoire of songs and stories. Her work in publishing Duncan's stories and in promoting him as a storyteller is, in part, responsible for his international reputation as a master storyteller and singer.

Though I don't exactly remember, I'm sure the first thing Duncan did when we arrived at his home was make me a cup of tea. I would later comment that Travellers never seemed to do anything, not even have a cup of tea, without having a cup of tea first. Duncan just laughed and agreed. I stayed with the Williamsons for nearly a week, sleeping on the couch. They insisted that I just make myself at home. This hospitality was no accident. I learned it was part and parcel of the Traveller way of life. At one point Linda summed up this sense of hospitality by quoting a Traveller saying: "Here is a people who have nothing, but if you had nothing and they had a blanket they would tear it in two and give you half." Kincraigie farm cottage was a cozy refuge from the blustery weather. We spent most of our time sitting in the main room before a huge open fire-

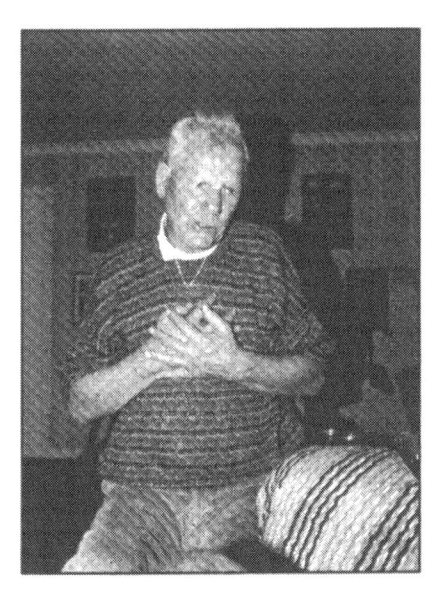

Duncan Williamson singing a ballad, 1993

place that served as a center of the home. The fire kept us warm and, because of strong winds blowing down the chimney, often filled the room with smoke as well. Duncan joked that he had burned up an entire farm in that fireplace because the wood we were using came from old farm buildings on the estate.

During my stay, Duncan and I told each other stories. As I listen to the tapes I made that week and hear the omnipresent crackle of the fire in the background, I am reminded of the magic of those days. One entry in my journal simply reads, "Roaring fire—more stories."

My introduction to Duncan's repertoire came on the very first evening, when he sang me ballads. As Duncan explained, ballads are simply stories told in song. Yet the boundary between story and song was blurred by the rich narrative context Duncan wove around the text of each song. These ballads evoked in me a vivid sense of the depth of the tradition I had encountered. He first sang "Sir Patrick Spens" (Child 58), a ballad set in the county of Fife that tells of a tragic sea voyage that Duncan says took place in the thirteenth century (Child 1965, 2:17–32). Yet Duncan's commentary on the ballad tied this event to the local landscape in such a way that it could have happened recently. Even more engaging, however, was the fairy ballad that Duncan sang next. As I listened to this ballad, I was enthralled. My mood was partly facilitated by Duncan's singing style. He sat close, holding my hand in his and staring into my eyes. His voice was rich, and his timing and melodic sense were subtle. The song seeped into my bones. In order to convey a full sense of Duncan's performance, I begin my transcription with the dialog that leads into the ballad and provides an interpretive context for the song.

Introduction

Lady Margaret[4]

DW And [this] tells a wonderful story about—
The problem is that these people who do these ballad, traditional ballads,
don't give you a clue what the original thing should be about—
And the problem was with this condition of England that. . .
these lairds in long gone time, in bygone years,
always had large estates in Scotland.
You know, large landowners?
And when a child was born,
they promised, "My child will marry your child
and keep the estate in the family."
You know?
"If I have a daughter and you have a son,
oh, they'll grow up and we'll marry them."
Supposing the children didnae love each other.
"We'll see that they get married to keep the estates in the family."
You know?

And one estate owner had a daughter,
and the other one had a son.
And the parents promised that when these children grew up,
they would marry each other
and keep the family estate together.

But lo and behold,
when this child was only just a small boy,
he completely disappeared.
He was gone.
He just vanished off the face of the Earth.
No one knew where he went to.
People believed he was tooken away with the fairies.
Right?
The fairies had took him.
They searched for [their] entire life,
but the baby boy was gone forever more.

The young woman grew up to be a young lady.
She knew the story;
she was promised a husband.
And the father died; and the mother died.
And the estate next to her became derelict,
because no one owned it.
She couldnae own it.

8   *Introduction*

She knew her . . . parents had died,
left her own estate.

But the next estate—.
But she always loved to walk into it,
across the borders from her own estate to the next one,
and pull hazelnuts,
which grew in abundance in her estate.

So, listen to the story.
That's a part of the story.
So, listen to the song.
So that you'll know what the story—

You see the problem is that when people goes up
and walks there and sings a traditional ballad,
they don't give the people a clue what the story's all about.
See the people doesnae understand.

But once you know part of the story,
it's only a story.
I told you part of the story.
Now you're gonna hear the rest.
It's all in song.
The voice is no good,
but the words are good—
either is the music.

DB The voice is good too.
DW But the words are really good
DB It's beautiful.

DW *Oh, Lady Margaret she sat in her high chambers.*
She was sewing her silken seams.
She lookit east and she lookit west
and she saw those woods grow green.

So, picking up her petticoat
beneath her harlin gown,
it's when she came to the merry green woods,
there she let them down.

Oh, she had not pulled one nut, one nut,
one nut nor scarcely three,
when the highest lord in all the countryside
came a-riding through the trees.

Lady Margaret

♩ = (approx. 60)

1st Verse:
Oh Lady Margaret she sat in her high chambers, She was sewing her silken seams. She look-it east and she look-it west and she saw those woods grow green.

2nd Verse:
So picking up her petticoat beneath her har-lin gown. It's when she came to the merry green woods, there she let them down.

5th Verse:
She said once-den time those woods were mine with-out a leave of yours. And I can pull those nuts, those nuts And I can bend those trees, those trees oh I can bend those trees.

He said, "Why do you pull those nuts, those nuts?
How dare you bend those trees?
How dare you come to those merry green woods
without a leave of me?"

She said, "Onceden time those woods were mine
without a leave of yours.
And I can pull those nuts, those nuts.
And I can bend those trees, those trees,
Oh, I can bend those trees."

So he took her gently by the hand,
and he gently laid her down,
and when he had his will of her,
he rose her up again, again,
he rose her up again.

She said, "Now that you had your will of me,
come, tell to me your name,
and if a baby I do have,
I will call him the same, the same,
I will call him the same."

He said, "I am an earl's son from Carlisle,
and I own all those woods so green,
but I was taking when I was young
by an evil fairy queen-n-n,
by an evil fairy queen.

"But," he said, "tomorrow night is Halloween,
and all those nobles you can see,
and if you will come to the five-mile gate,
it is there you can set me free, oh free,
it is there you can set me free.

"Oh, first they will come some dark, some dark,
then they will come some brown,
but when there comes a milk-white steed,
you must pull its rider down, down,
you must pull its rider down.

"Oh, first I will turn to a lion wild,
and then to a wicked snake,
but hold me fast and fear me not,

Introduction 11

for I'm one of God's own ma-a-ake,
I am one of God's own make.

"Then I will turn to a naked man.
Oh, an angry man I will be.
Just throw your mantle over me,
and then you will have me free, oh free,
Oh, then you will have me free."

So that night at the midnight hour,
Lady Margaret made her way,
and when she came to the five-mile gate,
she waited patiently-oh-ly,
she waited patiently.

Oh, first there came some dark, some dark,
and then there came some brown,
but when there came a milk-white steed,
she pulled the rider down, down,
she pulled its rider down.

Oh, first he turned to a lion wild,
and then to a wicked snake.
She held him fast and feared him not,
for he was one of God's own ma-a-ake,
he was of God's own make.

Then he turned to a naked man.
Oh, an angry man was he.
She threw her mantle over him,
and then she had him free, oh free,
and then she had him free.

Then cried a voice of the fairy queen,
oh, an angry queen was she,
saying, "If I had known yesterday,
oh, what I know today,
I'd took out your very heart's blood,
and put in a heart of clay, clay,
and put in a heart of clay."

So Lady Margaret on a white milk steed,
Lord William on a dapple gray,
with a bugle and a horn hanging down by their side,

>   it's merrily they rode away, away,
>   it's merrily they rode away.
>
> DW   And this was the baby she was promised when she was just a baby herself,
>   who was tooken away by the fairy queen.
>   Do you understand what I mean?
>   This was the baby that she was—that disappeared.
>   Who came back after many years later.
>   This is what you call—
>   Some people call it "Tam Lin."
>   We call it "Lady Margaret." (TS85001)

In addition to the ballads, Duncan told me stories during that week. The following story was one of my favorites, partly because it was short enough that I could learn it and tell it upon my return to the United States.

The Laird and the Crane

> Many years ago,
> there once lived this laird. You know?
> He had never married.
> And he had this large mansion in the village.
> And this laird was a great huntsman,
> and he liked to hunt and shoot.
> And whenever he hunted or shot something,
> he would always have a party
> and invite all his friends
>   to have a party
>   and a dance
>   and a sing song
>   and enjoy the meal that he'd shot, you know?
> He was a kind of a blowhard and a—
> He told tall stories, you know, to them.
> But they enjoyed this.
> But they also had a good feast and a good drink at his expense. [laughter]
> So, nobody seemed to worry.
>
> So anyhow.
> One day this laird walked early this morning,
> and sitting in the river by his house was a large crane—you know?—
> a heron,

sitting in the river fishing.
And you know when a heron sits in the river fishing,
it has a long wait, you know—
these birds with the long legs.
And sitting in the river is a wearisome thing,
for a, to wait till a fish passes by.
So, by sitting in the river for so long,
his legs gets tired.
So he naturally pulls up one leg
and rests it and stands on one leg.
And when that leg gets tired,
he lets that one down and rests the other one.
You know that's the way a heron does it, you know?
—so does the crane.

But, anyway,
this laird thought this would be a wonderful thing to shoot,
    and have a nice dinner,
        and have another party,
           invite guests and have another mair stories
              and mair sing songs, you know?
Shot the crane, [DW mimes shooting the gun]
    picked it up,
        took it back to his cot, to his mansion,
           walked round to the kitchen,
                and told the cook—
He says to the cook,
"My man," he said.
"Look," he said.
"I've shot a nice fat crane this morning.
And," he said, "I want you," he said,
"to cook this crane like you've never cooked it before.
I want it so delicious," he said,
"That youse never cooked it;
like nothing before in your life.
Because I have some guests for dinner
and we're going to have a nice lunch,
a nice party together,
some of my dearest friends.
And I want you to make this crane like you've never cooked it before."
"Very well," says the cook,
"I'll do that for you, master," he said.
"I'll do it for you."

So, true to his word,
the cook stripped the feathers off the crane

and cooked it like,
    with spices and herbs and everything that he could find
and made it so delicious
it was like nothing he had ever done before.
Special,
for the laird.

Then, just about time to take it in for the laird's lunch.
    Him and his guests were sitting in the dining hall.
      And they were smoking
        and drinking
          and laughing
            and telling jokes
              and tales, you know?
The laird rang the bell—

But before the laird rang the bell,
the cook thought to himself.
He said, "Look,
I worked hard on this crane.
And," he said, "I made the best job of it of all,
a wonderful job of it.
And," he said, "It looks so delicious.
If I send it in to the dining hall,
nothing will come back but the bones." [laughter]
And he lifted up the terrine—
you know these silver terrines?—
and there was the crane,
    lying beautiful,
      done to a turn.
Temptation got the better of the cook,
and he pulled a leg off the crane.
And he gobbled it up as fast as he could. [laughter]
And he put the lid back on.
And there lay the crane,
one leg.
Put the lid back on.
And then the laird rang the bell for the cook to bring in the lunch.

The cook carried in the terrine
and put it before the laird and all his guests sitting around.
They were having a good drink, you know?
And the laird had a wonderful story, you know?
"As I was telling you," he said,

"my friends," he said,
"and relations and guests," he said, eh,
"I have a wonderful surprise for you tonight,
for wir evening meal," he said.
"This morning," he said,
"I shot a wonderful crane," he said.
"And I got my cook to cook it
like he'd never cooked a crane before in his life.
And I hope you're going to enjoy this
like you've enjoyed nothing before in your life."

"Now," he said,
"I'll carve it for youse."
And he lifted up the lid,
and he looked in.
There was the crane lying,
one leg stuck up. [DW holds elbows into chest with one arm sticking up,
    in imitation of the one-legged roast]
When the laird saw this,
he slammed the lid back down
and demanded the cook to—
"Take it away!"
"I'll deal with you later," said the laird.

The cook was upset about this.
He knew he'd done wrong.
But, he sent in some roast beef
and something else for the supper.
And it was a very quiet supper.
But the laird wasn't very pleased.

And he, after his guests had departed,
he came into the cook.
And he said, "Look, my man," he said.
"You disgraced me before my friends tonight.
And I'm going to punish you severely for what you've done."
"But, master," said the cook,
"I've done nothing."
"I'm going to punish you," said the laird,
"because I've the right to."
And in these days they had the right to punish them.
"What have I done?" said the cook.
He said, "You sent in a crane to my table with one leg [laughter]
before my guests and insulted me."

"But, master," said the cook,
"a crane has only got one leg."
"Nonsense," said the laird. " 'A crane has only got one leg.'
Every crane's got two legs."
"Well," the cook said,
"maybe to you but not to me.
Every time I go for a walk or pass by a river and I see a crane,
it's always standing on one leg." [chuckle]
"Nonsense!" said the laird.
"Nonsense, my man," he said.
"I'm going to punish you!"

"Well, before you punish me," said the cook,
"you better prove it to me that a crane has two,
because the one you gave me only had one." [laughter]
"Right," said the laird.
"Tomorrow morning, before I punish you,
I'll prove it to you that a crane has got two legs.
I'll be in for you very early tomorrow morning.
And I'm going to show you that a crane has got two legs,
because there are many more cranes in my river.
And I'll show you that a crane has got two legs.
And then I'm going to punish you like I have punished no man in my life before."

The poor cook he lay in his bed all night.
And he was worried sick,
and knew that he had done wrong.
But he had gonnae suffer punishment
that the laird was gonna give him.
And he thought,
he racked his brains,
what to say on tomorrow morning to help himself?
But he couldna say nothing.

True to his word,
before breakfast the next morning,
in comes the laird once more.
Knocks the cook up and says,
"Come on, my man," he said.
"Today," he said, "I'm going to prove my point to you,
that the crane has two legs.
And then I'm going to punish you.
You'll never shame me before my friends again."

Took his gun with the cook
and walked down the river bank.

And sure enough,
there,
sitting once more in the river,
was another crane,

standing on one leg.

"Ha, ha!" said the cook.
"Look, master," he said. [laughter]
"Look, master," he said.
"There is a crane and," he said,
"it has only got one leg!"
"Nonsense!" said the laird, he said.
"That crane has two legs."
"Well," the cook says,
"I can only see one." [laughter]

Because the crane was standing on one leg.
True to his word,
the crane was standing on one leg.

"The crane has got two legs," said the laird.
"One," says the cook, "I can see."
"But, wait a minute," said the laird.
He took his gun and he placed it against a tree.
And he walked down to the riverbank.
[DW claps three times]
Clapped his hands like that,
as loud as possible.
And when the crane heard this,
the crane flew off and,
let down its other leg,
and flew off.

"Now," said the laird,
"did you see that when I clapped my hands?
It put down its other leg and flew off."
"Well," said the cook,
"what's your problem, master?" [laughter]
"The problem?" he said.
"What do you mean, my problem?"
He said, "Master," he said,

"If you had of clapped you hands at the dinner table," he said, [extended laughter]
"probably it would have let down its other leg,
and then you wouldnae have had all this trouble." [laughter]

And the laird started to laugh.
And the laird laughed
  and he laughed
    and he laughed
'til the tears ran down his cheeks. [laughter]
And the cook laughed.
And the laird came and he shook hands with the cook.
And he said, "You know, my man," he said,
"your wit has saved you," he said. [laughter]
He says, "That was the best laugh I've ever had in my life." [laughter]

And the laird and the cook became the greatest of friends.
And the cook spent his entire life with the laird,
all his days with the laird,
and became the laird's greatest friend.
But never again
did he ever touch another leg belonging to a crane.
And that is the end of my story. [laughter]

DB Oh, that's a good one. [laughter] (TS85005)

Duncan told me many other stories that week. Some were brief, like this one. Others were long magic tales such as "Jack and the Silver Keys" (see NAPPS 1991, 175–89; D. Williamson 1987b, 63–81) and "Hooch for Skye" (see D. Williamson 1991, 73–80). I do not transcribe these stories here, but I present examples of similar folktales in the chapters that follow.

Stories and Cultural Identity

As I listened to Duncan's performance, I knew that I had come in contact with a very rich tradition of storytelling. Since I was aware from reading folktales that variants of Duncan's songs and stories are found in cultures throughout the world, I began to see meanings in the stories that linked them to common human concerns and interests. I was intrigued by this relationship between stories and human life and wanted to learn more. The language of the stories and the references to the landscape around Kincraigie cottage, however, implied that the stories were somehow inherently Scottish. Yet, at that time, I was not familiar enough with Traveller culture to perceive the sometimes subtle and sometimes deep interconnections between the stories I heard and Duncan's personal and cultural identity as a Traveller.[5] Nevertheless, some of Duncan's performances did hint at the intimate relationship between the stories and the lives of those who remember, nurture, and retell them.

This relationship was particularly apparent in the songs Duncan composed himself. For example, one song Duncan sang me was "Yellow on the Broom," a song he composed for Traveller Betsy Whyte in honor of the publication of the first volume of her autobiography *The Yellow on the Broom* (2001). This song may at first appear to present vague and ambiguous images that evoke a feeling of longing and loneliness that might be part of anyone's experience. Yet for Duncan, this song has such deep ties to Betsy and Traveller life that he says it "tells the story about her whole life" (TS88006A). This claim makes sense in that Duncan has focused his song on key events in Betsy's life that are particularly meaningful for her. But in doing so, he has also selected symbols that capture one central struggle in the life of many Travellers. Specifically, he highlights the recurring conflict between the constraints associated with being housed in the winter months and the freedom that comes in the summer, when Travellers can move about and undertake those activities that bring both pleasure and independence. As such, the song, coupled with Duncan's commentary, offers a revealing glimpse into the experience of Traveller life.

> *Oh, come sit beside me, Maggie, lass,*
> *I hate to see you gloom,*
> *For I will take you from this place*
> *When the yellow is on the broom.*
>
> *Oh, to Loch Leven's bonnie glen*
> *Or to the River Spey,*

Yellow on the Broom

♩ = 63 (approx.)

Refrain:
Oh come sit beside me, Maggie lass, I hate to see you gloom. For I will take you from this place when the yellow is on the broom.

1st Verse:
Oh to Loch Leven's bonnie glen or to the River Spey. Where I can pearl fish, my love and there my pipes to play.

⌢ indicates elongation of note (not extended hold).

Where I can pearl fish, my love,
And there my pipes to play.

So it's put a smile upon your face,
I hate to see you gloom,
For I will take you from this place
When the yellow is on the broom.

When the Angus Hills are free of snow
And the swallow he is on the zoom,
For I will take you far away
When the yellow is on the broom.

Oh, to Loch Leven's bonnie glen
Or to the River Spey,
Where I can pearl fish, my love,
And there my pipes to play.

So it's put a smile upon your face,
I hate to see you gloom,
For I will take you from this place
When the yellow is on the broom.

But you see the problem was,
he, him being the Travelling People,
he took him and his wife to . . . an old house.
And they stayed there.
And it was breaking the woman's heart to stay in a house.
She wanted to be free
and go out and be on her way, you know?
And she was sad because she had to be housed up.
And her husband got sorry for her—
It all tells you in Betsy's book.

And he told her, he said,
"Look," he says,
"Maggie," he said.
"Don't be worried," he says.
"As soon as the summer comes
and the yellow is on the broom,
I'll take you away from here."
"We'll go," he says," "north," he says, "to the river."
And he says, "there I can pearl fish and play my pipes," he said.

He was a piper, you know?
. . . Bessie's father was a great piper,
one of the greatest among the Travelling folk. . . .

And he said—She tells all this in story, you know?
How her mother was so sad
because she thought she was going to stay in this house for the rest of her
    life.

>   And it was like putting a bird in a cage
>   because Betsy's mother was one of the original Travelling People. . . .
>
>   And he said, "Look,
>   I'll take you from this place.
>   But you must wait till . . . the snow goes from the hills
>   and the yellow comes on the broom."
>   That's the broom bushes gets yellow . . .
>   they turn the first of spring.
>   "I'll take you from here," he says.
>   "We'll pack up and we'll go."
>   And he says, "I can fish for pearl."[6]
>   He was a great pearl fisher, you know? . . .
>   And he, in his own life,
>   he had only settled down during the winter months
>   for the comfort of his wife and family.
>   And he couldnae wait for the spring.
>   And every time he came back
>   and seen his wife being so sad,
>
>   [sung] He said, "put a smile upon your face."
>   You play that for Betsy and you'll just,
>   you'll just be her friend forevermore,
>   you know what I mean?
>
> DB [laughs] All right. (TS85005)

The relationship between stories and Traveller lives was also particularly prominent in the stories Duncan called "Traveller Tales"—stories that were explicitly about events where Travelling People played a central role. These stories were not limited to a single genre, as Duncan comments in his introduction to the following story:

The Tinker and the Skeletons

>   This is one of the original Traveller tales.
>   As I was telling you,
>   there is many of them around,
>   some fact and some fiction and some true.
>   This tells a story again about another Travelling family,
>   on their way on the road as usual.
>   And they had six of family.

It was a man, his wife, and six of family.
And they were very poor,
they didna have very much.
They had a little donkey for to pull their possessions along the road.
And they traveled all day.
And they were very hungry.
And his wife had sold a little, a few baskets along the way
and collected a little bit of food.
And her husband said, "Look,
the first place we come to,
   we'll have to pitch a tent,
      and kindle a fire,
         and make some food for these children."
Because they were all very young children.

So they had never came this part of the country before.
It was a strange part to them.
And they came along this road.
And they came to this little field beside the road,
and there was no fences or nothing,
and there was a small stream running through.
And the man said,
"This looks like a nice place for to pitch the tent for the night.
And," he says, "there a place the kids can play after that in a wee field there.
And I don't think anyone will bother us for one night, surely."

So the man pitched his tent and—
But lo and behold,
he couldnae see a piece of firewood,
a bit of stick of any kind.
And he looked that way,
   he looked this way,
      he looked all way,
         but not a bit of stick.
He says, "I wonder where I'm going to get some firewood
to make some tea for these children?" . . .

Then he looks up in front,
across the old road,
and he sees a large dike.
And he sees the points of trees which looks rotten, you know?
The trees, the points of trees was rotten, you know?
He says to his wife, he said,

"If I climbed that dike and broke some of these sticks," he said—
"If I stood on the dike,
I could probably break some of the points of these trees off, rotten trees off.
And," he said, " that would do us for the night."

So it was a very high dike. Maybe, the dike was about ten feet tall.
But he manages to climb the dike.
There was no gate, just a dike.
And he stood up on the dike,
and he's breaking the points off the trees which grew behind the dike.
And when he looked out,
what he was standing on, Donald,
was an old graveyard.
A very old graveyard.
And it was surrounded by this high wall.
We call it a dike; you call it a wall.

But he stood breaking some of these sticks
and he's throwing them down on the roadside.
And then he looks,
and he sees a movement in the graveyard.
And he looks again,
and he sees these white things tossing and turning, you know,
like pieces of stick.
And they're circling; they're turning.
"Upon my soul," he said,
"I never seen the likes of that," he says.
He thought it was a sheep caught in the brambles, or something.
Because it was getting kind of gloaming, kind of dark.
"I better go up," he says,
"Maybe a sheep," he said,
"one of the farmer's sheep caught in a bramble,
and I'd better let it go."

So he jumps down the other side of the dike into the graveyard.
And he walks up for about ten or twelve yards.
And when he comes up—
Now, he had a bit stick in his hand that he forgot to throw over,
a piece of holly, holly sticks, you know?
And he's walking up.
And he looked.
"Oh, my God," he said, "it's holly."
And no Traveller will burn holly in any way.

And then he looks again.
And lo and behold:
three skeletons,
and they're fighting each other.
Three of them.
And they're wrestling
  and kicking
    and jumping
      and diving on top of each other
        and they're wrestling.
  And their bones is separating,
    and they'll go back together. [laughter]
  Heads is rolling in bits,
    and they'll go back together.
But this two which were taller than the small one,
seemed to be getting the better of the small one.
And they had him down
  and they're kicking him
    and they're beating him
      and they're pulling his head off
        and they're pulling his arms off.

And this Traveller man, being kind of fair, you know,
he says, "That's not, that's not fair," he says,
"even among skeletons.
Two to one is not fair in my way," he says. [laughter]
And he goes up with his piece of stick.
And he starts.
He says to the one who was down,
he says to the other two skeletons,
"That's no fair," he says.
"Let him up."
"If youse cannae fight fair," he says,
"I'll help him," he says.
Two to two is fair in my (?). [laughter]
And he started with a piece of stick. [laughter]
  And he fought the two skeletons.
    And he scattered the bones,
      and kicked them,
        and beat them.
And they disappeared.

And the one who was lying on the floor, the ground, got up.
And he stood straight.

And lo and behold, a change come over him.
There he was, back to normal.
A young, handsome man stood before him.

And he stood out,
and he held his hand up to the old Traveller man.
He said, "Look, old man," he says,
"That's a wonderful thing you done."
And the old man said, "What is it?" he said.
He said, "I thought you were a skeleton."
"But," he says, "I am.
But," he said, "I could never rest."
And the old man was mesmerized at this.
He says, "You could never rest?"
"No," he said, "I could never rest, because," he says,
"these two skeletons," he said,
"that was fighting me tonight, here," he said,
"are my two brothers."
"And," he said,
"wir father," he said, "was a farmer.
And," he said, "he was very rich.
And he left all his money to me,
being the youngest son (and these are my two brothers)
and because they were lazy and they wouldnae work.
And he left all the money to me
on condition that I don't give them a penny.
And before he died,
he warned me that something like this might happen.

"So," he said, "I took my money,
and I hid it in a well, every penny I owned.
And," he says,
"They took me,
and they killed me.
And I still wouldnae tell them to this day where it is. [laughter]
But," he said, "my soul wouldnae rest
because I never got fair play, two to one.

"But now," he says,
"two to two was fair tonight," he said,
"and my soul will rest in peace.
But," he says, "before I go away,
I'm going to tell you where my money is."
The old Traveller man was mesmerized.

Introduction   27

Now his wife's still waiting.
She was saying to herself,
"Where in the world is that old man of mine gone, over that dike?"
   [laughter]

He said, "You go back—
Which way did you come?" said the young man.
He said, "I came," he said, "through the village."
"Well, you go back to the village," he said, "tonight," said the young man.
"And," he said, "you'll see an old farm road going, leading up to a farm."
He said, "The farm's empty now,
there's nobody in it so don't worry,
nobody'll interfere with you."
He says, "Since I was murdered up there," he says,
"nobody will stay there.
And," he said, "before you come to the farm, you'll come to a large tree."
He says, "Step about twenty steps from the tree,
and," he said, "you'll come to an old well, a dry well," he says.
"There's nothing in it now.
Don't be afraid," he says.
"Climb down the well,
and," he says, "at the very bottom of the well," he said,
"you'll see a large stone.
Pull it out," he says, "and keep what you find there."
And like that, he was gone.

The old Traveller man stood and scratched his head.
And he wondered if he was hearing things
   or was he dreaming
      or sleeping?
But, he climbed back over the dike.

And the woman says to him, she says,
"You've been a long while away."
"Woman," he says, "be quiet."
He says, "Don't you say another word to me," he said.
"I had a terrible experience."
She says, "Where's the sticks?"
He said, "That's a graveyard in there.
And," he said, "it's holly.
And," he said, "you know, woman, I wouldn't burn holly," he said,
"for my father that's in his grave would I burn holly."
She says, "What were you doing?"
He said, "I was doing nothing. [laughter]

Nothing," he said.
He said, "I was searching for sticks.
But," he said, "I'll go down to the other way," he said,
"and I'll probably get you enough to boil your kettle."

So he went away down through the field,
and he managed to pick up wee bits of sticks.
And they kindled a fire and had some tea.
But he couldnae rest.
She says, "What's troubling you?
Is there something wrong?"
"No," he says, "no really.
There's no something wrong," he says.
"But I'll tell you something," he says,
"I think," he said, "I'll go back to the village."
She says, "What for?"
"Ach, well," he says,
"I think I'll go back to the village," he said.
"I seen an old farm back there," he says,
   "back the way," he says,
      "about a mile back the road," he says.
"And I want to see," he said,
"maybe there's some willows growing up the old road," he says.
And she says, "No at this time of night." [laughter]
He said, "I want to cut them at nighttime."
   Because Travellers always done this,
      because they knew how to do it at nighttime, even if it was dark.
   They just groped and felt for them
   and cut them, you know?
   It didnae bother them.
"Well," she says, "dinnae be too long," she said,
"because it's—I might be afraid to sit here by myself."
He said, "Don't worry.
I'll not be too long," he said.
"It's no very far back."

So, true to his word,
he walked back.
And he came to the, before he came to the village,
he came to the old road.
And he looked up and he saw the old farm.
It was derelict, empty.
He walked up the road,
   saw the large pine tree,
      walked across from the pine tree.

There was an old worn path,
  and there was the well,
    an old stone well.
And the stones of the well was all fallen in.
It was quite easy to get down.
He climbed down.
And right at the bottom there was a flat stone.
And he pulled it aside,
  and he looked,
    and there was a tin box.
And he pulled it out and he opened it.
And it was full of gold pieces,
two or three thousand gold pieces in it.
The box was rusty.
He carried the box,
and he says, "My God," he says,
"it is all mine."
And he climbed up the well,
took it (?) under his arm, and he walked back.

He just landed back.
His wife says, "Where were you?"
"Oh," he says,
"I was away back," he said, "to the farm."
She said, "Did you get some wands for to make a basket for me for the morning?"
"No," he says,
"there was nothing growing there," he said.
"It was just," he says, "weeds.
I thought it was, I thought it was wands but it wasn't."
She says, "What have you got under your arm?"
He says, "Just an old box," he says, [laughter]
"I want to hold some of my tools in."
See?

He said, "Have you put the children to bed?"
"Aye," she said, "they're all fallen asleep."
"Well," he says,
"cover them up with a blanket," he says.
"And kindle up the fire and make me a cup of tea," he said. [laughter]
She says, "You're no going to make me a basket for tomorrow,
for to sell along the roadway?"
He says, "Look,
you'll never need another, never need another basket." [laughter]

>   And he opened the box and showed her within,
>   and he told her the story I told you.
>   And these people were rich forever more.
>   And they never needed to worry about nothing else in their life again
>   because he had seen fair play done.
>   That is a true story.
>
> DB   That is a nice one.
> DW   So these are what you call real Traveller tales. (TS85006)

Duncan's performances of his own songs and Traveller tales gave me a taste of the uniqueness of Traveller identity and made me aware that Travellers were culturally different from other Scots. Yet, I did not understand the full significance of these cultural differences. Nor could I easily separate creative presentations of Traveller life recounted in some stories from the lived experiences recounted in others. In what way, for example, is "The Traveller and the Skeletons" a true story? Nonetheless, I began to wonder how stories could simultaneously evoke a sense of common humanity while maintaining ties to the unique cultures in which they are nurtured and where they thrive. My thoughts turned to the relationship between Traveller storytelling and Traveller lives. I wondered: who exactly are the Travellers, what kinds of stories do they tell, and what roles do these stories play in their lives?

Who Are the Travellers?

In order to answer my questions about Traveller storytelling, I realized I needed to learn about Traveller culture. It seemed only natural to ask Duncan about the Travellers. He answered my questions patiently:

> Well, Donald, . . .
> you wanted to know a little about the Travellers.
> Well, I can tell you as much about the Travellers as anyone else, I suppose,
> being one of them myself. [laughter]
> And eh, as my father was a Traveller
>   and my great-granny
>   and my great-great-grandfather
> have been Travellers all the days of their life before me. (TS85006)

At first I was puzzled by this comment. Upon reflection, however, I realized that Duncan was gently reminding me that answering questions about culture is a tricky business. My questions forced him to contemplate his experience and articulate the essence of his culture in words. Since it is rare for those who live a culture to reflect upon the underlying rules, patterns, and meanings that inform daily actions, this task might be difficult, even impossible, for most individuals. Yet, perhaps because Duncan is a storyteller and is well aware of the meanings and values in the stories he tells, he was able to answer my questions articulately and insightfully.[7]

Duncan also pointed out that answering questions about the Travellers is complicated for him because he is only one voice of many within a culture that values individual freedom.

> But you see,
> among the Travelling People in this country,
> every family is an individual family—
> even though they are connected.
> Even though they are a family,
> there's no bosses,
>   no law,
>   no king,
>   no nothing,
>   no union,
>   no nothing.
> Everyone is an individual.
> Everyone goes his own way.
> They meet when they can meet.
> Friends and relations meet when they can meet,
> and neighbors.
> And families meet and they spend time together. (TS85006)

This tendency toward individuality, or anarchy as Traveller Willie Reid later termed it, means that individual conceptions of Traveller culture may differ considerably from one Traveller to another. It is therefore difficult for one person to speak for other Travellers, and many are reluctant to do so. Yet there are many facets of Traveller experience, including the meetings and "time spent together" Duncan mentions, that motivate a feeling of common identity. This common identity is what allows careful generalizations about the Travellers to be made. I should note that throughout his life Duncan has been keenly interested in the stories and traditions of other Travellers. When he talks about Travellers and Traveller life, therefore, he tends to generalize beyond his own individual perspective. I have come to trust in his observations and portrayals of Traveller life because they have been corroborated time and again during my interviews with other Travellers.

From my discussions with Duncan, I realized that a further problem in understanding Traveller life lies in the fact that Traveller culture, like all cultures, is constantly being adapted to fit the needs of individuals in a changing world. Many Travellers have lived through a shift in this century from life with tents, horses, and outside campfires to life with automobiles, trailers, and propane stoves. Traveller occupations and migration patterns have also changed. Some people have settled and now live in houses. Yet, as dramatic as these changes may seem, they are but superficial differences in the outward appearance and activities of Traveller life. Underneath these changes is a continuity in the beliefs and values that lie at the heart of what it means to be a Traveller. Born in 1928, Duncan has lived through these changes and has a keen awareness of the value of what was being lost by the passing of the older generations. While he is perhaps less aware of the lives of younger generations of Travellers, his perceptions of the shifts in Traveller life have proved to be insightful.

Despite these potential problems, Duncan took my questions about Traveller culture seriously and gave me perceptive answers. He described the Travellers as a distinct group that has been present in Scotland for hundreds of years. Although Travellers maintain a separate identity from non-Travellers, Duncan said the two groups are economically interdependent in many ways. Travellers have survived over the years by selling non-Travellers handmade items, such as tin pots, horn spoons, and willow baskets; hawking carpets, furniture, and peat moss door to door; dealing in horses or secondhand cars; and providing farm labor or other necessary services to the non-Traveller community.

Most importantly, Duncan's comments suggested that the common feeling of identity shared by Travellers is in no way superficial but is part of a deeply engaging cultural tradition that binds Travellers to one another across space and through time. The pervasive influence of this cultural tradition became clear to me in a discussion about nomadism. The name "Travelling People" implies that Travellers are nomadic—and mobility and freedom are indeed highly prized by Travellers, as Duncan's song "Yellow on the Broom" suggests. But nomadism is only one facet of Traveller culture. For a variety of reasons, many Travellers now live in fixed housing. I asked Duncan about this:

DB Were there Travellers who really wanted to settle down
    or who didn't like the Travelling life?
DW Oh, hundreds of them settled down.
    Hundreds of them settled down.
    They gave up the Travelling life for good.
    Hundreds of them, down through the ages.
DB Right.
    And were they—
    Did they essentially just leave the Travelling People?
    You know? Because (?)
DW No, no, no, no.
    Even though they settled down,
    they were still classified as a Traveller.
    They never given up—
    They gave up the traveling part of the life
    but not the Travelling tradition.
    Do you see what I mean?
    They give up the traveling part.
DB And the Travelling tradition is the—
DW The Travelling tradition they still had.
DB —is the way of life?
DW Because they passed on to their sons,
    and their sons might, might not be a—
    the son might not want to travel.
    Say you give up.
    Say, "I want to go and stay in a house," right?
    Then, your son grew up.
    And he wanted—
    It was in his blood.
    He wanted to be a Traveller.
    See?

    I'll tell you a fantastic wee story.
    Listen to this. . . .

Away down in the West Coast, where I come from,
there was a gentleman.
And he lived in a large mansion, a great estate, you know?
And the Travelling People used to come and camp on his land.
And eh, he didna mind this.
He liked the Travelling People.
But he had only one problem that he hated in his life.
He used to admire all the Travelling children, you know?
And his wife could never have any children.

So one late night,
one of the Traveller women came to the door of the mansion house,
and she had a little baby in her arms and one by her hand.
And she was begging for something to eat.
And the lady of the house came out.
And she said, "Yes, I'll give you something to eat."
She says, "I've just had this newborn baby."
"How many babies do you have?" said the lady.
She says, "Ma'am," she says, "I have six."
And she says, "There I go," she said,
"I have got another one."

"Well," she said, "look," she said,
"Why don't you give me one of your children?
And I'll rear it up.
And I'll be good to it because I don't have a family."
"Oh, mister," she said,
"even though I have got six,
I wouldn't like to part with none."
"Oh, but," she says, "look,
he'll . . . never need or want for anything," she said.
"You can come and see him anytime, and you can—
if you just give me one of your babies
and I'll give you anything you want."

So the woman consulted her husband,
and finally they decided to give the lady one of the babies.
"And now," he said, "we will take it as wir own.
And we'll rear him up.
And he'll just be one of us."

So naturally,
the Travelling People went on their way.
And they left the wee baby,

Introduction 35

which was a wee boy,
and they left him with this lady and gentleman.

And they reared it up to be their own.
And they just loved it.
They gave it every attention in the world.
And when it was five year old,
the gentleman bought it a dog.
A beautiful golden retriever dog.

And one day,
him and the gentleman went for a walk with his wee son.
He was just his daddy,
he didn't know any better.
It was just his daddy
because he was only months old when they got him.
And, they went for a walk out on the estate.

And the dog was playing itsel
   and it ran out in the field
      and it picked up an old cow's horn,
         and it came back.
And it brought it back.
And the gentleman says,
"What have you got there, boy?"
He says, "Drop that!"
And the wee boy looked up.
And he ran over and picked it up.
"Oh," he says, "Daddy, it's a horn," he said,
"a wonderful horn," he said.
"Daddy, wouldn't that make a lovely spoon!" [laughter]
That is the truth.
And the gentleman just smiled. . . . [laughter]

DB Huh, that's interesting.
DW Yeah.
     "Daddy, say, wouldn't—"
     It shows it was in his blood, you see?
     "Wouldn't it make a lovely spoon?" he said.
     Because his father used to make spoons, you see?[8]

     So there you get the same thing of—
     Supposing his father had left the road
     and took up a house of residence

and stayed there for twenty years.
Some of his sons would want to go on the road, right? . . .
So you've got that in many families.
That's what keeps it going.
If one or two can keep, from each family, can keep the tradition going,
that's all that's needed to keep the values of Travelling folk alive
at the present moment in Scotland. (TS85006)

Duncan's story is a testament to the strength and resiliency of Traveller cultural traditions. The story implies that Traveller culture is not about surface appearances. It is about deeper ways of perceiving and understanding the world. Keep in mind, however, that this story is a creative presentation. Duncan uses the image that Traveller culture "is in the blood" to make an emphatic point about the depth to which Travellers experience their culture, but it would be a mistake to take either this statement or the story literally to mean that Traveller identity is in some way genetically inherited.[9]

This story illustrates something more than the pervasive influence of Traveller culture, however. When viewed in context as part of our dialog about Traveller identity, it hints at the role stories play in the daily lives of Travellers. Duncan presumably told this story at the moment he did because it effectively captures the essence of what it means to be raised as a Traveller. Over the years, I realized that Duncan and other Travellers often resorted to stories as a way of getting me to understand puzzling issues about Traveller life and Traveller identity. As I reflect back on my experiences in Scotland, it is the stories that come back to me most vividly. As I now try to understand issues of Traveller identity, it is in the stories that I find answers. But my point here is not simply that Travellers find stories to be an effective way of communicating about difficult topics to an ignorant outsider like myself. The more I work with the Travellers and learn about their lives, the more I understand that stories are an integral part of Travellers' interactions with each other. They are used as a form of entertainment, a vehicle of education, a way of reminding themselves of who they are, and a way of knowing or comprehending experience in the world. In short, Duncan's story hints that Traveller stories and Traveller lives are deeply intertwined.

Identity and Conflict: "If I Had My Life to Live Over Again, I Would Be a Traveller"

Additional dimensions of the connection between Traveller stories and Traveller lives became clear to me as I learned about the broader contexts of Traveller life. During our visit, for example, Duncan also talked about the problematic relationship between Travellers and non-Travellers. I learned from his comments and stories that many outsiders view Travellers as pariahs and frequently discriminate against them. I also learned that non-Traveller social policies and practices affect Traveller lives. Yet, I did not understand the full complexity of the Traveller/non-Traveller relationship until long after this visit, when I started reading academic articles, government documents, and popular writings about Travellers and Traveller culture. I quickly realized that the portrayal of Travellers in these works was often at odds with what I knew about Travellers through my own experience. Nonetheless these readings, and sometimes the misrepresentations they embodied, provided me with a sense of the broader social, historical, and political contexts that are essential to understanding who Travellers are, the relations between Travellers and settled folk, and especially the full significance of Traveller storytelling traditions. I therefore sketch the outlines of these contexts as background for the stories and analyses I present in the chapters that follow.[10]

Outsiders have many names for the Travelling People of Scotland. They call them *tinkers* because some Travellers used to make and sell tinware, the term *tink* being linked to the sound of hammer on tin (Grant and Murison 1974, 9:338–39). In common practice, however, the term "*tinker*" or "*tink*" is used as an ethnic slur and is therefore avoided by many Travellers. Their nomadic life inspired names such as the *Gan-aboot folk* (the going-about folk) or the *mist-folk* (Whyte 2001). They are also called *The Summer Walkers* because of seasonal work patterns (Neat 1996, xii). A few scholars use the term *tinkler-gypsies*—a term that emphasizes possible ties to the Gypsies found in England and other parts of Europe (e.g., Henderson 1992, 229; McCormick [1907] 1973). Even the label *Traveller* is problematic. While many Travellers accept this term as a relatively neutral label, others are troubled by the way it reduces their culture to a function of nomadic lifestyle. They are therefore thinking about adopting their own term, *Nachins*,[11] as a way of avoiding the problematic meanings of outsider terms.

Nobody knows exactly how many Travellers there are in Scotland. A 1969 government census distinguished Travellers from other groups by adopting a broad working definition of those to be counted as

tinkers, gypsies or other travelling people who live in caravans, tents, huts or shacks, or possibly are squatting in derelict or abandoned property. In general this group can be regarded as socially isolated from the settled community. They rarely take a regular job and make their living by a variety of seasonal work, by collecting and dealing in waste material such as scrap metal and rags, dealing in other commodities, log or firewood cutting and some hawking or begging. (Gentleman and Swift 1971, 7)

A 1992 census used the 1969 description, but noted that there have been some changes in Traveller life since that time:

Nowadays there may be fewer people living in tents, other than at particular times of the year, and possibly fewer in shacks. Since 1969 many local authorities have provided official caravan sites for travelling people and many of the families who are on these now stay there for long periods of time. . . . Ways of making a living have also changed to some extent, although they are still almost entirely based on self employment. Activities may now include the laying of tarmac driveways and small roadwork contracts, and the selling and/or painting of farm and house gates. Many travellers now have little or no occupation and may be largely dependent on some form of state benefit, but the community covers a broad social and economic spectrum. (Gentleman 1993, appendix II)

The 1992 census concluded there were some 750–800 Traveller households, or approximately 3,000 individuals, actively travelling in Scotland (Gentleman 1993, 14). But this census explicitly excluded Travellers who, for whatever reason or for whatever length of time, were living in fixed housing. This census was also criticized for severely undercounting the Traveller population (e.g., Save the Children 1995, 1996a). In 1991, Thomas Acton, Professor of Romani Studies at the University of Greenwich, estimated the actual population of Scottish Travellers, including those living in England, Wales, or Northern Ireland, to be 17,000—a figure that includes approximately 5,000 individuals who are nomadic

(Acton 1993, 2). For Scotland alone, Acton estimates a total population of 15,000, including 4,000 nomads (2).[12]

While outsider names and census criteria differentiate the Travelling People from non-Travellers based on occupation, habitation, and lifestyle, they do nothing to capture the uniqueness of Travellers as a cultural group. This approach is typical of attempts by the settled community to conceptualize the boundary between Traveller and non-Traveller identities. In fact, non-Travellers frequently perceive a contrast between the two groups that is based more on stereotypes or beliefs about how Travellers deviate from the norm of settled society than on any appreciation of cultural difference. Many settled folk consequently view Travellers as a lazy, thieving, dirty "other," as a "social problem to be dealt with" rather than as a valuable component of Scottish cultural diversity.

These misperceptions of Traveller identity are nothing new. They are part of a pattern of discrimination against Travellers that has unfolded over hundreds of years and that has frequently made Travellers the focus of legal and social policies that threaten their way of life.[13] For example, an entry in an encyclopedia of the law in Scotland is illuminating in terms of exclusionary policies that were in place in the 1600s. Under the term "Egyptians," a label that includes Travellers, appears the following entry:[14]

> In almost every nation in Mediaeval Europe severe enactments were passed against Egyptians or gipsies. The habits of these Oriental wanderers were lawless and demoralising. France, Germany, England and Spain enacted laws which ordained that Egyptians should be banished from these countries. Following the example set by these nations, the Scottish Privy Council in 1603 made an order that the whole race of Egyptians should quit Scotland by a certain day and never return, under pain of death. This order was made a perpetual law by the Act of 1609, c. 13, and numerous trials and capital convictions subsequently took place under the Act. At first the mere fact of a man being an Egyptian led to his conviction of a capital crime; afterwards the court required, in addition to proof of this fact, evidence that the accused had actually committed a theft or other crime. (Chisholm 1897, 383)

Fortunately, local officials often recognized that Travellers provided valuable services in their communities and therefore did not prosecute them (see Fraser 1992, Departmental Committee on Tinkers in Scotland 1918, 7).

A second response to Travellers can be characterized as confinement—"the authoritarian, and generally violent, integration of Gypsies into the surrounding society" (Liégeois 1987, 98). Under these policies, a number of Travellers were punished through "transportation to the New World and forced labour in factories and labour colonies" (Gentleman and Swift 1971, 10). In a similar vein, it was common up until the 1950s for Traveller children to be removed from their families and placed in industrial schools.[15] Because this practice severed all ties between the child and Traveller culture, few ever returned to their families or the Travelling life (TS92022).

Current policies attempt to deal with the perceived "Traveller problem" by assimilating Travellers into mainstream society. This process is legitimated by denying Travellers cultural or ethnic identity (Liégeois 1987, 106-8). Once purified of any but residual traces of some old and fragmented culture, Travellers become wayward citizens in need of help. Help comes in the form of increased social programs and regulations that are intended to guide the "misfits" back into society.

The denial of cultural or ethnic identity is made possible, in part, by the general acceptance of ethnocentric attitudes that fail to treat Travellers and Traveller culture as equal participants in the modern world (see Fabian 1983). Examples of these beliefs abound. An early government report, for instance, suggests that Travellers are "an immigrant race representing a stage of human development different from that current in the society into which they intruded" (Departmental Committee on Tinkers in Scotland 1918, 22).

The academic literature on Travellers also carries a lingering notion of cultural and temporal stagnancy. This is particularly prominent in some early arguments about Traveller origins.[16] Without going into detail, I can characterize two proposed origins of the Travellers: that they are the "heirs of a caste of nomadic metalworkers who rose to play an important and integrated role in High Celtic Society," and that they are "heirs of the aboriginal hunter-gatherers who settled in northern Europe in the Neolithic period" (Neat 1979, 42; cf. Henderson 1992, 229). While such origins may give the Travellers historical status, or some claim to aboriginal rights, these arguments also suggest that Travellers maintain an archaic quality that explains their inability to integrate themselves with the modern world. Timothy Neat develops this theme of stagnancy by suggesting the "parallels that can be drawn between the Highland travellers and the Paleolithic Peoples" and concluding: "If the Highland travellers are not descendants of pre-agricultural, aboriginal Britons, their lifestyle and their psychology retain remarkable similarities" (Neat 1979, 42). In his recent book *The Summer Walkers* (1996), Neat presents a slightly different picture of Travellers by celebrating their creativity and adaptability: He describes the Travellers as "heirs of a vital and ancient culture" and suggests that they "bridge time and space like art itself" (vii).

Romanticizations of some past golden age of Traveller culture similarly contribute to the belief that Travellers are not full participants in the modern world. Some facets of Traveller culture, such as their storytelling and ballad-singing traditions, may be venerated as works of art, but these arts are viewed as survivals of a now stagnant or decaying culture (cf. Reid 1997). By way of illustration, consider the closing lines of an article titled "Scotland's Colorful Tinkers" in *The Highlander*, a magazine for Scots in America:

Today the classic tinkers of Scotland have all but vanished. There's a breed of folk who call themselves "travellers" who turn up for the berrypicking and others ape the old time Gypsies when it suits them, to extract money from the public. But the tinkers who sat by road, loch, and burn mending tin pans have gone and with them the colorful ballads which told of their colorful mysterious ways. (Lamont-Brown 1994)

This comment denies any meaningful connection between current-day Travellers and a vague but idyllic past—as if all remnants of this past culture have vanished in the mists of time. Similarly, during a visit to the exhibit on Traveller culture in the Highland Folk Museum in Kingussie*—amid signs that lauded the old days and commented on the rapid changes in Traveller life and occupation in recent years—a museum guide told me, "The Travellers used to provide a valuable service to the community. They were respected for that. People were glad to see them. But the tinkers these days are a menace to society" (Field notes 4/25/93).

---

*Kingussie is about 40 miles south of Inverness.

It is in the arena of law and public policy, however, that Travellers are purged of any remnant of cultural identity. Consider the definition of Travellers proposed to the U.K. Secretary of State for Scotland in the third report of *The Secretary of State's Advisory Committee on Scotland's Travelling People* (a definition effectively adopted in the Local Government and Planning [Scotland] Act 1982). This definition, which parallels language used for Gypsies in earlier court decisions and in the Caravan Sites Act of 1968 (England), identifies Travellers as "persons of nomadic habit of life, whatever their race or origin" (1982, 17). While it might be argued that this definition results from an attempt to avoid problems in determining who is or is not a "true" Traveller for application of policies, as Sir Alfred Munnings argues with respect to similar language regarding Gypsies in the English version of the law (Munnings 1984), the definition effectively eliminates consideration of cultural identity as being relevant to policy decisions that directly affect Travellers (cf. Liégeois 1987, 106; Acton 1993, 16).

Yet this definition does more than deny Travellers their cultural identity. It also reduces the uniqueness of Traveller lives to their choice of a nomadic lifestyle. From this perspective, it becomes possible to conceive of a policy through which Travellers may be cured of nomadism and assimilated into mainstream society. This goal is made clear in a consultation document on the reform of the Caravan Sites Act 1968. Under a heading "Encouragement towards Settlement and Permanent Housing," there appears the following comment:

The process of settling down and possibly transferring into traditional housing may not be easy for people who are accustomed to a nomadic life-style. Accordingly, the Government believes that it may be necessary to provide advice on education, health and housing which encourages gypsies and other travellers to settle and, in time, to transfer into traditional housing. (Department of the Environment 1992, 13–14)

Implicit in this comment is the idea that the difference between Travellers and non-Travellers is one that may be remedied by properly educating Travellers. Note also the ethnocentrism present in the assumption that settled housing is "traditional housing."

These laws and policies are but a small sample of the discrimination

Travellers face on a daily basis. This discrimination is enabled by beliefs that deny the Travellers their cultural or ethnic identity. It is played out in terms of laws, government policies, and popular attitudes that apply pressure on Travellers to give up their culture and assimilate into mainstream society. It must be remembered, however, that any affirmation or denial of Traveller identity is played out not in some abstract realm of discourse but in Travellers' face-to-face interactions with settled people. Travellers directly experience the effects of government policies and of the prejudices that often generate these policies. They are frequently forced to deal with beliefs and behaviors from both citizens and government representatives that range from discrimination to harassment to violence.

Given the discrimination that is frequently a part of their lives, it is not surprising that some Travellers decide to cloak, or even abandon, their Traveller identity and "pass" as settled people (Whyte 1990, 87; TS93019; Gentleman and Swift 1971, 81). Those who choose to do this may live in houses isolated both from other Travellers and from the folks next door. They also live in constant fear that they will be discovered for who they really are.

Despite pervasive problems, many other Travellers have no desire to assimilate into the non-Traveller world. A number of those I interviewed echoed a comment Duncan Williamson made while discussing Traveller life with a group of Americans interested in storytelling:

> I'll tell you something.
> I've been to both sides of the street.
> I've dined and wined with lairds and dukes.
> And I've met many intellectuals all over the world.
> And if I had my life to live again,
> I would go back to be a Traveller.
> But this time,
> coming around the second time,
> I'd be a damned better one. [laughter]
> And that's the truth." (TS87019)

The choice to maintain their identity and cultural heritage, however, often leads Travellers to isolate themselves from non-Travellers. As a consequence, contact between Traveller and non-Traveller groups takes place only when demanded by economic necessity or where mutual respect re-

A Traveller van camped on the shores of Loch Fyne, 1998

sults in trusting relationships. In this way, Travellers minimize the direct influence of outsider attitudes and beliefs and create an environment in which Traveller culture can be nurtured in association with other Travellers. Traveller nomadism might, in fact, be understood as a means for maintaining isolation and safety. If threatened by violence, Travellers have the option to avoid conflict by moving down the road—although this option is increasingly limited by laws that restrict options for legal camping.

Isolation has fostered a strong sense of shared identity among Travelers. Betty Townsley, for example, noted she would never mistake a Traveller for a non-Traveller. She said she could easily pick out a single Traveller from a crowded street in the town of Cupar, no matter how well disguised he or she was with fancy clothing (TS92025). Identification among Travellers goes well beyond physical appearance, however. It builds on perceptions of similarity in experience, belief, and value.

While Travellers isolate themselves from settled communities as much as possible, it is important to recognize that they cannot and do not live in total isolation. Travellers are surrounded by the settled community and survive in relation to it by exploiting the cracks in the settled economy. Travellers therefore do not shield themselves from knowledge of non-Travellers. Instead, they seek it out, believing that understanding non-Travelers is essential for their own survival. This knowledge, however, is carefully contextualized in ways that clearly mark non-Traveller behavior as undesirable.

It is my suggestion that, in addition to the functions of entertainment, education, identity, and comprehension of experience listed in the last section, Travellers use stories as a way of responding to the social, political, and historical issues that affect their lives. For example, Travellers use experiential or fictional stories to remind individuals of who they are, who they are not, and what it means to be a Traveller (cf. Basso 1979). Similarly, Travellers use stories that contrast Traveller and settled beliefs as a way of negotiating identity and difference with outsiders. Travellers additionally use storytelling as a symbolic medium for playing with differences in belief and thereby understanding how settled people think and make sense out of their world. This gives Travellers an edge in dealing with non-Travellers and provides resources for responding to conflict between the groups. In these ways, storytelling functions not only to strengthen the bonds between Travellers within their own communities but also to challenge outsider views and to maintain Traveller autonomy and identity in the face of pressure to assimilate into settled culture.

Lives Shaped through Stories

At one point during our week together in 1985, Duncan quoted a comment Hamish Henderson made about his own work with the Travellers:

> He said, "You know I was away up (at?) Inverness,
> and I was there with some of the Travelling Stewarts."[17]
> And," he said, "I stayed with them for over a week.
> And enjoyed every moment of it.
> And I come back to Edinburgh, and," he says,
> "I come back to my flat in Edinburgh,
> and I saw the flat dark and lonely," he said.
> "I wanted to drop everything
> and go back to the Travelling Stewarts." (TS85006)

When I left Kincraigie farm cottage, I understood how Hamish felt. Yet this visit was only the beginning of my acquaintance with the Travellers.[18] It was also the beginning of the journey of transformation that brought me into the academic life I had never expected to lead.

I arrived at my home in Seattle, Washington, with an appetite to learn more about folktales and traditional storytelling. I read what I could find on storytelling and Traveller culture. Then, in 1987, I enrolled in the Graduate Summer Institute in Folklore at the University of Washington—an experience that provided me with an introduction to folklore theory and an orientation to the academic study of folklore.

In the fall of 1987, I organized a tour for Duncan and brought him to the United States for a series of events with the Seattle Storytellers' Guild and storytelling sessions at East Tennessee State University and the National Storytelling Festival in Jonesborough, Tennessee. During his visit I asked Duncan many of the questions I had formulated during the Summer Institute and recorded a dozen hours of stories, ballads, and interviews.

I traveled back to Scotland in 1988, stayed with Duncan for about two weeks, and got to know other Travellers, including Betsy and Bryce Whyte, Willie and Bella MacPhee, Stanley Robertson, and Elizabeth Stewart. My tape recorder did not get much rest.

In 1989, inspired by my interactions with Travellers, I quit my job at the University of Washington and entered the doctoral program at the Folklore Institute at Indiana University in Bloomington. Questions about the relationship between stories and the lives of storytellers remained at the center of my interest throughout my work at the institute. Although I expanded my knowledge of traditional storytelling to new cultures, the Travelling People of Scotland, and Duncan Williamson in particular, remained an essential focus of my research. Consequently, I returned to Scotland in 1992–93 to undertake a year of field research on Traveller storytelling. Further fieldwork with Travellers took place in 1994, 1995 and 1998. Sue Grizzell, my wife, accompanied me on many of these trips.

During this period, one milestone of my academic journey was reached when I finished my doctoral dissertation, "The Negotiation of Meaning and Identity in the Narratives of the Travelling People of Scotland" (1996a). Yet, because my work with the Travellers is based in friendship and a very real desire to understand who they are, my work to understand the Travellers did not end with the dissertation.

Since my first meeting with Duncan, my goal has been to understand the multifaceted relationship between Traveller stories and Traveller lives. But research is a lot like storytelling. A story lives only in the telling, in the exchange between teller and listener. Where storytellers tell stories, academics write books. It is our way of synthesizing experience and insight and presenting the results for public examination. This book is therefore a synthesis of my experience and understanding of Traveller storytelling practices.

Because it is not possible to capture the full diversity and complexity of Traveller storytelling within the confines of a single book, I enter the world of Traveller storytelling through the words, stories, and songs of Travellers I met during my field research. This approach allows me to accomplish several overlapping goals. First, by presenting transcriptions of interviews and performances, I bring the reader face-to-face with Travellers' own voices and the practice of Traveller storytelling. Second, I use these transcriptions as examples that open into discussions exploring the interconnections between storytelling and Traveller life. While each performance is unique in terms of participants, functions, and meanings, I believe that the examples I present hint at the broader ways in which Travellers' lives are shaped through stories and Traveller stories are shaped by the lives of their tellers. Finally, I explore insights these performances offer about the process of storytelling in order to develop a theoretical base for understanding storytelling as a unique mode of human communication. It is my hope that these ideas may be usefully extended beyond the Traveller example to offer insight into the place of stories in human communities and our identity as human beings.

Throughout the chapters that follow, keep in mind that my understanding of Traveller storytelling is a product of my own experience as guided by the synthesis and insight of the Travellers I worked with during my research. During my time in Scotland, I sought out Travellers, observed their interactions, recorded their stories and ballads, and asked them questions about their lives and storytelling practices. I made recordings during events ranging from gatherings where the storyteller's primary focus was on interactions with other Travellers to interviews where I asked questions and was the primary audience for any storytelling that took place. One context is not more authentic than the other, since ethnographic research necessarily involves an exchange wherein individuals from differing cultures or groups collaborate on trying to understand each other.[19]

Edith MacGregor, Isa Sutherland, Eckie Sutherland, Jimmy Williamson, Nancy MacDonald, and Sue Grizzell, 1988

A number of the Travellers I worked with, and whose voices are heard herein, I met through Duncan Williamson. Some are closely related to Duncan, others are not. Some consider themselves to be storytellers, others do not. These individuals are of widely varying ages and experiences. I did not make recordings with everyone I met. In some cases I did not want to impose a tape recorder into our conversations. At other times, I was more an observer than an active participant in the discourse interaction. Although I may not reproduce their words here, these voices influenced and confirmed my understandings of Traveller life and culture. While I got to know some Travellers as friends, stayed with them at times, and worked alongside them for brief periods, I never tried to "go native" and become a Traveller. Nor did I try to hide my interests and research goals.

Since I do not present a chronological account of my research, it is useful in advance to clarify the identity of a few key storytellers who are found in these pages. I also give approximate ages for these individuals during 1992–93—the time of my most extensive fieldwork in Scotland.

Duncan Williamson was in his mid-60s at this time. Jimmy Williamson (in his 40s) is Duncan Williamson's oldest son from his first marriage, to Jeannie Townsley.[20] Jimmy Williamson and Nancy MacDonald (30s) live on the Dumbarton caravan site near Glasgow, surrounded by her parents and a number of other close relatives. They have two children: Elizabeth Donaldson (20s) and young Jimmy or Bimbo (teens). Nancy's sister Isa (50s) also lives on this site and is married to Eckie Sutherland (50s). Duncan's oldest daughter from his first marriage is Edith Williamson (40s). She is married to one of the many Willie MacPhees, and they live in a cottage near Perth. Their daughters are Tracy and Donna (both in their early 20s). Betty Townsley (40s) is Duncan's second oldest daughter from his marriage to Jeannie Townsley. Betty now lives in Ireland.

Less closely related to the Williamson clan are Betsy (who was in her 60s when she died, in 1988) and Bryce Whyte (late 70s). Bryce still lives in a council house he shared with Betsy in Montrose, on the NE coast. Betsy's autobiographies, *Yellow on the Broom* and *Red Rowans and Wild Honey*, are honest and revealing and provide insight into both her life and Traveller culture. Bryce is an excellent singer and storyteller in his own right.

Willie and Bella MacPhee (in their 80s) are well known throughout Traveller circles and to non-Travellers interested in the folk revival. They live on the Doubledykes caravan site near Perth. Willie is best known as a piper, but he is also a wonderful singer and storyteller. Two of Willie's songs are collected in Ewan MacColl and Peggy Seeger's book *Travellers' Songs from England and Scotland* (1977, 186, 295). Sheila Douglas has published several of Willie's stories in her book *The King o' the Black Art* (1987) and a brief biographical account of Willie, including several of his songs, in *The Sang's the Thing* (1992).

I believe I present a view of Traveller storytelling with which my Traveller friends would agree. Yet, as I noted earlier, Traveller culture is not homogeneous but characterized by anarchy and individualism. Consequently, I do not intend the insights I present to be understood as representative of some uniform Traveller practice. Yet, the comments of those I interviewed do reach beyond our immediate interaction and hint at the practice of Traveller storytelling in general terms. By allowing their voices to speak in this book, I intend to retain the rich detail of the specific and some sense of generalization about that which lies beyond my immediate experience.

1. "That's Not a Crack; That's a Story"

An Overview of Traveller Storytelling Traditions

I encountered many puzzles in trying to understand Traveller storytelling. For example, during a conversation with Traveller Nancy MacDonald, I asked if she, like her husband Jimmy Williamson, had been raised on stories. She said, "No," and explained that it was not until she met Jimmy that she started hearing stories on a regular basis. Consequently, I did not pursue questions about the role of stories in her childhood. Yet, a month or so later, Betty Townsley commented that one of the best tellers of "old cracks" she had ever heard was Willie MacDonald. She said I really should visit him and make a recording. Since Willie is Nancy's father, I was confused. Similarly, when I asked Nancy if she told stories, she said "No." I was somewhat puzzled when minutes later I was recording wonderful, engaging stories from this woman who said she was not a storyteller. These apparent contradictions dissolved when I realized I had fallen into the trap of expecting Travellers to share my academic vocabulary for understanding and categorizing their storytelling traditions.

In the abstract realm of theory, I understand storytelling as a unique mode of human communication. Storytellers use symbolic language to replay events in such a way that listeners can follow the symbolic stream as it unfolds and can re-create, even re-experience, the event being narrated (Braid 1996b, 1998a). In my broad conception, the events replayed in story may be personal experiences, stories heard from others, expressive lies that play with "what really happened," fictional constructions, and so forth. Since cultural groups may understand and use the common medium of stories differently, it is only by examining how a given group uses and understands stories that the functions and meanings of the stories, and therefore the relationship between stories and the world of lived experience, can be fully understood.

With regard to Traveller storytelling, my initial confusion arose from not understanding the distinction Travellers make between *crack* and *story*. *Crack* is a term Travellers use to label a wide range of conversational expressions including jokes, riddles, speech play, and a number of narrative forms. People crack to each other, exchange cracks, or talk of having a good crack. Not every conversation is an exchange of crack, but when the conversation becomes animated and witty, when play augments referential communication, when the element of performance becomes highlighted, it is *crack*.[1] Stories that are termed *cracks* are based in real-world events, no matter how stretched or distorted they may have become in the act of performance. In this sense, stories of personal experience, tall tales, ghost stories, and even expressive lies fall squarely into the category *crack*.

Story is a term Travellers use to refer to what folklorists normally label by the academic terms *folktale* and *magic tale*. These are narratives that both teller and audience recognize as fictional in content. While characters and settings in the stories may be modeled on the real world in which teller and listener live, the stories do not ask that listeners interpret them as reporting events in the real world. Stories often animate worlds that differ significantly from the world of lived experience: Animals may speak, witches may cast spells, horses may fly, and cooking pots may walk of their own accord.

From this perspective, when Nancy said she did not hear stories growing up, she meant she did not hear many folktales. She did hear crack constantly. It is therefore not surprising that she is a wonderful teller of cracks in her own right. I doubt that many Travellers would deny hearing or telling cracks on a regular basis. However, many Travellers have not invested the time needed to learn and become fluent at telling the longer folktales, and so they deny being storytellers. Yet some Travellers do take an interest in learning these stories and enjoy retelling them to a wide audience of those who love to hear them.

Understanding Traveller storytelling is further complicated by the fact that the distinction between *crack* and *story* is not rigidly observed throughout all my discussions with Travellers. Consider, for example, the following exchange that took place during a recording session with Eckie Sutherland and Jimmy Williamson, in which our focus was explicitly on the distinction Travellers make between *crack* and *story*. After telling an anecdote about a widely acknowledged teller of folktales, Eckie Sutherland continued:

ES   There are not really many that I know going about now tell stories, except (?)
JW   But, if you think about it, everybody does.
ES   And everybody does, aye.
DB   Well, yeah.
      You see, it depends what you call *stories*.
ES   That's right. (TS98013)

Perhaps Jimmy's acknowledgement that everyone tells stories is a concession to my academic system of classifying narratives. It may also reflect his recognition of the underlying parallels in communicative form between crack and story. Yet, other Travellers similarly used the term *story* in a way that included both crack and folktale. In order to prevent possible confusion, I will use *story* as a general term that refers to both categories of narrative discourse. Where the distinction between folktale and crack is relevant to understanding the meaning of my consultants' words, I will clarify the intended meaning as I introduce quotes.

This chapter provides an introduction to the world of Traveller storytelling and especially the genres of crack and story by focusing attention on the occasions when Travellers tell stories and the kinds of stories they tell on these occasions. To a certain degree, what emerges from my interviews is an idealized or romanticized view of Traveller storytelling traditions that downplays the reality of recent changes in Traveller lives. This picture emerges because connecting with a meaningful past is an essential component of how individuals in all cultures create a sense of who they are (see D. Hymes 1975a, 353–55). Many Travellers I met belong to older generations and feel that their way of life has fallen apart or will fall apart with "the way things are going." Younger Travellers are well aware of the experiences of their parents and older relatives and carry stories of "how life used to be" as essential components of their own identity. When I ask Travellers to reflect upon the practice of Traveller life and culture, it is therefore not surprising that they respond with both observations of the present reality and comments about a traditionalized past that may no longer exist. I would expect nothing different from participants in any culture.

This chapter is organized around four overlapping facets of Traveller storytelling traditions. In the first section I investigate the place of storytelling in the daily lives of Travellers and focus attention on the contexts where storytelling takes place. Here I also explore the continuities in storytelling traditions that persist despite the significant changes in Traveller life over recent years. In the second section I look at the genre of crack and give examples of the kinds of stories that are grouped under this label. The third section deals with folktales and examines the place of fictional stories in family and public interactions. Within this section, I highlight the nature of storytellers and the contexts of folktale performance. In a final section, I situate Traveller storytelling within the wider interaction between Travellers and non-Travellers. I argue that Traveller storytelling traditions have not developed in total isolation. Despite Travellers' tendency to keep to themselves, they have always existed in relationship to the surrounding culture. Traveller storytelling traditions must therefore be viewed as a product of mutual influence and exchange between Travellers and non-Travellers.

I. Campfires, Visiting, and Ceilidhs—The Contexts of Traveller Storytelling

Travellers tell stories in sessions ranging from informal chats to ceilidhs (pronounced KAY-lees), gatherings where there is an explicit focus on performance. When I asked Duncan Williamson about storytelling sessions during his days on the road, he painted a detailed picture of when and how these performances might take place.

DB The other thing I wanted to ask you about is the storytelling sessions.
    I mean, you'd sit around the campfire in the evening. . . .
    Were there special times that stories were told,
    or did it just happen all the time?
DW Well it was especially when . . . you got together.
    You come into a camping site,
    and you probably met some members of the family
    or some strangers you had never seen for a while. . . .
    They would say,
    "Come and put your tent up beside mine.
    One fire will do us."
    And then they would start away cracking about . . .
       where they'd been,
       and who they'd seen,
       where such and such a Traveller was,
       and what like places they'd been,
       and where the roads had traveled,
       and what like the situation was that place,
       and what direction you're going,
       and where did you come fae.
    That would start it.

    And then,
    when it got a bit later,
    it would come to stories.
    They'd say,
    "Here, wait a minute.
    I'll tell you who I met yesterday.
    I met such and such,
    and he told me a great story I never heard before."
    And you would say, the weans* would say, "Oh, a story."
    We would all gather around, you see?
    In close.
    And maybe the old, the man would say,
    "Well, this is a great story.
    I heard this one.
    I never heard my faither tell this yin before."
    Could be a Jack Story could be ony story.

---
weans (pronounced WAYNES) = children or young children

And everybody was listening to the story.
And you'd tell this yin.
And then maybe the man who'd been sitting there . . . said,
"Well, I'll tell you a story."

Because that was the idea.
If someone told you a story,
you'd always got to tell one back.
That was the custom.
Whether you liked to or no.
It was expected of you. (TS87013)

Implicit in Duncan's idealized portrayal is both a sense of the way crack and storytelling permeate Traveller social interactions and a sense of the progression in content and types of stories that might take place during visits. At first, the talk focuses on the pragmatic details of campsite arrangement and the relationship between the participants in the interaction. From here, the participants start telling cracks that move from news of friends and relations to relevant experiences in the world to future plans. Ultimately, the talk shifts to entertaining folktales. Duncan also frames this exchange in customary terms, noting the expectation that one story will be answered by another. While Duncan's example focuses on storytelling around an open fire, a practice more typical of years gone by, I frequently observed a similar progression of storytelling during my fieldwork when Travellers visited with each other around a kitchen table.

Visiting and sharing stories and crack with others is an important aspect of Traveller life. For instance, Bryce Whyte commented that if work necessitated an isolated camping location, Travellers might walk for miles to visit one another: "When my father was a young man, they would . . . on a Sunday, go maybe three or four miles on to another camp where there was some other body and have a news with the men" (TS92031; cf. Whyte 2001, 183). Willie MacPhee noted that visiting was a regular event.

DB Did it used to be that the folk you'd visit
    would just be the folk you'd stop with?
WM Many years ago . . . they would travel,
    travel for miles to go and see one another.

>   Say, I'm stopping here,
>   and maybe some other body is maybe five or six mile away.
>   Well, naebody would think nothing of just walking—
>   of course, there was nae motors or nothing then—
>   just walk there to there,
>   [have] a chin-wag,
>   a crack,
>   and then come back again.
>   On a Sunday, every Sunday. (?)
>   And that's what they used to do in these times tae many years ago.
>   They would go from the one camp to the other and tell stories to one
>   another. Maybe folk from this place would go away there
>   and maybe spend five or six hours telling stories up there.
>   Or maybe the following Sunday (or that?),
>   they would come here and they would tell stories back here.
>   You see?
>   That was the way it workit.
> DB That sounds lovely.
> WM Aye. It was a great idea. (TS93028)

When gatherings of Travellers were large, Bryce Whyte suggested that each family would have their own camping site but that there was also a great deal of community interaction:

> DB When you used to travel around
>   and, um, meet with other people and have camps . . .
>   what happened?
>   Did they have . . . one big fire in the middle that people would come to? . . .
> BW Well, you could do that, . . .
>   but . . . the most of them,
>   when they had their own families,
>   they had their own . . . places where they could pitch their tents up. . . .
>   But at night, at night
>   we used to maybe come to the one great big fire and,
>   build a great big fire,
>   and all the men used to, eh, stand round the fire.
>   And all the women used to get chatting together . . .
>   mostly away on their own.
>   And the men chatted among themselves. (TS92029)

Bryce also alludes to the fact that men and women associate in separate groups. This gives an insight into Traveller storytelling that I return to shortly.

Overview of Traveller Storytelling Traditions   57

What emerges from this series of comments is a vision of a culture where stories and storytelling play a central role in social interaction. Yet these comments should not be understood to imply that all Travellers tell identical stories or even that they relate to storytelling in the same way. I briefly illustrate the diversity of Traveller storytelling practices with regard to three issues: the interest of some Travellers in seeking out and learning stories, the differing kinds of storytelling appropriate to specific events, and the role of gender differences in storytelling.

First, it is not the case that all Travellers are equally interested in stories. Duncan Williamson said that there might be several fires on a given evening around which people with different interests were gathered. At one fire the discussion might center on the bagpipes. At another fire there might be a focus on pragmatic aspects of work. These groupings might shift during the night, "and maybe before you were finished you were all sitting round the same fire" (TS87014).

Where individuals were particularly interested in hearing and retelling folktales, they might seek out well-known tellers. Duncan Williamson, for example, talked about walking long distances at night to hear the masterful storytelling of Old Johnny Townsley.

DW But if you got a name as a good storyteller,
    people would come from far and wide for a story.
    I . . . [remember] . . . me and my brother Jock
    walking ten miles to listen to an old soldier, Johnny Townsley.
    He's dead now.
    Traveled ten miles, at nighttime—five going and five back—
    just to sit and to listen to him tell a story.
    See what I mean?
    Instead of going to the pictures or going to the pub,
    we walked five miles each way, each direction.
    We knew where his camp was.
    And we sat there and listened to stories, him telling a story.
DB Would other people be there, or would you just show up at his family camp?
DW Other people would come, too.
    Other people would come from another direction. . . .
    There was no such thing as,
    "Oh, we'll go and visit old Johnny tonight."
    It just happened.
    We just went there.

We got there and maybe there was somebody else there.
See, they had come, too, for the same reason as we did. (TS92034)

I told Eckie Sutherland about this comment, and he simply said, "Oh, aye, you would walk more than that to listen to him, I am telling you" (TS98013).

Second, not all storytelling events follow the same pattern or evoke the same kinds of stories. For example, Bryce commented that different kinds of stories might be told at family fires than are told at the larger fires around which many families gather.

DB When would the stories and songs happen
and how would that happen?
BW Well . . . in the long winter nights,
if you went up to some of the older ones and say,
"Come on, tell us a story,"
they would . . . just tell you the story,
because there was nothing else to dae. . . .
There was nae TVs or nae things like that, you know?
And, eh, they . . . just were glad to get the people in about.
And maybe have a . . . a cup of tea or—, you know?
And tell them stories, and that's just,
and tell them about things that they used to do,
and how they met their wives and,
and, eh, how they went about their business, and—
They told us all that.
DB Would that happen at the more—
at the family campfire rather than the great big one then?
BW Oh, well, it was mostly at their own campfire.
They never, eh,
they never said that when they were talking to the rest of the Travelling men.
They used to talk about, eh, different things, you know?
And, eh, but it was mostly about what they used to do
and about going to farmers,
farmers and working and about horses and things like that, you know?
DB So, about their own experiences?
BW Yes, about their own experiences. (TS92029)

Bryce hints at not only a wide range of stories but also a wide range of functions for storytelling performances. In small family gatherings, he suggests, storytelling is a medium for conversational exchange, entertainment, history, and enculturation. At the larger fires, storytelling seems to take on pragmatic functions that have to do with the problems of work and interaction with non-Travellers.

Similarly, not all visits have the same goals. In the Scots language, the word "ceilidh" means "an informal social gathering among neighbors, with or without singing, playing instruments, story-telling etc, spontaneously performed by some or all of those present" (Robinson 1985, 89). As used by Travellers, this term is normally reserved for visits where there is an explicit focus on entertainment. Ceilidhs may be preplanned or spontaneous. Visits might, in fact, evolve into ceilidhs, and in this sense visits and ceilidhs might best be considered as two points on a single continuum involving the increasing focus on performance. Ceilidhs typically move beyond crack to include instrumental music, song, and ballad. For Duncan, ceilidhs are fundamentally participatory. His rule is "tell a story, sing a sang, show your bum, or out you gang" (cf. Whyte 2001, 22). Ian MacGregor said his family similarly encouraged participation as keyed by the phrase: "Tell, sing, or bing.*"

Third, gender differences must be explored for a full understanding of Traveller storytelling traditions.[2] In the comments just quoted, for instance, Bryce Whyte talked of men and women chatting together in different groups. During one interview, Betty Townsley similarly noted that it is still common for men and women to gather in segregated groups. When families camp together, she said, "a lot of them goes inside the trailers, but a lot of the men will kindle a big fire up. And they'll stand and talk for hours and hours and hours outside. And the women will bring tea out to them" (TS920025). This comment should not be interpreted as devaluing women because they serve men tea—a point made clear by an English Romani woman when she commented that she might take tea out to the men at the fireside, but only because that meant the men had no reason to disturb the truly important conversation of the women inside the trailer.[3] Nonetheless, it raises questions about how the stories and storytelling differ because of gender.

------

bing = Traveller cant for *go*

Presumably, the content of the men's and women's talk and storytelling are different. Willie and Bella MacPhee acknowledged this difference after a question from Thomas Burton, an American folklorist doing research in Scotland:

TB Did the men and the women tell
WM Different stories?
TB Different kinds of stories?
WM They would, aye.
    I suspect they would.
BM They all had different kinds of stories.
WM The women does that to the very day,
    to this very day [laughs].
BM [laughs]. (TS92022)

Betty Townsley gave some insight into the nature of this difference during a conversation about changes in Traveller storytelling in recent years. In talking about the kinds of stories men tell when gathered in their separate groups, she suggested that their cracks might reference different ranges of experience for men and women.

You know, like they would tell stories,
what happened to their fathers.
You know?
Not fairy stories.
But say, "My daddy told me this that some such thing happened."
You know?
And they'd tell stories all night about their different fathers' experiences, what they told on, see?
Because men's got a lot of stuff like that their daddies passed on to them that the woman doesn't hear about. (TS92025)

Implicit in this comment is a multichannel view of oral transmission in which men and women pass on different kinds of experience to those of their own gender.

Questions of gender also arise with respect to folktale performances. When I heard about the great folktale tellers, I heard about as many women as men. The repertoires of these tellers also seem to be balanced in terms of the kinds of stories they tell. Yet there are some stories considered to be specifically targeted at one gender or the other. Where the well-known Jack Tales focus on the adventures of a young man, both Duncan Williamson and Stanley Robertson talked about another category of stories that follow the adventures of young women (TS92034; TS93006; TS93014). These stories were told with the hope that children would identify with protagonists of their own gender and grow up like the characters in the story. Edie Williamson and her daughter Tracy, for example, talked about stories with female protagonists, like "Mary Rashiecoats and the Wee Black Bull" (D. Williamson 1987a, 62–77) and "Mary and the Seal" (D. Williamson 1992, 115–26), that were favorite stories in their own childhoods.

Despite the focus on the past in the preceding comments, it would be a mistake to believe that the importance of storytelling in social interaction has diminished as a result of recent changes in Traveller lives. Stories are so deeply entwined with Traveller interaction that there is little fear of their dying out. There are, in fact, strong continuities between the storytelling around the campfire in years gone by and the storytelling of the present day. Duncan Williamson implied that any changes are merely superficial and mask an underlying continuity in storytelling practice:

> Oh, we don't have wir great outside fires [and] . . . carry ons any more.
> But still in their little caravans and the little caravan sites
> they have always close-knit family get-together[s] for the storytelling sessions.
> And they'll say,
> "This is a story, I remember my old grandfather telling this one."
> "This was one of my mother's old stories."
> "Minding my old uncle telling me this one."
> And that's the way it goes on.
> And then maybe the next time it'll be on somebody else's caravan.
> And these stories will go on forevermore.
> That's the way it was with the Travelling People.
> And I hope it remains like that for a long, long time to come. (TS87001)

Yet, despite the continuities, there have been changes in the kinds of stories that are told in interactions. Jimmy Williamson worries that many of the folktales are in danger of being lost:

Four generations of a family gathered together: Nancy MacDonald, Elizabeth Donaldson, Jimmy Williamson, Halie Donaldson (in Jimmy's lap), and Duncan Williamson (playing a jaw harp), 1998

DB And do you think most other folk have forgotten the stories, then?
JW I think so.
DB Because, I mean,
    if I came over to you and asked if you knew any stories,
    you'd say, "No."
JW [laughs] Well, I mean,
    I'd probably say no,
    but I'd probably know a few, you know what I mean?
DB Yeah.
    Do you think that is true of a lot of other folk as well?
JW Definitely.
    Well, it's just like a person living in isolation and not speaking the language.
    I mean it'll eventually go.
    The stories never get used. (TS93025)

At another time, Jimmy commented that many Travellers still enjoy listening to stories when they get a chance to do so.

JW I still like listening to a story.
    I still like it.
    As long as it is being told.
DB Yeah, yeah.
    But are there many folk that you know that do enjoy that?
JW Oh, I think that everybody does.
    I think nearly all.
    If there was—
    If they could all get somebody to tell them more often.
    I think they would all, everybody would listen.
DB Well, I know, like Eckie has told Bimbo stories.
    I mean, is Bimbo the only one who is interested in listening to him or—
JW I don't know.
    I mean, there—I mean,
    I think everybody's got a sense of embarrassment now telling stories.
    Used to be they never had
    because they used to put up a fire and tell them. (TS93017)

These comments should not be interpreted as a death knell for folktales among Travellers. It may simply be that the public occasions for folktale performance are dwindling and that these stories, as is the case in other cultures, are retreating into the world of family storytelling except where they are displayed on the revival stage. Jimmy acknowledges that folktales are still being told within his family, but he suggested that this was a product of the interest in stories he inherited from his father and has passed on to his own son (TS93017). Similarly, Betty Townsley, Duncan's daughter, tells me that she told stories she heard from her father to her own children and that her son is "telling his wee girl now" (TS92025). I also know of others who are still telling the folktales within the family, but I have no data that allows me to conclude how widespread this practice may be.

In some situations fictional storytelling survives quite well. Edie Mac-Phee and her daughter, Tracy, said that fairy stories and ghost stories are still told among Travellers, especially when they are gathered around fires during the potato picking or at other times on the road when people are camped together (TS93026). At other times Travellers still gather to tell stories and sing songs at ceilidhs in someone's trailer or house.

Storytelling traditions that focus on crack do not seem in the same danger of disappearing. When I asked Betty Townsley for her opinion on how storytelling has changed over the years, she answered:

BT It's a lot different today, I think.
    They still tell stories, but it's in the trailer.
    But it's not, it wouldn't be fairy stories or stories anymore.
    It would be like real-life experiences now,
    how to cope with everyday problems.
    And if you've got a bad problem and you can't get over it or can't get (done?),
    or whatever it is,
    I mean, you'll go in the trailer,
    and maybe five or six men will get together and they'll sit and talk it.
    And tell them if they had the same problem.
    You know what I mean?
    And how to deal with it.
    And if you go to an area, where there have been bad police or that—
    and how to deal with that.
    Do you know what I mean? . . .
    And the women will do the same thing about their life, you know?
    The women's life.
DB Yeah, unhuh.
    In a different trailer?
BT Mhmm. (TS92025)

While Betty's comment implies a shift in the kinds of stories that are told, it also confirms a continuity in the practice of telling of personal experience stories and cracks in Traveller interactions.

Travellers still welcome any opportunity to get together and crack. Every time I have seen Travellers gather, there is intense verbal exchange. Some Travellers specialize in humorous cracks, others relate stories of the old days, and still others prefer ghost stories.

Yet some Travellers do feel that the isolation of modern life—and especially the physical isolation of government sites and the easy mindlessness of television—have set barriers to social interaction and have therefore interfered with the spontaneity of verbal exchange.[4] Eckie Sutherland, for example, feels Travellers have become "hermitized" (TS98003). The desire for interaction and crack is still there, however. Nancy MacDonald noted that when they left the government site where they live:

Overview of Traveller Storytelling Traditions

NM And you are away maybe for a fortnight or three weeks or whatever.
    At night you'll go out and kindle a big outside fire
    and everybody will sit cracking round it.
DB Mhmm.
ES Aye, even if you take your television with you.
NM That's what I am saying.
    And you'll make a kettle of tea,
    and everybody will sit outside,
    and they'll have a cup of tea,
    and they'll have a crack.
JW Mhmm.
NM And they'll sit there
    till maybe about twelve o'clock or one o'clock. (TS98003)

Even at the site, anything out of the ordinary serves as an excuse to break down the barriers to interaction:

NM I have seen us here though,
    we went away and got a, ken, a big 40-gallon drum, eh?
    And Jimmy went and chopped holes into it, him and Eckie.
    And they put it out the back
    and put it onto stones
    and went with sticks and kindled a fire.
    And within half-an-hour, everybody in the site was there.
JW It was a focal point.
ES It was a focal point, aye.
JW A fire is a focal point.
NM When you kindle a fire,
    you get plenty of crack. (TS98003)

Eckie Sutherland noted that the fire need not be terribly exciting to be used as an excuse for a gathering:

ES I've seen about thirty folk standing round a burning boot,
    where that was the last thing that was to be burned. [laughter]
    And they stayed because that was there.
    Because the fire was there. (TS98003)

What these comments on storytelling reveal is the close integration between Traveller stories and Traveller lives. In a very real sense, Travellers live, eat, and breathe stories. While the genres, functions, and meanings

66 *Overview of Traveller Storytelling Traditions*

of Traveller stories may have changed over time, Traveller competency and interest in stories as a form of expression and as a way of knowing the world maintain strong continuities with the past.

II. "Give Us Your Crack"—Stories Based in Lived Experience

Thus far I have only implicitly suggested the kinds of stories that might be told during visits. As I noted in the introduction to this chapter, Travellers make a primary distinction between crack and fictional folktales. While the kinds of stories told during any given visit will depend on the interests of the people who are present, crack permeates these interactions. In this section I therefore give an overview of the overlapping categories of stories that are referenced by the term *crack*. In the next section I fill out this overview by focusing on folktales.

When I asked Duncan Williamson about the kinds of stories other than folktales that might be told around the fire, he answered:

DW All kinds of stories, Donald,
    all kinds of stories:
    family tales,
    Burker stories,
    there were stories for every occasion.
    You know what I mean?
    Anyone had a story to tell.
    There are stories of experiences with bad farmers,
        good farmers,
            greedy farmers, ...
                miserable farmers.
DB So you learned a lot about who you might meet on the road?
DW Yeah, that's right.
    And you told stories about other Travellers
    to somebody you might meet up with.
    You know what I mean?
    And there were—
    ghost stories were very important, ...
    and Burker tales,
    stories of spirits,

Overview of Traveller Storytelling Traditions 67

```
        and stories about things they seen.
        I mean, (I see . . . ?)—
DB      Experiences?
DW      Experience stories, aye. (TS92034)
```

Duncan's comment points to a wide range of stories that as a folklorist I would term *personal experience narratives*, *memorates*, or *legends*. What distinguishes these stories from folktales is their connection to the world of lived experience.

By way of illustration, consider the following story that emerged when I was visiting Jimmy Williamson and Nancy MacDonald in their trailer on the Dumbarton caravan site in 1994. We were discussing midges, an almost microscopic flying insect that inhabits wetlands and the ocean shore in Scotland. Although midges are quite small, their bites are painful. Since they attack in clouds, they can drive you quite mad. Nancy commented that the only cure for midges was "a gale force wind." She continued:

```
NM      I remember a time that we went up to go to South Uist,*
        me and you and my father and mother, mind?
JW      Mhmm.
NM      We went and we were, we went through Skye.
        And we bade† at this bit at the roadside.
        And they got up early in the morning.
        My father and mother had a tent, right?
        And they got up early in the morning,
        and the midges started, eh?

        And my father caught—
        My father had a pickup like that.
        My father just caught the camp,
        throwed it in the back of the pickup, [laughter]
        never bothered to pack it or nothing,
        just throwed it in.

        And we went right to the top of a hill, eh?
        And we started to make tea,
        because there was a wind blowing.
```

---

*South Uist is one of the islands in the Outer Hebrides of the NW coast of Scotland.
†*bade* = stayed

68   *Overview of Traveller Storytelling Traditions*

>   And he took the tent out.
>   He said, "I'll have to pack this tent up," he said,
>   "because if we are going on a boat," he said,
>   he said, "it looks really bad."
>   Ken, it being rumpled in a knot in the back of this motor?
>   He says, "I'll have to take this tent out and fold it up."
>   He took the tent out,
>   and there were that many midges in it,
>   we were eaten with the midges that was inside the tent.
> DB Oh, dear.
> NM You have no idea what like it was, eh? (TS94002)

In her storytelling, Nancy uses words to replay a past experience that embodies the horror of midges. Her performance presents this event in such a way that I can expand my own knowledge of midges with regard to Nancy's experience. As a folklorist, I would term this a personal experience narrative and suggest that Nancy chose to replay this incident because it is relevant to our discussion, because it makes a persuasive point about the nature of midges, and because it allows us all a chance to vent our anxieties on this subject.[5]

Personal experience narratives are frequently told in Traveller social interactions. As is common in other communities, Travellers use these stories as a way of bringing individual experiences into focus in the performance interaction so that they may be shared, evaluated, and interpreted as resources for the community. These stories may function to amuse, horrify, entertain, or warn. Personal experience narratives are also a potent medium for communicating about worldview and identity (see chapter 4).

Family Stories

One step removed from personal experience narratives are family stories. These stories focus on the actions and words of family members. I heard many such stories, especially when I was sorting out family relationships. These stories go beyond identifying the degree of family relationship, however, to provide an experience of essential moments in the life of the person featured in the narrated event. Because tellers often know multiple stories about their close relations, these stories tend to create an experiential mosaic of different facets of the individual. While family stories may originate as personal experiences, they usually circulate well beyond the original teller.

The following family story, for instance, was told to me during a discussion with Nancy MacDonald, Jimmy Williamson, and Eckie and Isa Sutherland that focused on memories of the old days.

NM Jimmy's Uncle Geordie used to do some fishing, eh?
IS Oh, my.
ES Oh, my God, he was a (?).
NM He used to take—
He was staying beside us at Lochgilphead.*
And we had tents, ken barricades eh?
And he used to get up,
and he would dress hisself in this, the best of claes,
and he would have this wee case,
and he would go out on the road,
and he would thumb a lift.
And he would get dropped off at Furnace.
And he would go into the wood, dress hisself in his old claes.
He would go into the burn,
and he would snare out about maybe ten big salmon.
ES The Furnace burn, aye.
He kent every pool.
NM And he would take them, take his work claes off,
put on his dry claes again.
He was really dressed like a gentleman, you know what I mean,
with these claes and everything on.
He would wrap the fish into the old claes,
   put them into the suitcase,
      zip it round,
         and then he would go back out onto the road
            and thumb a lift back to Lochgilphead.
Then he would go to the hotel, and he would sell them. [laughter]

His Uncle Geordie used to do that all the time.
Because he come back one night and he given us one eh?
I only took the weeest one.
The weeest one was about four pound.
And I took the weeest one.

---

*Lochgilphead is a town on the shores of Loch Fyne in Argyll.

70 Overview of Traveller Storytelling Traditions

　　　　He offered me one of the fish eh?
　　　　And I said, "Just give me the weeest one you got."
　　　　And he gave me the weeest one, and I cooked it mind?
ES　Oh, there will never be another Geordie.
NM　That's what he used to do.
　　　　He used to do that at least twice a week.
ES　There will never be another Geordie. (TS98003)

　　This story focuses on Geordie and his skill at poaching salmon with ease and style. On one level the story is entertaining, a key attribute of many cracks. Yet the story serves a number of other functions as well. On a second level it highlights not only the wit and passion of Uncle Geordie but also, by implication, the wit and passion that is characteristic of the Williamson family, and perhaps all Travellers. On a third level the story functions as a key to the memory of Geordie the human being, friend, uncle, and relative. This comes through clearly when Eckie Sutherland says, "There will never be another Geordie." In this sense, this brief story functions as a link to broader memories. Not surprisingly, more stories about Geordie and his unique exploits followed Nancy's telling.

　　This connection between story and memory is not unique to stories about Uncle Geordie. Both personal experience and family stories frequently serve not only as a vehicle for memory but also as an anchor to which other memories can be attached.

Newsing

　　Another category of crack focuses on current or recent events. These are the kinds of stories that Willie MacPhee suggests follow the pattern "Oh, did you hear what happened to such-and-a-body?" (TS92022). These stories sometimes relate what has happened to friends and relations and thereby serve to update the connections between people who may not have been able to see each other for some time. These stories might also replay important events that listeners were not present to experience directly. People telling these stories are said to be newsing or having a news. Newsing stories might be built on personal experiences or on stories heard from others.

　　For example, the following story was told to me during a discussion

Eckie Sutherland, 1998

about settled attitudes toward Travellers because I was not present to experience the event it recounts:

ES That incident happened down at, eh, Strachur.*
   What do you call that pace where Louie and Laurie had the hotel?
JW Strachur?
ES Aye, just past Strachur. . . .
   And eh, Eckie and eh, Big Willie, I think it was, Eckie, Eckie Johnson,
   they were coming back,
   and I'm sure it was from Big Willie Burke's funeral at (Greenock?).
   And they went into Louie and Laurie's pub and they—
   Oh there were a lot of toffs† there, all the tourists was in.

---

*Strachur is a small town near the head of Loch Fyne.
†*toffs* = upper-class or wealthy individuals

And the hotel was packed full of toffs.
I would say 70 percent of them was English,
maybe 10 percent Americans and other ones.

And eh, they had a drink,
and Eckie asked if they could play a tune.

So they played the pipes a couple of times, a couple of tunes.
And this guy come over, you know, and he telled them.
He said, "Listen," he says, (?)
"you'll have to tell those damned Tinks to get out of there," he says,
"because we, what we really want," he says,
"is some peace and quiet.
We came to Scotland for some peace and quiet,
not to hear that horrible noise."

So the barman says, "Right boys.
Stop the pipers."
He says, "Right.
You, you, you, you, you, what about you?"
Oh, there were quite a lot of them complained.
"Right," he says,
"get your luggage.
Get out."
Put the whole lot out of the hotel.
"And anybody else who doesn't like the bagpipes," he says,
"or doesn't like the Scots people enjoying theirselves
or doesn't like Travellers in here," he says,
"Out."
I mean he is the (?).
He says, "Out of my hotel."

And the hotel didna stop that night.
We bade into it to the following day before we left.
We were away in the rooms and everything all night.
But John Cook was there,
and eh Big Willie, Andrew, and eh quite a few others of us.
There must have been twenty Travellers. (TS98013)

By retelling the story, Eckie gives me a concrete example of one non-Traveller who values Travellers and includes them in his conception of Scottish identity.

Newsing stories like this are significant because they broaden the experience of listeners to include events they have not personally witnessed. Where the stories tell about family and friends, these stories also provide one of the threads that links Travellers together over time and space.

Ghost Stories and Burker Tales

Experiential stories about supernatural or supernormal experiences are also a part of crack. Duncan Williamson nicely summarized both the kinds of stories that might fall into this category and the role of these stories among Travellers when he commented:

> Some said they seen the Loch Ness Monster
> some said they seen the Broonie,[6]
> some said they seen a ghost . . . and
> some said they heard the fairy music,
> you know what I mean?
>
> You cannae condemn these people because you don't know.
> It could have happened. (TS92034)

Folklorists call these stories *legends*, or *memorates*, if they are first-person stories. As Duncan notes, legends are grounded in the events of the lived world in the sense that they are believable, they "could have happened." The uncertainty as to whether the events did or did not happen is the essence of legends (Dégh 1991, 30; Oring 1986, 126). Legends challenge listeners' understanding of the world and suggest listeners may need to modify their beliefs and worldviews in order to understand the narrated events.

Within this larger domain of legends, Travellers often refer to ghost stories and Burker stories as separate categories. On one level, some truly believe in the stories they tell.

JW   I can remember one night like that up near Aberfeldy.*
     You ken old Johnny MacKenzie . . . ?
ES   Aye.
JW   Mind him that got the hand cut with the fan on the motor?

---

*Aberfeldy is a town 20 miles NW of Perth.

ES Aye.
JW We were camped right beside the two twin trees at Aberfeldy (?).
    You know the twin trees?
    And they stopped by.
    And they were at it.
    I mean ghosts to them was real, weren't they?
ES Oh, aye.
JW They saw ghosts everywhere.
    To them, ghosts was real.
DB Mhmm.
JW And the stories he was telling that night (oh).
    My father, he got the fire going,
        and the kettle going,
            put all the weans to bed,
                chased us inside,
                    locked the door.
    And all th(?) at the fire.
    The lot of them was at the fire,
    my Uncle Jimmy, my father.
    And I sneaked out to listen at the fire. (TS98013)

On another level, it is not the believability but rather the play of performing these stories that creates the engaging experience for listeners:

ES But oh, it was great when you listened to the old Travellers.
    My granny, God rest her,
    when she was telling a story,
    especially about the Burkers and that,
    you would see them creeping in closer and closer to the fire, [laughs]
    really getting terrified of the darkness outside.
    But, usually the ghost stories even,
    I mean it was so—
    You could see through them a mile away,
    the ghost stories. [laughs]
JW Aye, but you still liked to listen to them.
ES And you still liked listening to them. (TS98013)

I recorded a number of ghost stories from Travellers during my fieldwork. While no one text can represent the variety of ghost stories Travellers tell, the version of "The Tinker and the Skeletons" I transcribe in the introduction is a well-known ghost story that has been polished by many tellers over the years. Other ghost stories report personal experi-

Overview of Traveller Storytelling Traditions 75

ences. A case in point is the following story I recorded from Eckie Sutherland:

ES   That devil's den is (?).
There's something not right about it.
The devil's (den?).
Ken Stockie, Stockiemuir?
Me and Isaac and, eh no Isaac, it wasnae Isaac.
Me and Adam, aye and Isaac,
the three of us.

I had this lorry (?) an old Bedford,
and I had it tuned to perfection.
And eh, every day, every day through the day,
I had this motor going perfect.
And I mean perfect.
  I had the points set to perfection,
    valves set to perfection,
      everything going nicely.
And eh, we were going over to an old railway at—
to lift some stuff. [gather scrap]

So.
As we headed down the hill,
we were coming down, just tae the devil's den—
  And you ever see thon kind of nights, kind of misty?
  but we'd been dry weather for about a week or ten days,
  and there were a kind of mist rising up.
And as I come down round the corner,
I seen this thing standing at the side of the dike.
There were an opening going—
it must of been a gate at one time—
going through the dike.
The dike's about seven feet high.
This thing was standing along side of it,
and I, I could see the face was just a blur.
Because it was, touch wood—
I was always blessed with good eyesight, do you ken what I mean?—
it was standing,
with a big long thing that seemed like a robe over the top of it.
And it was standing with a kind of white face and—
You could just make this white shape out, and do you know what I mean?

So, eh.
I says eh, [weak laugh]

I changed into third and (?) . . .
I changed into second. [laughs]
Said, "What is that, boys?"
"What is what?"
"Did you see that man standing there in the—"
You could see it in the headlights quite plain.
"Cannae see any man."
Isaac says, "I cannae see any man."
But I put it down like that,
and the tires spun! [loud laughter]
And I shot away on.
Never seen it (nae more?).

So, eh.
On the road back, I didnae come back that way.
I circled round by Strathblane,*
come back another way up,
through Strathblane and up the steep hill.
He said, Adam, "What was—"
"Ah it was nothing.
It was nothing at all," I said.
"It was just a shadow," I said.
"It was nothing."
I wouldnae admit to anything, you ken?

So, eh.
About a week later, we were coming back the same road.
Down the hill.
I was driving again!
Headlights on full, main beam,
watching this bit.
Nah, nothing (?).
And uh,
"Adam!"
"Isaac!"
"Adam, Adam, Adam!"
"Isaac!"
And Isaac and Adam were shaking one another.
"What is that?
What is that?!"
NM You never seen it?
ES "That's the tallest man in the world!"

---

*Strathblane is a town just north of Glasgow.

NM You never seen it the second time?
ES Nothing, no.
I couldn't see nothing. [long pause, laughs]

So again,
ZZZOOOM! [laughter]

And Adam asked me,
"What WAS that?"
I said, "I never seen nothing!"
"You're fucking lying," he says,
"you never seen nothing." [laughter]
I says, "I'm no lying!" I says,
"I never saw nothing!"
He says, "You DID see it!"
I says, "I seen it the last (day?) and youse laughed at me."
"I never seen it tonight."
He says, "You're a liar!"
He says, "I saw it, and Isaac saw it."

I said, "A fisherman?"
He says, "What are they going to fish?
Dry burns?"
The burns was dry, completely dry, you ken what I mean?
"Well," I says.

So.
He says, "Wait,
we'll stop on the way back and see how high it is."

So.
Isaac could just put his hands on the top of the dike.
Adam's wee enough, five foot ten inches, five foot eleven inches."
He could just put his hands on the top of the dike.
He says, "That man was abeen* that."

So.
"Look for his footprints." [laughter]
He says, "You bastard."
He says, "You saw it."
I said, "No.
Honest to God, I never saw it the second time."

---

*abeen = above

78 Overview of Traveller Storytelling Traditions

> But what it could have been, you ken,
> it could've been some kind of reflection—
> It could've been anything.
> But [laughs]
> I never saw it the second time.
> But Isaac and Adam saw it.
> I never liked that road to walk on after that. (TS98004)

Eckie's story has all the classic elements of legend. He narrates a troubling experience that neither he nor his companions understand. He also invites us to consider the narrated events and try to puzzle out what actually happened, as he does in his comments at the end of the story or as listeners must do in hearing "The Tinker and the Skeletons." Like many ghost stories, this story is partly entertainment and partly serious. We laugh at the absurdity of the situation. Yet, the story also serves as a way of questioning and challenging beliefs about the world. Are ghosts real? If so, what do we need to know about them to better live our lives? Should we avoid this particular stretch of road? Should we keep our vehicles perfectly tuned so we can be ready to make a speedy escape? If ghosts are not real, what are we missing that might explain these puzzling experiences?

Burker stories are a special class of legends, found only among Travellers (see Henderson 1970). These stories generally tell of narrow escapes from "Burkers," or body snatchers, who purportedly travel the countryside to collect fresh bodies for medical research. The name derives from the historical figure of William Burke "who was hanged in Edinburgh in 1829 for selling murdered victims to Dr. Knox's anatomy school" (Henderson 1992, 223–24). Some Travellers said their ancestors felt they were particularly at risk from Burkers because the combination of Traveller nomadism and non-Traveller dislike of Travellers meant that Travellers would neither be missed nor cared about in situations of foul play.

During an interview Duncan talked of how Burker stories were sometimes told as warnings for children to stay close to camp and to be suspicious of strangers. Yet the stories go beyond this function in terms of the way they relate actual events that place adult Travellers at risk. Consider the following story Duncan told during our conversation (For additional Burker tales see Douglas 1987, 103–5, 150–51; Williamson 1983 143–52):

I remember my father telling me a true Burker story.
This is true.
Because . . . they did steal Tinkers' bodies, they did.
For early medical research, they did.
Because, you see, Donald,
the Travellers were not registered.
No one knew how many there were.
Do you see what I mean?

And if they took a body,
whether it be a man, woman, or child,
they were never missed.
The Travellers never reported it.
There were no cases took to law.
And if they needed a body for medical research,
then they just (?) "We are going to get a Traveller."
Do you see what I mean?
Sometimes it was two or three Travellers.

But anyhow.
My father telled me this wonderful little story.
I don't know if it is true or not.

But anyhow.
There were a group of Travellers,
a man and his wife and a family, four or five of a family.
Away down on the West Coast, a long time ago.
They had special places to camp on, you know.
And these were the days of horses and coaches.

Now.
Every coach that passed by to the Travellers was taboo,
maybe a mail coach
or maybe a family going home late at night.
"Burkers!"
When they heard the horses' feet.
There was no cars.

But one particular camping site,
The coach—
Now the thing was,
if it passed by once,
it passed by twice,
the same coach,
then they got a little wary.

If it passed by and didn't stop,
"Och," they'll say, "it is maybe something."
But if that coach went by
   and then came back again
     and back again,
then they got wary.
What was they after?
What was he doing?
Why was he passing so much by their tenting site?

But anyhow.
This group of Travelling People was camped by a,
in a camping site away down the West Coast.
And this coach passed by,
three men sitting up in the front.
And when they came where the Travellers was camped—
   because their camp was by the side,
   and they had an out campfire—
they slowed the horses,
and they didn't stop.
They slowed the horses,
and all looked at the Travellers.
And the Travellers all looked at them.
It was daylight.
It was not dark,
And they went on.

Then about half an hour they come back again.
And they looked at the Travellers.
And the Travellers looked at them.
Coach went on.

They come back again the third time.
The Travellers said, "It's Burkers."
See?

Now.
The Travellers always kept little dogs for keeping their pots supplied,
you know, rabbits,
kept little dogs.
They always kept the little dogs tied up,
in case they would go away and get lost, wander
or somebody would steal them.
Because these dogs were very special to them.

They had a little greyhound, a little whippet.
He was a little killer, you know.
He was deadly for rabbits.
And the family loved this little whippet.

Now.
The Travellers when they had an outside fire,
they always kept pots and pans lying out in the grass, you know?
Washed them and put them in little places in the grass.
They always kept these pots, homemade pots.

So.
They said, "That's Burkers."
The man went, and his wife, and he took the blankets,
and he went off into the wood,
away and left the tents,
left the fire burning.
They would be safe in the wood.
Nobody could find them in a big thick wood.

My father told me this story a long time ago.
And he said it is a true story.
Maybe it was a man and his wife and maybe four or five kids,
and maybe a sister or something,
maybe an old aunt stayed with them.

Off they went to hide theirselves in the wood,
because it was beginning to get dark.
And then they looked,
and they saw the lights of the coach coming along again.
When the coach came to the fireside, it stopped.
And they could see through the wood.
The men climbed down from the coach.
Another two came out from the back of the coach, that was in the back.
You know these coaches were very big.
They saw them come into the campsite.
They saw them throwing up the tent covers,
throwing out everything.
They searched that tent.
The Travellers was gone.

But the Travellers sat there all night long, till morning.
They knew nobody would touch them in daylight.
The coach waited at that tent site for about, at least an hour.

And then it was gone.
Climbed back in the coach and was gone.

So the Travellers, when the daylight came,
maybe seven o'clock or eight o'clock in the morning,
they come down from the wood to their campsite.
The camp was in a mess.
Everything was scattered, high and low.
Pots and pans was kicked around the whole place.

And one man says, "Where's my wee dog?"
"Where's my wee dog?"
"Where's my wee dog?"
They went over to the rope where the wee dog was tied.
They forgot to loosen the wee dog.
And one woman went over,
and she gasped in amazement.
For she had a big pot,
and there was the wee dog with its throat cut
and head, stuck head into the pot.
They cut its throat and stuck its head into the pot.

That's true.
My father told me that many, many times. (TS92022)

Whether or not listeners believe that Burkers actually roam the countryside looking for fresh bodies, the stories warn that danger may come from the settled world. Burker tales like this one remind Travellers that there has been a long history of discrimination and violence against Travellers. They may also be used to instill a healthy fear of outsiders in Traveller children. These stories therefore reinforce the desire for isolation and strengthen the sense of shared identity in Traveller communities.

Lies

While cracks have firm grounding in the events of the lived world, this does not mean they are purely factual. A degree of artistic play is an expected part of the process of telling cracks. This creative element was clearly acknowledged in an interview with Jimmy Williamson and Eckie Sutherland.

ES   But when they start talking about like some wee thing like that,
a wee incident like that—
JW   Somebody will (woop?) eh? [gesture of stretching]
ES   That's right.
JW   That happens constantly.
ES   And it goes back and forward,
back and forward,
back and forward.
Later on it gets embroidered,
and stretched, [laughs]
JW   [laughs]
ES   And widened. [laughter] (TS98013)

As experience stories are progressively stretched and widened they blur into the genre of expressive lies where the teller deliberately bends the truth and plays with the coherence of the narrated events.

Similarly, tellers of lies might play with truth by portraying events that happened to others as actually happening to themselves:

DB   Would people then tell their stories about what somebody else had experienced?
DW   They would tell their stories.
And I've heard stories told by a person
who heard a story from another person's experience
and put theirself in it.
DB   Oh, I see.
DW   See what I mean?
That happened many times.
I mean, you would tell me a story that happened to you.
The next time I met somebody else,
I would tell them that story happened to me.
And you get the same story happened to a lot of people.
You see what I mean?
So you knew in your own mind,
that this is just a story
because it couldn't have happened to everybody. (TS92034)

Willie MacPhee noted many Travellers were fond of joking with each other and "swearing on all that was holy" that exaggerations or lies were true (TS93028). This practice should be seen as part of the play with language that permeates Traveller interactions. Eckie and Jimmy insisted that this expressive lying was not intended to be malicious.

DB   Well, now, another kind of story that I've heard told a lot
     are the, the sort of the
     sort of the people telling tall tales
     or stretching the truth a little bit and so on.
ES   Oh they did they certainly do that.
JW   [laughs]
ES   [laughs] Tall tales.
DB   Is that all in fun?
ES   It was in fun, aye.
DB   Just entertainment.
ES   Entertainment value only. (TS98013)

When I asked about the kinds of tall tales or lies Travellers might tell, Duncan Williamson told me about old man Townsley, saying he was "the biggest liar ever." He said Townsley told a story about a time he was burning the brush left behind from a logging operation:

> He made a big pile of ash one night.
> The next day he came back to re-light the fire and burn more,
> when a huge bumblebee, "the size of my thumb," flew into that pile.
> [Cough, cough, cough.] He coughed.
> He swore he could hear that bumblebee cough. (paraphrased from field
>   notes 4/17/93)

Duncan related another story Old Man Townsley told about a man playing golf.

> He placed a ball on a tee and stood ready to drive.
> The ball spoke to him,
> "No, not like that. . . .
> Calm down.
> Steady yourself."
> The man listened for half an hour,
>   and finally put his club in the bag,
>   and walked off,
>   leaving the ball there.
> Because he couldn't face hitting a ball that had been talking to him.
>   (paraphrased from field notes 4/17/93)

Overview of Traveller Storytelling Traditions

Eckie Sutherland similarly recalled how events might be stretched in the telling. In talking about a long journey, Eckie said the teller might comment:

> When they walk along the road,
> the stanes was making holes in the soles of their feet,
> the birds was making nests on the crown of their heads. (TS98013)

As an illustration of how tellers might exaggerate, Eckie then recounted one of the stories that he heard from Jimmy's Uncle Jack.

> He telled me one night he was up at Campbelltown,*
> and he was lying in his bed.
> He says, "Me and Mary was not long together," he said.
> And he says, eh, "We had been out working all day.
> Come back at night, and we lay down," he says.
> "I was lying in my bed," he says.
> "I could feel my heart," he says,
> "going thump, thump, thump."
> And he says, "I lay for a good while," he says.
> "But it must have been about half-an-hour lying," he says,
> "listening to my heart
>   beating away,
>   beating away."
> And he says, "All of a sudden it stopped." [laughter]
> "My heart stopped," he says,
> "completely stopped.
> So I roared to Mary,
> "Mary, Mary, Mary,
> my heart's stopped!"
> She got up.
> "NO, JACK!"
> And that was it.
> The heart started again, he said.
> That was it. [laughter] (TS98013)

Expressive lying was so much a part of playful interaction that it sometimes became difficult to tell when something was a lie and when some-

---

*Campbelltown is a town at the southern end of the Mull of Kintyre in Argyll.

86 *Overview of Traveller Storytelling Traditions*

thing was intended as a factual presentation. I asked about how distinctions could be made.

DB How do you tell when somebody is telling you the truth then?
ES You cannae. [all laugh]
ES You can't do that.
    I'll tell you that much.
DB Or do you just have to know the person?
JW Know them.
    You know them.
ES You have to know the person.
JW Know them, aye.
ES Usually if they swear into it.
JW Aye.
ES If they swear,
    say, "My hand to God" or
    "As sure as death" or
    something like that—
DB Yeah.
    Then you know it is a true story. (TS98013)

While expressive lies build on a stretching and widening of events to the point where they transcend the believable or even the possible, these stories still present themselves as having a grounding in the world of lived experience. It is for this reason that expressive lies are included as crack. Yet, in a very real sense expressive lies bridge the gap between experientially based stories and the world of fictional stories. It is to this realm of fictional storytelling that I now turn attention.

III. Folktales—The Realm of Fiction

The second major category of Traveller stories is folktales, stories that are explicitly framed as fictional accounts. Since these stories are usually quite long, I do not present sample texts in this section, but see "The Laird and the Crane" in the introduction, "The Traveller and the Hare" in chapter 2, "The Fox and the Crow" and "Cinderella" in chapter 3, "The Fox and the Dog" in chapter 4, and "The Black Laird and the Cattleman" and "The Boy and the Blacksmith" in chapter 5.

Folktales differ from cracks in that they make no claim the events they replay have actually happened at some past time. Yet these stories do relate to the world of lived experience in the sense that places and characters are often modeled on the narrator's own experiences (Dégh 1972). Duncan Williamson, in fact, makes the claim that the best folktales are the stories that perhaps have never happened but "could have happened" in the sense that they do not diverge too significantly from the patterns of daily life (TS92034).

A second factor that distinguishes folktales from cracks is the length of the story. This distinction came out clearly in a discussion with Jimmy Williamson and Eckie Sutherland.

DB Well, I remember when Jock Burke came in the other night.
    I mean he was full of short little stories like that.
JW That's, that's continual all the time.
    He does that all the time.
    That's just classed as crack though.
    That's not classed as stories.
    That's just classed as crack.
DB But there are stories as part of that crack.
JW Aye, aye.
ES Aye.
DB But where do you see the line with stories?
    Stories are the longer ones?
    Would you call this story a story? [the crack about Jack's heart transcribed in the previous section]
ES No.
JW It is just crack.
ES No, that's just a crack.
JW Aye.
ES No, a story goes on maybe for (two hours?)
JW If you asked him for stories,
    stories to him is the wonder tales like the long saga things, eh?
DB Right.
ES Two hours or three hours I seen a story go on.
    I have seen me sitting for about a fortnight. [all laugh]
JW Getting a bit.
ES Aye, you'd get a bit one, you'd maybe get about an hour a night.
    And then the following night,
    you were keen to get everything done to get the rest of that story.
    It was a serial.

> And it went on for about a week.
> Maybe ten days.
> And that's no exaggerating.
> That's genuine. (TS98013)

This exchange highlights a possible third attribute of folktales: that they are sometimes told in installments. Where newsing stories or family stories or legends urgently communicate vital information, folktales serve to entertain or teach in less immediate ways and therefore may be spread over time.

One important audience for Traveller folktales has always been children. This is especially true with storytelling that takes place within the family. In the Williamson family, stories permeated the daily routine and formed an integral part of adult/child interactions. Betty Townsley, Duncan Williamson's daughter, commented, "Daddy used to toast us bread on the fire, on the front of the fire . . . and he was busy telling us a story or doing something when he was toasting us bread. And we really liked it" (TS92025). She went on to say that she also heard personal experience stories and folktales stories while spending time with her grandmother.

BT   My granny, my daddy's mother . . .
       she was great at telling stories.
DB   Again, just at bedtime or—
BT   No. . . . She used to stay with us.
       And, eh, Granny would, in the morning,
       she would come up and I would do her hair.
       She says, "Will you comb my hair?" . . .
       She had blond hair similar to mine you know? . . .
       And she says, ". . . Can you do my hair?"
       And I said, "Can you tell me a story Granny?"
       as I combed her hair.
       And sometimes she would tell me stories
       about way back when she workit in the castle in Inverary,*
       and all the things that happened there.
       And other times she would tell me stories, fairy stories. (TS92025)

Edie MacPhee, Duncan's oldest daughter by his first marriage, talked of how her father spread stories throughout the day by telling them in installments:

---

*Inverary is a town at the head of Loch Fyne in Argyll.

EM Well, when . . . he started working at Kincraigie,
    he was working with cattle.
    He was a cattleman.
    And I think I was about 5, maybe.
    I was at school . . . and, eh, maybe about—
    Dinner time come—
    he was working on the harvest—
    he would tell us a bit of a story.
    At nighttime he would tell us the rest of it, sort of thing.
    That's the way it would go.
DB How long would they last?
    Would they go over days and days or—
EM Mostly two days, maybe two nights.
    That's the way of making it interesting, you see,
    to keep us occupied.
DB Would he sort of leave you at a very important part in the story?
EM Aye, you know what like he is, eh?
DB Yeah.
EM He'd get you to an exciting bit
    and then he would stop and say,
    "Oh, I'll tell you that tomorrow," or,
    "I'll tell you that when I get back from work." (TS93025)

Betty similarly talked about how Duncan would tell bedtime stories:

BT [He] . . . used to sit down and tell us stories.
    And he always telled us stories in like a sequence,
    one every night.
    Same story, but a part every night. . . .
    What we used to do is . . . give us all something to eat. Right?
    And eh, he would put us all sitting down [or] . . .
    he would put us all to bed,
    and he would maybe sit on the log at the front.
    And he would tell us these different stories.
DB Right.
    And how would he stop for the night?
    I mean would he just—
BT He would say,
    "Well, kids, youse get to sleep tonight and, eh,
    I'll tell you the next part tomorrow."
DB Would he get to an exciting part and kind of leave you hanging there?
BT Mhmm. (?) sort of cliff-hanging bit. [laughs]
    It was nice.
    It really was lovely. (TS92025)

Yet children are not the only audience for folktale performances. Where families work together, stories might be told for the benefit of both children and adults. Betsy and Bryce Whyte remember hearing stories told during the work of the potato harvest (SA75.107). Eckie Sutherland similarly recalled hearing a man named Johnson tell stories to keep the workers, and especially the children, engaged and working during the turnip thinning:

ES He was an old man,
 well, he wasn't an old man,
 but at the time I thought he was old.
 He would be 'round about 35 or 40 maybe.
 And we were thinning turnips in the fields.
 And he would tell stories,
 start and tell stories from the top
 and keep everybody working beside him,
 all the young ones,
 keep them going up and down the field.
DB So, was he working while he was doing that?
ES Aye he was working and telling stories. . . .
 And, eh, that way, we couldn't,
 we had all the kids,
 my sisters and nephews and nieces
 and them all that was working in the field.
 He would tell the story,
 and everybody worked to keep up with him to hear the story.
 And, eh, my father and mother was there as well.
 But this is how he told the stories.

 And he'd maybe tell us a story at the start of the field,
 and you would only get about the half of it to the other side.
 And then, after that, I mean, you had to start again.
 But, when that started first
 I wasna old enough to thin turnips,
 so I just walked along side of him.
 That was a long time ago. (TS98013)

As comments I presented earlier suggest, folktales are also told among adults when they are camped together. During one interview, Edie MacPhee suggested that a good deal of adult storytelling takes place after the children are put to bed.

EM	We were put to our beds
	and the adults would sort of get round the fire
	and they would tell stories to each other....
	I know there was adult stories.
	Did he ever tell you about that?
	Did my dad?
DB	He said some of that, but he, you know,
	he said a lot of the same stories he is telling now were the adult stories.
EM	Aye.
	But they were, you know,
	like they were put different ways, you know?
SG	A little more racy as they say?
EM	Aye. (TS93025)

She said these "adult stories" weren't "allowed for the kids."

Not all Travellers are interested in the same kinds of folktales, however. During one conversation Duncan Williamson said that some Travellers specialize in telling certain kinds of stories:

DW	Somebody told ghost stories, famous for telling ghost stories.
	Somebody was famous for telling Burker stories—
	even though they actually took place.
	But the way he could tell it about the, tell a Burker story.
	And I mean they really enjoyed him telling Burker stories.
	Somebody told Jack Tales.
	See what I mean?
	And there's a wee man his,
	well my oldest lassie is married onto his son.
	And you know the nickname they called him?
	"The Pot o' Gold."
DB	"The Pot o' Gold?"
DW	That was his nickname
	because he always told stories about where,
	there was always found a pot of gold at the end of the story.
DB	Ahaa.
DW	And they nicknamed him "The Pot o' Gold."
	His name was Isaac Stewart and he was a great storyteller. (TS87013)

He went on to say that some Travellers who actively pursued folktales developed reputations because of their skill in telling these stories:

> There was some people who were respected as good storytellers,
> apart from the rest.

> No[t] everyone told stories.
> Not everyone told stories.
> But when old Johnny Townsley
>   or old Sandy Reid
>   or old Johnny MacDonald
> was around the campfires
> and they started to tell a story,
> everybody listened.
> Because they knew their business they knew their job.
> They loved stories.
> They collected stories. (TS87013)

Those, like Johnny Townsley, Sandy Reid, or Johnny MacDonald, who take a particular interest in folktales actively seek out other tellers and swap stories. Willie MacPhee noted that this is a primary mechanism whereby these stories are learned and shared among family groups:

> You see . . . most of the stories Duncan . . . [knows] . . .
> he heard them from his folk, you see . . . and from other people.
> And most of the stories that I know,
> I heard them from my people.
> But, eh, they were just the same type of stories.
> Because all the Travellers . . . went from one to another
> and telled one another stories.
> They'd say (to you?),
> "Oh, did you ever hear this yin?"
> and then (that's how?) "Oh, I heard that yin,
> You'll have to tell me another yin." [laughter]
> "Did you hear this yin?" (you know to him?)
> "Ah, no.
> Och, I heard that yin.
> Ach, that's an old story that.
> I heard that already.
> Think on something else."
> So this was the way they learned their stories. (TS92029)

Some insight into why Travellers might want to learn and retell folktales comes from Duncan Williamson's own motivation to do this:

> So I was interested, you see. . . .
> I was collecting everything I could find.
> Because I knew in my mind that someday,

because I was young,
people would die and (?) take their stories with them to the grave.
And I didn't want their stories and songs to go with them to their grave.
Because my old granny used to sing to me when she [sic] was very young and tell me stories.
Well, my granny died.
There was a big loss in my life
because there were no more stories of the old people around any more.
So I said,
"I'm going to set out.
I'm going to find all the old Travelling People—
not the young Travelling People,
I had little time for the young even though I was young myself—
find the old Travelling People
who has got the sort of knowledge of things that I want to find."
So, I stayed with them,
   I worked with them.
      I visited them.
         I carried on brought them a little drink and—
but no recording—
a tape recorder running in my head. (TS93015)

Duncan says he learned many of his best stories from people like Johnny Townsley, Sandy Reid, and Johnny MacDonald. He also credits his father and grandmother for passing on many wonderful stories and ballads. I believe one of Duncan's best traits as a storyteller is his ability to listen. He recognizes the value of each individual Traveller he meets as well as the value of the stories passed on within that person's own family. For example, Duncan's children told me how he spent time with Maggie Cameron, a Traveller who was much older than he was, taking her to the shops or on other errands so he could exchange stories with her and learn what she had to teach him about the ways of the older Travellers (TS92025).

Because they are fictional, folktales are often assumed to be a simple form of entertainment. For the Travellers these stories do entertain, but this does not mean the stories are no more than an amusing diversion. Entertainment is serious business. Tellers might use storytelling performances to generate states of mind or emotions in the listeners—such as wonder, contentment, confusion, or amusement—in order to serve a variety of functions. Duncan Williamson's description of the role of stories in Traveller life makes this point explicitly:

> When we walked on the roads in the cold winter's day,
> and we were wet and tired and hungry . . .
> When we got to a camping place at night,
> we were miserable and tired.
> But once the tents was up,
>   the fires was kindling,
>   we had a little to eat,
>   got wirselves dried,
>   and then it become story time.
> The thought of everything else,
> the thought of the day's torture was gone
> 'til the next time again.
> After a good storytelling session everybody was happy. (TS87001)

The ability of storytelling performance to influence the listeners' state of mind arises partly through the content of the specific story and partly through the intimacy that is part of the performance process. Nancy MacDonald illustrated this process nicely when she talked about how her son Jimmy, who is perfectly capable of reading stories out of books and knows his father's stories "word by word," nonetheless prefers oral storytelling. As Nancy concluded: "He'll just tell you, 'I'm no wanting a story out of a book. I want yin oot of your mooth' " (TS93018).

A second function of folktale performance is education. Consider the following comment from Duncan Williamson about the kinds of stories that would be most appropriate for children of a certain age:

Between the ages of three and five, a Traveller child hears stories about animals, such as the fox, the rabbit and the birds—stories in which animals can speak. From the very beginning a child is taught to be gentle and kind to animals, to love and respect creation. For everything a Traveller needs to know can be learned from nature: in their own environment in their own way, animals can take care of themselves.

The older child, from the time he is about six, hears many stories where the hero is called Jack—tales of fortune and tales of cleverness. In these stories Jack may be lazy and appear daft, but he is not too greedy or cowardly or bad. . . . Devil stories, ghost stories, and Burker tales are most suitable for children beyond the age of ten.

Between the ages of twelve and fourteen, Traveller children are considered mature. Socially that means they are permitted to sit around the fire and listen to anything: then they are expected to sit like men and women, tell their own cracks [short, loosely formed stories on any subject] and longer stories. (quoted in D. Williamson 1983, xviii)

Duncan comments eloquently on the importance of the educational function of stories within his own life:

When I come to a puzzle and I cannae see my way around this puzzle I think back on the stories my father told me and try and analyze what he told me in these bygone days, and there's always a solution. Because thinking back on these tales I can find a solution. (quoted in L. Williamson 1981, 71)

His awareness of the educational value of stories is, in fact, what motivated Duncan to teach his own children through storytelling:

I would like my daughter to gain the same knowledge my father taught me . . . it's telling her how to live in the world as a natural human being. . . . number one my father told me not to be greedy. Number two, he taught me not to be foolish. Number three he taught me not to be daft or selfish *by stories*. . . . He was teaching us to be able to understand by his tales what was in store for us in the future. (quoted in L. Williamson 1981, 70—emphasis in original)

Others, such as Aberdeenshire Traveller Stanley Robertson, spoke similarly about the broad education that took place through Traveller stories. He said he was receiving not only amusement but also language, literature, and history through the ballads and stories of his folk (TS93013).

Some of the younger Travellers I got to know said the education they received through stories included both deeply held values and beliefs and pragmatic knowledge of how to survive in daily life. Betty Townsley, for example, said stories she heard "taught you to be good and be trustful and not to tell lies and things," or "don't be greedy and help" (TS92025). She also said that fictional stories could impart pragmatic understanding of the lived world. In speaking of the stories her Uncle Jimmy told her, she said:

BT He was telling stories about farm work.
    You know what I mean?
    So you're actually getting taught but in story.
    Does that make sense?
DB So even, . . . like horses and how to deal with horses you were learning

BT Mhmm.
    or stories like how the boy would maybe shoe the horse.
    And you were listening to this.
    Say Jack, for instance, had a problem with a horse.
    And he's telling Jack how to fix the horse and how—
    Well, if you come across the same problem—
DB You've got it right there.
BT See what I mean?
    You know what I'm getting at.
    It's actually trying to teach you
    but not to sort of bossing you. (TS92025)

Betty's comment suggests that the educational process involved in storytelling is one that leaves it up to listeners to take what they want and need from a given telling. In chapter 2, I will develop a model that demonstrates how the lessons and meanings of storytelling performances are very much the product of the listener's interpretive process and are not fully proscribed by the narrator.

While it might be argued that the educational content of the traditional folktales is out of date with respect to Traveller life in the modern world, Duncan Williamson would not agree. He believes that human beings have changed very little over the centuries. During a discussion of the wisdom in stories, Duncan commented:

> You see the problem is that even today,
> though we have come so far forward in our life in the twentieth century,
> we still do the same things that was done over nine hundred years ago:
> We eat,
>   we sleep,
>   we drink,
>   we make love, right?
> We fight,
>   we argue,
>   we steal.
> Nothing has changed.
> We look for money,
>   we are greedy,
>   we're selfish,
>   we are ignorant,
>   we are stupid.
> The same things that have gone on for nine hundred, over a thousand years.

Nothing has come forward.
We're more modernized,
  and we have got cars and airplanes and things.
But that is just a means of transportation.
But the actual things that means the most important to your life
is the things that was still around of today. (TS93015)

It is in this sense that centuries-old stories provide a medium Travellers use to teach deeply held values and understandings of what it means to be both a human being and a Traveller.

Folktales serve other significant functions in Traveller lives as well. For example, folktales provide both a literal (in the sense of the co-presence of tellers and listeners) and symbolic (in terms of the content of the stories) thread of continuity that binds Travellers to each other in community. Similarly, the fictional world of folktales provides a fertile medium for negotiating identity and belief about the world. I do not develop and support these ideas here since I do so in chapter 3 and chapters 4 and 5 respectively.

IV. The Intersection of Traveller and Non-Traveller Narrative Traditions

Although Travellers mostly tell stories to other Travellers and non-Traveller presence at storytelling performances might be seen as a product of scholarly or revivalist interest in Traveller traditions, it would be a mistake to presume that Traveller storytelling traditions were completely isolated from non-Traveller circles before the present time. After all, Travellers have lived in relationship with non-Travellers throughout their lives. An examination of the overlap in Traveller and settled folktale and ballad repertoires, for instance, suggests that there has been ongoing interaction and exchange between the two groups (e.g. Henderson and Collinson 1965; Douglas 1985).

During one interview, Duncan Williamson proposed that stories might find their way into Traveller circles by way of friendly visitors:

Well, as I told you,
where the Travellers got some of their stories from was—
Maybe they're sitting at a campfire by the side of the beach
   or maybe a hill road,
      maybe in an old quarry somewhere,
         kind of derelict land.
And some old crofter or some old shepherd,
coming back from the pub late at night,
would wheel his bike down and place his bike on its side.
Maybe he made an excuse to come in for a light,
and said, "Hello, how long have you been here?" and,
"Are you comfortable tonight?"
And they would say,
"An old gadgie."*
Maybe he had a bottle of whiskey.
And he'd sit doon and,
"Would you like a drink?"
Well naturally the men wouldnae refuse a drink, you know.
And eh they would sit down.
And one crack would lead to another,
and they would say,
"Maybe the old gadgie kens a story?"
They were always interested in a story.
Travellers always (?) for stories, do you know what I mean,
so's they could pass them on the next time they met.
It was a great thing to have a strange story that somebody never heard.
That was a great thing.
Because stories were told so often
that naturally the Travellers got used to the same person
   telling the same story a lot of times. . . .
So they would pull as much out of the old crofting man as they could.
The kind of stories he heard when he was a child. . . .
They didnae want to know about the man. . . .
They wanted the stories he had learned, you ken,
the traditional stories, oral telled by his grandfather,
telled by his uncle. (TS87013)

As noted in the previous section, Duncan was keenly interested in stories since he was a young man. He actively collected stories from Traveller storytellers. Yet Duncan was also interested in stories told by non-Travellers. He speculated that his interest in these stories was awakened

---

gadgie = Traveller cant for *man*

beginning at age 14 in Argyll when he worked for several years with Neil MacCallum, a non-Traveller stonemason and drystone diker:

> I think what started off with me, Donald,
> was when I took up employment with this old crofting man, Neil
>   MacCallum,
> and worked with him,
>   and talked to him,
>   and heard some of his tales.
> Then I said to myself,
> "I've heard manys of stories from my father.
> I've heard many stories from my uncle
>   and my aunt
>   and my grandmother.
> And if I am going to be interested in stories,
> there must be other stories just as good as mine among the non-Travellers."
> So I start collecting stories from the non-Travellers.
> And when I came to a session around the campfires,
> I could tell a story that they never heard.
> And that's what made me popular in the stories. (TS87013)

Duncan's interest in stories causes him to seek out new stories from non-Travellers whenever he has the chance to do so. To illustrate this point, his daughter, Edie MacPhee, talked about riding with her father while he was on his rounds gathering scrap metal. She said Duncan would often tell stories to non-Travellers as part of his ongoing business interaction and suggested these storytellings not only enhanced his ability to get scrap but also encouraged his sources to tell stories of their own (TS93026). She said this practice provided him with "fresh material" for his storytelling within the Traveller community. Duncan also credits many settled crofters for teaching him their stories (for example see Williamson 1985 and 1992).

Duncan's interest in the folklore of non-Travellers is not unique, however. Many stories and especially songs have similarly come into Traveller repertoires through encounters with non-Travellers. Sheila Douglas, for example, notes that John Stewart learned one of his stories from his father, who in turn learned it from a old storyteller he met during a visit to Ireland (1987, 9). Belle Stewart remembers her father sought out and learned two of his ballads from a plowman at a farm where he worked (MacColl and Seeger 1986, 31). Willie MacPhee told me he learned several of his songs from non-Traveller performers or even commercial recordings (TS92018). In her thesis on Traveller ballads Linda Williamson even identifies country and western songs, and especially Jimmy Rogers songs, as one popular category of Traveller singing traditions (1985, 58).

Print sources have also played a role in the influx of stories into Traveller culture. Despite the general assumptions that Travellers are illiterate, many read and may have learned stories from books. For instance, Duncan talked about his grandfather's brother, Sandy Williamson, who died about 1890. Duncan knows from family stories that Sandy knew how to read and that he owned many books, including a copy of the *Arabian Nights*. He said that Sandy would sometimes sit with others around the fire and read them stories (TS93005; SA76.112).

Stories also flowed from the Travellers to the settled populations. Evidence of this comes from early folktale collectors who were well aware of Traveller storytelling abilities. Collector Joseph Campbell includes two stories in his collection *Popular Tales of the West Highlands* ([1860] 1983) that he attributes to John MacDonald, a "travelling tinker." Of John MacDonald and his son, Campbell comments: "They do not simply tell the story, but act it with changing voice and gesture, as if they took an interest in it, and entered into the spirit and fun of the tale" (179). He laments not being able to collect more stories because "the wandering spirit of the man would not let him rest to dictate his story" (179).

Scholars studying Gypsies at the turn of the century also made forays into Traveller culture in Scotland. Although their interest was primarily historical (e.g. MacRitchie 1894), linguistic, or sociological, they at times paid attention to stories. Andrew McCormick, for example, relates several folktales from an elderly Traveller woman in his book *The Tinkler-Gypsies* ([1907] 1973). Francis Hindes Groome includes a chapter titled "Scottish-Tinker Stories" in his book *Gypsy Folk Tales* ([1899] 1963). Several more texts can be found in early volumes of *The Journal of the Gypsy Lore Society* (e.g. McCormick 1908).

The awareness of Traveller storytelling traditions sometimes extended to the general population. Duncan told me about one incident that took place in the village square in Tomintoul, a village 60 miles west of Aberdeen. He arrived at the square, set up camp, and within minutes schoolchildren were throwing rocks at the tent saying, "Send out the old man and we'll no bother you." Old Johnny MacDonald, a man Duncan lauds as one of the great Traveller storytellers, had been camped in the village square before Duncan arrived. He was a favorite storyteller among Traveller children. He had apparently earned a similar reputation among the village children (see also SA76.066).

The very public presentation of Traveller culture that has taken place through the folk revival in Scotland has opened the door to general awareness of Traveller storytelling and singing traditions (see Munro 1984). This revival has also led to increased scholarly interest. Researchers from all over the world now visit some Travellers and create performance opportunities during recording sessions or during the spontaneous ceilidhs that may develop from these visits. The community of folk performers in Scotland often finds excuses to hold gatherings or ceilidhs that might include Traveller and non-Traveller performers as well as interested scholars from around the world. I had two such ceilidhs at my own home during my fieldwork year. During one ceilidh at Duncan Williamson's house the international crowd of nineteen people included five well-known Traveller performers. During the course of this event Willie MacPhee was moved to comment: "at one time the tinkers was rubbish" that "sixteen years ago they [non-Travellers] would have never dreamed to come into a tinker's place like this" but "people recognize us today" (TS92040).

Several Traveller tellers have become popular among both teachers and schoolchildren because they are hired to bring Scottish oral traditions into the classroom. This practice has also raised the awareness that Traveller schoolchildren, who are often outcasts in the eyes of their classmates, might be similarly competent storytellers. After telling the story of "Jack and the Ax" during a family gathering I attended, young Jimmy Williamson, Duncan's grandson, talked about how he came to tell stories to his classmates when he was in primary 2 (age 7). He told the story "Jack and the Ax" to his teacher:

Willie MacPhee sings during a ceilidh in the author's cottage, 1993

> I telled the teacher [that story], ken,
> just by herself when, when I was getting my meat,*
> And—
> or we were doing gym.
> And she telled everybody to sit down, right?
> And she went and got a chair.
> And she brung it oot.
> And I thought she would maybe bring one of the teachers or somebody in.
> ME she wanted to sit in the chair. [laughter] (TS93012)

The increased flow of stories between Traveller and settled cultures is ongoing. While the effect of this transfer on either culture cannot be determined without focused research, I believe Traveller storytelling performances provide a means through which Travellers can present aspects of their cultural identity to non-Traveller audiences. This exposure to Traveller stories may challenge some non-Traveller stereotypes of Traveller identity and may eventually lead to greater understanding between the groups.

---

*meat = food, lunch

2. "It Could Have Happened"

Storytelling, Identity, and Worldview

As I have already argued in this book, Traveller stories, songs, and ballads are not an isolated category of "things Travellers know." There is a deep interconnection between Traveller stories and Traveller lives. One place where this connection is particularly apparent is in the relationship among stories, worldview, and identity. Understanding the nature of this connection, however, requires a closer look at what I mean by the terms *worldview* and *identity*.

At the outset, it is important to note that personal and cultural identity are not somehow synonymous with superficial artifacts of lifestyle. For example, Travellers living on the road, on government sites, or in fixed housing may all equally share the same cultural identity. Instead, I believe that both personal and cultural identity fundamentally involve a continuity in perception of similarity or difference between self and other (see Burke 1969, 22; Erikson 1968, 50; Dundes 1983, 237–39; Mathisen 1993; Oring 1994). In this sense, identity is a perception based on ongoing interaction among people over time. Central to perceptions of identity is an awareness of how others engage the world as expressed through their words and actions. A person who is perceived to approach or interpret the world in a similar way is perceived to have a similar identity. Someone who is perceived to approach and interpret the world differently is perceived to have a differing identity.

I will use *worldview*[1] as an inclusive term to refer to the underlying factors that shape how a person engages the world. Worldview depends on the underlying ideational systems, belief systems, or "webs of signification" (Geertz 1973, 3-30) that community members develop over time through the unfolding of individual experience with the world in relation to community interaction. Though not determinative, worldview is an influential resource that informs an individual's perceptions, interpretations, and constructions of meaning and therefore shapes how he or she interacts with and engages the world. In this sense, the premium Travellers place on freedom and autonomy, and the choice they make for family over economic success, can be said to be expressions of Traveller worldview. Ultimately, then, perceptions of identity are based in perceptions of similarity or difference in worldview.

It does not follow, however, that a perception of difference in worldview leads to understanding the origins and implications of such a difference. Because the ideational systems, belief systems, or webs of signification on which worldview is based remain unquestioned at a deep level of "common sense," it may not be apparent that individuals interpret fundamental aspects of the world around them in very different—and equally viable—ways. Consequently, when individuals in one culture try to understand those of another culture, differences are often perceived ethnocentrically from within the framework of the individual's own worldview. The outsider view of Traveller culture discussed in the introduction is a case in point. This view builds on a valid perception of difference in identity but attributes this difference to the belief that Travellers are failed citizens, social deviants, or survivals from an earlier stage of human evolution.

Several key properties of worldview, and by implication identity, follow from my definition. First, in proposing that worldview is formed through the unfolding of individual experience with the world in relation to community interaction, I mean to imply that worldview, and therefore identity, only exist as emergent personal constructs that are shaped through interactions with other people over the course of time. These personal constructs are not necessarily systematic or coherent but pragmatic, providing an essential framework that is as complete as it needs to be to orient individuals to their world and to their community.

Second, and as a corollary of my first point, by virtue of differing experiences, interests, and needs, individuals will form differing constructs of worldview. Listeners may therefore make sense out of a given event in different and divergent ways, even when they are members of the same community. As a consequence of these differences, individuals will formulate and will be perceived to have unique personal identities.

Third, while worldviews are personal constructs, they are not formed in isolation. It is therefore possible to talk about worldview as being shared by the members of a community because personal constructs may be formed, negotiated, and attuned through a continuity of interaction among individuals. Where attunement does take place, individuals may come to identify with a social or cultural group and contrast this cultural identity with that of outsiders—whether those outsiders are perceived as individuals, as members of distinct communities, or as homogeneous groups.

Finally, worldviews are not comprehensive or immutable. Because an individual's worldview is pragmatically formulated, it is only as complete or coherent as his or her experience has required it to be. Consequently, worldviews are open to being reformulated as needed in order to account for new experiences. By this I do not mean to imply that worldviews are superficial or easily changeable. Worldviews are deeply intertwined with the perception of meaning. They are rooted in a continuity of experience that begins at birth and integrates both personal experience and symbolically mediated associations with other people and ancestors. New experiences, however, may challenge the completeness or coherency of an individual's worldview. If the challenge is strong enough and there is sufficient adaptive benefit, these experiences may precipitate a reformulation or reattunement of the person's worldview.

Keep in mind that worldview and identity are deeply intertwined. Identity, as a perception of similarity and difference in worldview, is influenced by already existing constructs of worldview. At the same time, perceptions of identity over time are part of an individual's experience in the world and will therefore have a formative influence on worldview. Constructs of identity and worldview must therefore be understood to emerge through reciprocal influence as an individual ongoingly engages the world. Consequently, where new experiences challenge and precipitate a reformulation of worldview, they also may cause individuals to reformulate their identity and their sense of relationship to others.

Because stories provide a symbolic medium for representing, sharing, and questioning experiences, it is my suggestion that they afford a potent means for challenging and attuning individual constructs of worldview and identity. In this sense, stories are deeply implicated in shaping the beliefs and perceptions that situate individuals with respect to other people and to the world in which they live. Note that stories need not replay "actual events" in order to be used for negotiating worldview and identity. As I argue here, following a storytelling performance is an experience in itself, and this experience may serve to challenge existing constructs of worldview and identity.

In this chapter I therefore begin my investigation of the connection between Traveller stories and Traveller lives by exploring the relationship among storytelling, worldview, and identity. First, I present insights that arise from viewing storytelling as performance and argue that storytelling must be understood as an emergent and creative process wherein performers adapt traditional resources to create meanings and accomplish goals within a specific performance event. In order to clarify this process, I analyze a performance by Duncan Williamson of "The Traveller and the Hare," a traditional Traveller folktale. In particular, I direct attention to the way Duncan creates a multilayered performance experience that engages listeners in a demonstration of the relative validity of Traveller and settled worldviews.

I next focus on the listener's experience of *following* and extracting meaning from storytelling performances. I suggest that this process is experiential in nature and parallels the way we understand experiences in the lived world. I argue that it is the experiential nature of this process that makes storytelling a powerful medium for understanding experience and therefore for negotiating worldview and identity.

In a third section, using a second performance of "The Traveller and the Hare" by Duncan Williamson, I examine how performers can adapt traditional stories to address specific needs of performance events. In this performance, Duncan uses his competency as a storyteller to respond to audience criticism both by spontaneously creating an additional layer of meaning in the story and by intensifying the artistry of his performance.

Finally, since worldviews and identities are formed over time and integrate a wide variety of experiences, I argue that individual storytelling performances must be understood as distinct moments in the ongoing process that takes place in formulating worldview and identity. While the symbolic nature of storytelling enables individual performances to contribute to this process in significant ways, understanding the full relationship between stories and lives requires attention be directed beyond individual performance events to consider the influence of multiple performances over the course of time.

Storytelling as Performance

My conception of the relationship among storytelling, worldview, and identity builds on a reorientation in folklore study from viewing stories as fixed texts that have been handed down over the generations to viewing stories as performance—a perspective that highlights the dynamic qualities of storytelling as social interaction.[2] Approaching storytelling as performance focuses attention on the "doing" of stories or, as Richard Bauman puts it, the "situated use of folklore in the accomplishment of social life" (1989, 177). This sense of performance emphasizes how stories are used as "equipment for living" (Burke 1941). It also highlights the fact that oral stories cannot exist independently of tellers, listeners, and situated performance events, except perhaps as an individual's memory of a past performance event. Any analysis of the function and meaning of a storytelling must therefore address not only the text of performance but also the identities and motivations of the participants in the interaction, the situational and cultural contexts of the event in which they are performed, and the dynamics of the event itself (see Malinowski 1953; Bauman and Briggs 1990, 66–72).

Approaching storytelling as performance also focuses attention on the nature of the communication that takes place. Here performance is understood as:

a special, artful mode of communication, the essence of which resides in the assumption of accountability to an audience for a display of communicative competence, subject to evaluation for the skill and effectiveness with which the act of expression is accomplished. (Bauman 1989, 177; see also Bauman 1977 and D. Hymes 1975b)

Framing a communication as performance directs attention to how the communication is carried out above and beyond its referential content. This framing therefore foregrounds the poetics of the performance and offers the act of expression as "available for the enhancement of experience, through the present enjoyment of the intrinsic qualities of the act of expression itself" (Bauman 1977, 11). This sense of performance therefore highlights the creativity and competency of performers in shaping the exchange that takes place with participants in the performance event.

From a performance-centered perspective, therefore, attention to how a story is told is critical to understanding what it means and what it does. The meaning of a given story will emerge out of the performance interaction. The traditions of a community, therefore, must be viewed as resources that can be adapted through individual creativity to the needs of a performance event. For example, the narrative motifs, themes, and genres passed down through the generations may have culturally recognized meanings and associations that can be creatively used by performers to create new meanings or to interpret current events in the lives of tellers and listeners. Dell Hymes has in fact argued that tradition itself must be understood to be the product of an active process of "traditionalization" through which individuals in the present create and actively maintain the connections to a meaningful past that are essential to personal and social life (1975a, 353–55). In this sense, performers might choose to repeatedly perform specific stories as a way of traditionalizing values, experiences, or events in their lives.

Similarly, the function of a given story will arise out of the performance interaction. Performers may use storytelling to entertain, teach, question what happened, challenge beliefs, shape identity, and so forth. An analysis of a given storytelling event must therefore include an analysis of the artful strategies tellers use in accomplishing their goals in that event. These strategies may involve competent play with basic elements of story such as time, reference, and coherence; the suggestion of meanings through formal patterns created in performance (see Burke 1953; 1969, 57–59); creative adaptations of stories in performance; or the patterning of stylistic elements of the communication.

Performance-centered approaches also call attention to the formative role of the audience in shaping and evaluating the performance. Who is present at a given event, what is happening in the event, and how the audience responds will all influence what stories are told and how the stories are told. Traveller performances among community members, for instance, will call forth differing kinds of stories and story content than will performance interactions that include outsiders such as folklorists or government officials. Listeners also play an active role in evaluating and interpreting performances. Each audience member may therefore come away from a given storytelling with a unique sense of the meaning and function of the performance.

With regard to the relationship among storytelling, worldview, and identity, then, performance-centered approaches warn that stories do not simply replay a static expression of worldview or identity. Given the creativity and emergence of performance, tellers can use stories as a fertile symbolic medium not only for representing but also for transforming conceptions of worldview and identity.

As an example of this process, I turn to a performance by Duncan Williamson of "The Traveller and the Hare," a traditional Traveller folktale. I recorded this story during a visit to the United States that I arranged for Duncan in the fall of 1987. The story was performed on 15 October 1987 during a public concert that took place in Kane Hall at the University of Washington. The concert was advertised as an evening of "Traditional Stories and Ballads from Scotland" and featured Duncan as sole performer. During this event Duncan knew he was performing for a group of people who, though familiar with the storytelling art form, were not necessarily knowledgeable about Scotland or the Travelling People.

The Traveller and the Hare

1   The local Travelling man, like myself,
    travelled through Scotland for many years.

He had never married,
and he didn't have any family.

5   And one day he was far away in the West Highlands
when he took a thought to himself,
and he said to himself,
"You know, I'm getting old.
    And I've traveled far.
10   And I've seen many things.
But what have I got for it?
Nothing!"
He said, "I'll have to do something.
I can't go on like this."

15 And he's walking on talking to himself.
He said, "You're terrible.
You haven't a penny to your name.
All you have is the clothes that stand on your back.
And you're hungry."
20 Talking away to himself.

Then beside the wood he came to a little field.
And in the field sat a great big brown hare.
Eating away at the grass, you know? [mimes wiggling of hare's ears with
    index and middle fingers]

And he stopped.
25 And he looked at the brown hare,
and he smiled to himself.
He said, "At last,
I've found my fortune."
And the hare sat on,
30 eating away at the grass.

He said, "I'm going out to that field,
    and I'm going to catch that hare.
        And I'm going to take it to the butcher
        and sell it, for two-and-sixpence."
35 "And," he says,
"With that two-and-six I'm going to the local market,
    and I'm going to buy mysel a little pig.
        And I'm going to breed with that little pig,
        and I'm going to get some more pigs,
40   and I'm going to sell them."

And the hare's still eating away at the grass,
paying no attention.

And he says, "Then I'm going to start myself a little piggery
and get many, many pigs."
45 And the hare's still eating away at the grass.
[mimes wiggling of hare's ears] [laughter]

"And then," he says,
"I'm going to get myself a nice young wife to run my pig farm." [laughter]
[mimes wiggling of hare's ears]
50 Paying no attention to him.

"And," he says,
"Then I'm going to get two lovely young boys,
and I'm going to grow them up to work for me.
By this time, I'll be retired, and I'll have plenty of money."
55 And the hare is still eating away at the grass. [quiet laughter]

"And," he says, "These boys will be lazy / they'll not be lazy.
Because I'll (?) and make them work hard.
And they'll not lie in their beds in the morning and sleep.
GET UP YOUSE LAZY BOYS!" [shouted]
60 And the hare got such a fright,
it was off. [laughter]

And he watched it disappear in the distance.
And he said to himself,
"Well," as he turned away,
65 "It could have happened." [laughter and applause] (TS87016)

Duncan's performance of this story suggests a number of interconnected interpretational frames that are created as the story unfolds (Goffman 1974, 82). In order to understand how meaning is evoked in the performance of this story, it is necessary to explore these frames and their relationships to each other. The largest frame I consider (Frame A) is that of the concert event itself. This is the frame in which the story is being told. I refer to this frame alternately as the narrative event (see Bauman 1986, 2) or the performance event. This frame is clearly marked by the physical arrangement of the space, the event advertisements, and my behavior and comments in introducing Duncan. These markers set up the expectation that Duncan will assume responsibility for a display of communicative competence in the genres of storytelling and ballad singing. The frame invokes conventionalized understandings of what behaviors are expected to take place and how to interpret those behaviors (understandings that are sufficiently similar in Scotland and the United States). These conventionalized understandings become resources that are available to Duncan to use or to manipulate in his performance. It is within this frame that Duncan performs the "Traveller and the Hare."

In his performance, Duncan uses his formal patterning of the story and his management of temporal references to suggest three further nested interpretational frames. Lines 1–5 introduce and frame the narrated event (Frame B), the event that is replayed through the words and actions of the story (see Bauman 1986, 2–6). The content of line 5 locates the narrated event as taking place "away in the West Highlands" of Scotland. This event is projected to some unstated time in the past through the use of past tense (Silverstein 1976). Duncan further contextualizes the "hero" in line 1 by making the comment that he is a Traveller "like myself." This brief comment invokes the audience's entire knowledge of Duncan and the Travellers, including knowledge gleaned through the event publicity, the concert introduction, and Duncan's performances of and comments about Traveller folklore. This knowledge is a resource listeners use in understanding the narrated event.

A third frame (Frame C) is keyed by the metanarrational comments in Lines 7 and 20 (Babcock 1977, 68). Metanarrational comments are not strictly part of the story but involve the storyteller stepping out of the narrative frame and commenting directly to the audience about how to interpret what is going on in the story, the performance process, or the relationship between performer and audience.[3] Here, these comments key the present tense dialog as being the Traveller's comments to himself within the narrated event. Lines 8–19 take place within this frame and serve to contextualize the narrated event by giving details of the Traveller's age, history, poverty, and hunger. Throughout the performance, frames B and C maintain their relationship within the story. But a temporary reframing takes place (Frame D), one that is crucial to the efficacy and meaning of the story. In lines 31–59 the Traveller in the narrated event spins out a daydream of how the hare in the field will prove to be his fortune. These thoughts are presented in future tense as actions the Traveller is going to do, but they are also expressed with a certainty and detail that suggest these events are actually occurring for the Traveller in the story. This sequence of events is contrasted with the presumed actual state of events (Frame B) in the narrated event by the parallel descriptions of the hare in lines 29–30, 41–42, 45, 49–50, and 55 (e.g. "And the hare sat on, eating away at the grass"). These descriptions suggest to the listener that the Traveller's projected future actions are a creation of his own mind and frame the Traveller's thoughts as a "self-deception" (see Goffman 1974, 111–16) to be contingently accepted as actually taking place for the Traveller as the story unfolds. The repeated descriptions of the hare also act as a metanarrative commentary on the absurdness of the Traveller's self-deception by creating a tension between the earnestness and detail of his vision and the fact that the hare, long since sold to the butcher within the Traveller's reality, continues eating calmly, paying no attention to the Traveller (see especially lines 42 and 50). Gauging from audience reaction, this tension provides one source of humor in the performance. The Traveller's sudden shout in line 59, "GET UP YOUSE LAZY BOYS," scares the hare off and thus discredits the self-deception by removing its one tenuous link to reality. The fantasy world (Frame D) and the frame of the narrated event (Frame B) collapse together leaving the Traveller as alone, poor, and hungry as he was in the beginning of the story. The audience laughs. The Traveller, deprived of the wondrous results of his dream, is calm and reflective as he comments in lines 64–65: "Well . . . it could have happened." The audience laughs again.

This story is more than a humorous anecdote, however. As already noted, the identification of the main character as a Traveller asks each audience member to contemplate his or her knowledge about Traveller identity as contextualizing information that may be useful in understanding the performance. Because audience knowledge of Traveller identity lies outside the narrative event, this identification suggests a connection between the commentary within the narrated event (Frame C) and the lived, "real world" in which the narrative event (Frame A) takes place.

The use of direct speech in the performance further supports the possibility of such a connection between the story and the real world. While lines 7 and 20 indicate this speech reports the words of the Traveller in the narrated event, this speech ambiguously coexists as present tense speech in the performance event and as reported speech from the narrated event (Jakobson 1960, 370–71). Since Duncan comments in line 1 that the Traveller in the story is "like myself," the uncertainty of reference in direct speech raises the possibility that the Traveller's comments are not purely fictional but that they accurately reflect the experience of some Traveller who is "like" Duncan.

This potential relevance of the commentary to the "real world" is further supported by the opening of the story. Lines 1–4 do not frame this performance as a folktale but leave open the possibility that it should be interpreted as a true experience narrative.

The contextualizing information, the use of direct speech, and the possible status of the story as a true experience blur the distinction between the world of the narrated event and the world of "real events." These aspects of the performance suggest an alternate interpretive frame in which the narrated event is not only a fictional event performed for the amusement of the audience but also a serious commentary on Traveller identity, choices, and values that transcends the boundaries of the performance event. After all, "it could have happened," or has the potential to happen to some Traveller in the future.

Depending on the listener's understanding and cultural background, the logic of this commentary on Traveller identity will be perceived differently. To Travellers in the audience and those who have an understanding of Traveller culture, the actions of the Traveller in the story are those of an individual who has abandoned Traveller worldview and accepted settled worldview. This interpretation is supported by a number of features of the performance. For instance, Traveller culture is based on very close ties between individuals, especially at the family level (Neat 1979, 40; Rehfisch 1961). The fact that this Traveller has chosen a solitary lifestyle indicates that he is behaving in a marginal way with respect to Traveller norms. Further evidence of this shift in worldview comes from examining the criticism the Traveller directs at himself in the narrated event. While self-doubt might be a normal response for anyone who has lived with the pervasive discrimination Travellers endure, the Traveller's disappointment at having made nothing of himself is informed by a logic that derives from settled non-Traveller beliefs. Consider the Traveller's decision to pursue pig farming and a life of comfort and security. This choice is based on future-oriented planning that permeates American and perhaps European worldviews (Dundes 1969) but is not a part of Traveller worldview. Travellers prefer to focus on the present rather than make tenuous plans about the future (TS93017). They prefer freedom and mobility to security and comfort (see my analysis of "The Fox and the Dog" in chapter 4).

The Traveller's choice to abandon Traveller worldview in favor of settled worldview creates an opportunity Duncan uses to demonstrate the relative validity of Traveller and non-Traveller worldviews. As he unfolds the story, Duncan comments on the Traveller's choice of settled worldview by following the Traveller's proposed life plan to its absurd conclusion. The illusion of comfort and security is humorously revealed to collapse at the slightest provocation—here the shout that scared off the hare—thus simultaneously pointing out the absurdity of settled worldview and vindicating Traveller worldview. In lines 60–61 ("And the hare got such a fright,/ it was off") the Traveller is returned to his senses—literally to his eyes and ears in the narrated event. In the "real world" frame he regains his cultural senses as he reflects on the previous events from the perspective of Traveller worldview. His detached comment, "Well, . . . it could have happened," reasserts his acceptance of the uncertain future that is implicit in Traveller worldview.

For Travellers in the audience, this story may therefore function as an entertaining vehicle for teaching or reminding listeners about Traveller beliefs and worldview. On another level, if the story is heard as a critique of those Travellers who have chosen to abandon their Traveller heritage and live in houses as if they were settled folk, the story might serve as a warning about how easily Traveller culture can be lost. From this perspective, the final line becomes an expression of relief that the Traveller was returned to his senses just in time to avoid actually going through with living his life in the non-Traveller way.

A non-Traveller audience member may perceive a slightly different argument emerging from the potential connection between the narrated event and the "real world." To a settled person it might be plausible that people living with poverty, uncertainty, and hunger would feel that they have wasted their lives. It might make sense that someone living such a life might wish for change. It might seem logical to long for the security of a house, a stable job, and a family—things that (typically) can be gained only through investment and sacrifice. Given these assumptions, the story follows what seem to be sensible decisions for bringing Travellers into the modern (i.e., non-Traveller) world. But, through a logic that parallels that just described for Traveller audiences, the performance reveals that these decisions lead to absurd conclusions, leaving the Traveller no better off than he was at the beginning. In the performance I have transcribed here, Duncan may have intentionally used the story logic as a way of educating his American audience about the differential identity between Travellers and non-Travellers.

My argument that this performance embodies a serious cultural commentary is supported by comments from Duncan himself. During an interview he commented: "The moral was, never let it happen to you" (TS92038). Duncan's conception of the story's logic emerges from our discussion:

DB Well, the thing I wonder in that story, too, . . .
    his plans to settle down and have a pig farm,
    isn't that sort of a non-Traveller thing to do?
DW That's a non-Traveller idea.
    But you see that he had been traveling and not doing any work.
    He had wanted something . . . better than what the Travellers had,
    which his teaching had taught him.
    He had saw many pig farms in his travels,
    how they were comfortable, settled down.
    He probably went and begged food from pig farmers,
    and saw them, the pigs.
    And because he had come to that conclusion
    that here was the time that he had to change,
    had to change,
    he didnae say to his self,
    "Oh, I'm going to go back once again to the Travellers,
    to my Travelling family.
    I'm going to find myself a wife,

and marry her,
    and start all over again."
He was going to start off that particular moment,
from that moment on,
because he had made a big mistake.
He should have done what he was taught to do when he was young.
Now he was forty years old.
There's no way back.
Right?
DB Right.
DW So therefore he had to start and begin again.
DB And he sort of chose the wrong way to start?
DW He chose the wrong way to start.
That's what was the prob[lem].
He chose the wrong way to start.
DB So he chose the settled way to start?
DW That's right.
That's the idea.
That's the idea of the story. (TS92038)

My point here has been to show how attention to the full dynamics of storytelling viewed as performance can give insight into the function and meaning of a given storytelling. As I have argued, this requires a careful examination of not only the story text but also how the story is told and what audience members bring to their interpretations of the storytelling. From this perspective, both the humor of this story as fictional event and the underlying exploration of differences in cultural identity that is used to argue the validity of deeply held cultural beliefs should be understood as intentional aspects of meaning in Duncan Williamson's performance of "The Traveller and the Hare." The potential for the story to embody these meanings partly emerges from the structure of the story as it has been passed from one teller to another. Yet it is through his careful performance and especially through his formal patterning of the story, structuring of interpretive frames, and management of temporal references that Duncan suggests these meanings to listeners.

Following and Experiential Meaning

No matter how carefully Duncan structures his performance of "The Traveller and the Hare," however, he cannot determine the meanings listeners carry away with them. Listeners do not passively receive meaning. They actively interpret meaning for themselves as they interact with the performer in the performance event. A complete analysis of this performance must therefore take into account the process whereby listeners formulate their own understanding of the function and meaning of storytelling performances.[4]

Understanding how listeners formulate meaning in a storytelling performance requires a shift to a phenomenologically oriented perspective that explores how listeners *follow* or experience the performance as it unfolds in time. The conception of following I present here builds on a comment by Duncan Williamson that a listener tries to anticipate where a story is going: "You're a step ahead of the storyteller. Because you want to know what comes next" (TS87013). It also builds on W. B. Gallie's discussion of what it means to "follow" a story (1964, 22–50) and my conviction that listeners try to make sense of a performance in a direct parallel to how they make sense of any other lived experience (see Braid 1996b).

In following lived experiences, individuals engage with events in the world and try to make sense of what is happening. Sense-making is a dynamic process that draws on beliefs, worldview, and past experience. It builds on expectation, since interpretational choices are contingent on their ongoing usefulness in making sense of the unfolding present. The sense-making process is also emergent, in that individuals are constantly updating, reinterpreting, reforming, or abandoning their "understandings" as needed and as required by subsequent experience.

Following a storytelling performance involves a similar process. As the full complexity of the performance event unfolds within their present awareness, listeners engage with it as they would with any lived experience and seek to make sense of what is happening. Since a central component of this experience is the story itself, attention will be directed to understanding the narrated event and its relevance to the performance interaction.

Two generally accepted qualities of story are particularly relevant to understanding the nature of the listener's experience of following. First, stories embody a temporally ordered sequence of events. Michael Toolan, for example, tentatively defines narrative as "a perceived sequence of non-randomly connected events" (Toolan 1988, 7). Similarly, the first part of Labov and Waletzky's classic definition of narrative centrally implicates this quality: "Narrative will be considered as one technique for recapitulating experience, in particular, a technique of constructing narrative units which match the temporal sequence of that experience" (Labov and Waletzky 1967, 13; cf. Labov 1972, 359–360).[5]

The second essential quality of story derives from the realization that stories are more than simple sequence or chronology (see White 1987, 1–25). The sequence of events in story is selected, interpreted, or organized in a way that transforms the sequence into a coherent and meaningful whole. In Toolan's definition of narrative just quoted, for example, he notes the sequence is "non-random." Labov and Waletzky argue that sequence is motivated and organized by an "evaluative function" (1967, 13). This characteristic is also implicitly at the heart of the suggestion Aristotle makes in his *Poetics* that stories have a beginning, a middle, and an end.

Following a story is an ongoing experiential process in which listeners follow the sequence of the story as it unfolds, at any given moment trying to integrate the performed coherence, emerging narrative information, formal features of performance, and dynamics of the performance interaction into a coherent and meaningful sense of "what is happening." Note that the performed coherence of the story need not derive from any objective reading of events in the world but is a synthesis of the performer's perception and presentation of the event as intended communication. The coherence apprehended by the listener, while guided by the performed coherence, is very much a product of listeners' own experiential processes—a point I develop in chapter 5.

Following a story is not a linear process. Listeners must follow a story as it unfolds, accepting wild and unpredictable contingencies as long as the story shows them to be "acceptable after all" as it moves toward an unpredictable conclusion.[6] Gallie points out that a story "is as much a journey as an arrival" (1964, 67). This journey of following requires active participation:

In following a story we must always keep our minds open and receptive to new possibilities of development, new hints, clues and leads, up to the very last line: besides exercising our intelligence in making routine predictions or seeing complicated but definite lines of continuity, we must be ready constantly to reassemble and reassess different possible relevances, links, dependences, still unexplained juxtapositions. (Gallie 1964, 43-44)

Following a story therefore involves a repeated synthesis and resynthesis of the perceived narrated events in an attempt to comprehend the narrative course and thereby grasp the coherence that informs the story and gives it meaning.

It is possible to argue that the validity of story as a way of knowing comes from "having followed" a story (Mink 1978, 144). Stories can indeed function and have meaning as wholes that are abstracted from performance (cf. Bauman and Briggs 1990, 72-78). In this sense, there is value in talking about the "point" of a story (cf. Labov and Waletzky 1967; Polanyi 1985). The point refers to features of the whole of a story and its relation to the surrounding discourse. In a similar way, it is perfectly valid to consider what a story is about, as I do with regard to the texts I present later. But none of these distillations gives a complete understanding of what a story means, or how a story means, to a listener. If meaning resides entirely in some distillation of story, why bother to listen to a story twice? Why not just give the distillation in the first place instead of telling the story?

I suggest that significant meaning is generated in the active process of following a story—in the ongoing endeavor to follow narrative threads and contingencies, grasp the narrative coherence, and make sense of what is going on at any given point in the unfolding story. While the organizing principle that gives story coherence may be seen as atemporal, the process of following or comprehending is experiential—an active process that takes place within time. The listeners' effort to make sense of the story is crucial. Through this process they are led tentatively to accept or experience the performed coherence of the story. Following a story is an experiential process that can generate states of mind—or more dynamically, flows of thought—that engage the listener. These states of mind and flows of thought may arise from both individual constructions of sense-making and from the sequence in which these constructions unfold in time. These states of mind and flows of thought are constitutive of what I term *experiential meanings*.[7] By using the term *experiential* I intend to invoke a parallel between the meanings generated through following a storytelling performance and the full range of meanings available to human beings.

With respect to Duncan's performance of "The Traveller and the Hare," the experientially grounded process of following the performance is what makes the story a particularly potent vehicle for communicating about the difference in identity between Travellers and settled people. Listeners are first introduced to the figure of "the local Travelling man" in a manner that invites sympathy and curiosity as to who he is and what will happen to him. As his performance unfolds in time, listeners must try and integrate the emerging story information, formal elements of the performance, the dynamics of the performance event, and the interpretational resources they have brought with them into a coherent understanding of who the Travelling man is, where he has come from, and where he is going. This interpretive process includes attention to the narrative event. Listeners must endeavor to comprehend why Duncan has chosen to tell the story and what the intended function and meaning of this particular performance might be.

I have argued that one key meaning in this story is generated through the pig-farming fantasy that Duncan spins out in Frame D. At the point this frame is developed in the narration, listeners must contingently keep track of several distinctly framed narrative threads until the performance provides enough information to resolve "what is going on." Frame B, in which the narrated event takes place with the tired Traveller watching the grazing hare, provides the basis for the first narrative thread. A second thread is evoked in Frame C, where the present-tense dialog ambiguously coexists as part of the developing action of Frame B and as commentary that transcends the narrated event by referencing Frame A and the real world of Traveller/non-Traveller interaction. When Duncan introduces a third thread through the pig farming fantasy (Frame D), neither its relationship with respect to Frames B and C nor its meaning with respect to the overall story is clearly defined. This uncertainty means that listeners must simultaneously keep track of all three narrative threads as potential story lines that must be followed and anticipated. Listeners must work to find coherence within each thread and between threads until the ambiguous connections between these threads can be resolved into a coherent and meaningful understanding of what is going on.

Because the process of finding coherence in the story is an experience in its own right, listeners draw on their own knowledge and experiential resources to try to understand what the Traveller is feeling and thinking so they can project what will come next. In this search to comprehend what is going on, listeners actively engage with the story—giving rise to states of mind or flows of thought. When the Traveller shouts, "GET UP YOUSE LAZY BOYS!" and the hare runs off, the ambiguity between Frames B and D is finally resolved. Yet the contrasting states of mind and flows of thought evoked in the process of following these two threads are very real. The resolution in the story is therefore accompanied by a parallel experience of resolution in terms of listeners' thought processes. By suggesting paths for the listener to follow, the formal patterning of the story "sets up" contrasting states of mind that are resolved at this moment in the story. The performance therefore influences listeners' experience and therefore the meaning they derive from this experience.

Yet this resolution between Frames B and D still does not resolve the ambiguity as to whether the reported speech in Frame C references Frame B (the narrated event) or Frame A (the performance event). The possibility is left open that story meanings are intended to comment on aspects of differential identity between Travellers and non-Travellers in the real world. If listeners make this association between story meanings and the real world, the meanings evoked in the process of following add an experiential component to their interpretation of Traveller and non-Traveller identity.

Following a storytelling performance is an experience in its own right. Listeners try to extract coherent meaning from this experience exactly as they would from any other lived experience. There is, however, one crucial difference between lived experience and storytelling performance. In following a story—in constructing coherent states of mind, or flows of thought—listeners are led by the performed coherence as they pull together the narrative threads in order to make sense out of the story. From this perspective, a significant part of Duncan Williamson's competence in performing "The Traveller and the Hare" involves an understanding of how listeners extract meaning in following a story. His performance artistry is a resource that enables him to suggest experiential meaning through how he selects, performs, and unfolds the sequence of the story. By encoding insights about the differential identity of Travellers and non-Travellers into his performance, Duncan can therefore suggest an experience of this difference to members of his audience. In following this performance, listeners are led by, and contingently accept, the performed coherence as they work to find meaning in the performance.

Yet listeners' experience of this process will be their own. The coherence listeners perceive in following Duncan's story will be a synthesis of the performed coherence and the coherence that is formed through their own experiential process of following. The meanings listeners create in following Duncan's performance are therefore not passively accepted but a direct product of their own interpretive processes. These meanings are experiential resources listeners can take away from the performance events in the sense that these experiences can be thought with and thought through in ongoing attempts to understand the world. It is in this sense that following a storytelling performance is an experience that may influence constructs of worldview and identity. It is also in this sense that Traveller stories and Traveller lives are intimately connected.

Creativity and Emergence in Performance

In the summer of 1988, I was in Scotland at a ceilidh in Duncan Williamson's living room. During the course of the evening, Duncan started to tell "The Traveller and the Hare." But this time he stumbled over one line of the story, most likely because he had "quite a dram on him" as they say in Scotland (as had many others who were present), and opened himself up to the mocking laughter of the ceilidh participants. Undaunted, Duncan managed to regain control of the audience and continue his story with a virtuosity that not only more than made up for his infelicitous mistake but also simultaneously commented on the laughter's implicit critique of his drinking.

Duncan's performance provides an opportunity to explore not only how the function and meaning of a given storytelling can emerge in the course of telling but also the creative role of the narrator in adapting traditional resources to address the needs of a given performance interaction.[8] I therefore focus attention on how Duncan transforms his normal performance of the story in the 1988 ceilidh by increasing the artistry of his telling and creating an additional layer of meaning as a response to audience criticism.

The evening when Duncan retold "The Traveller and the Hare" started with a relatively formal public performance in the town of Strathmiglo, in Fife. After this event was over, most of the performers and their friends returned to Lizziewells farm, Duncan's home at that time. Soon, the living room was filled with family, friends, and the tins of ale and bottles of whiskey that they had brought with them.

Because this ceilidh took place in his living room, Duncan felt that it was his responsibility to see that the event went well. As informal master of ceremonies, Duncan often called upon individuals to perform a story or ballad and rarely took no for an answer. In his requests Duncan frequently extolled the person's competence in performance. When ballads or stories were being performed, group attention was focused on the requested performance. At other times, instrumental music filled the air, holding the attention of some but allowing others to drift off into small group conversations.

One fundamental ceilidh rule that evening seemed to be that everyone must have their trochs, or drinking glasses, full to the brim with an alcoholic beverage at all times. Presumably this was in celebration of the earlier successful ceilidh and the presence of so many friends in his living room. As host, Duncan took the role of policing the liquid level in glasses. The cry "Is anyone needing their trochs filled?" came from Duncan somewhat regularly. Those who did not have to drive that evening had no excuse for an empty troch, as Duncan teasingly let them know. Apart from the mechanics of keeping glasses full, the topic of alcohol consumption permeated a great deal of conversational and performance time.

Storytelling, Identity, and Worldview 125

Many songs, stories, jokes, and even speech plays about drinking were performed as the evening progressed.

In order to capture the mood of the ceilidh and especially the persistent focus on alcohol, I transcribe here a segment of conversation that came shortly before Duncan's performance. Since I am primarily interested in content, I have transcribed only the main thread of the conversation and have ignored some voices where they are masked by louder voices with similar intents. DW = Duncan Williamson; WM = Willie MacPhee; BW = Betsy Whyte; RK = Robin Kuller; SD = Sheila Douglas; SG = Sue Grizzell.

DW   Whose troch is empty?
      And then we'll hae another song—from Sheila.
      Oh, a wee song from Betsy for a change. Eh?
      Whose troch is empty?
      Bella, your troch is empty.
      Willie? [DW looks from person to person and troch to troch]
WM   No thanks, I've had enough.
DW   You're asleep.
      Ted's not getting any more. [laughter]
      Your troch are okay.
      And, eh, Gavin? You're fine.
      And you're sitting all right.
      And Ted—you're no going anywhere, so where's your troch?
      Donald and Sue's no going anywhere tonight.
      Neither is Alec or (?).
      And Sheila Douglas is no going to drive tonight.
      So.
      Alex you're, you're just free.
      So.
      Anyway, it's my, It's my troch.
      I—I—H—I, my own troch!
      I forgot about mysel!
BW   It's your ain troch.
DW   I was so interested in other people, I forgot about mysel.
      Wait 'til you hear this.
RK   Well, there's no much in that one.
DW   Ah, it's no much.
RK   Are you going to sing a song for us?
SD   Betsy, Betsy.
SG   Let Betsy sing, Duncan.

SD Something about the silly old man.
DW Aye, Betsy is going to sing us a song.
SD I like that one.
BW I was going to sing "The Isle of France."
SD Well, sing that.
DW Oh! "The Isle of France."
    Go on, "The Isle of France."
BW It's a ballad, you know.
    Mind, I'm no singer.
SG Yes you are!
DW Ahhh. You're just kidding yourself.
    You're no kidding us, all right?
BW [Starts singing "The Isle of France"]

As the applause was dying down from Betsy's song, Duncan took control of the ceilidh talk in his role as emcee and, with the attention of the group, began to tell "The Traveller and the Hare." In the transcription that follows, I use italics to preserve the distinction between the two voices that emerge when the Traveller argues with himself. These voices were clearly distinguished in performance through recognizable shifts in vocal quality and facial expression.

The Traveller and the Hare—1988

1   Wonderful, Betsy, Wonderful! [applause continues]

    Okay.

    So.
    The old Travelling man had traveled far that morning.
5   He was alone.
    He'd traveled far and wide.
    He was hungry.
      He was down and out,
        and he was poor.
10 His shoes were coming through—
      his soles were coming through the shoes of his feet /
      toes was coming through. [gentle laughter builds in intensity]
    He was hungry.
    He never had a BITE ALL DAY LONG. [As laughter increases in intensity, Duncan raises his voice so he can be heard.]

15   He says to himself, [As the laughter dies away, Duncan's voice returns to
      normal.]
      "*Something must be done about you chap.*
      Something must be done about you chap," he said. [laughter]

      So he stopped.
      He said, "Listen.
20   *Consider yourself.*"
      Talking to his self. [laughter still gently in background]
      He said, "Who do you think you are talking to?" /
      He says, "*I'm talking to you.*" [laughter]
      "Me?" he said. "You are talking to me?"
25   He said, "*Oh, I'm talking to you.*"

      He said, "Listen.
      You never did a honest day's work in your life.
      "Oh," he says, "*you work at the farms.*
         You get a couple of shillings,
30   *and you blow it,*
              and you go on,
                 and you travel on."
      He says, "*You know, you're coming up forty?*"
      "Well," he says, "maybe I am."
35   "*You're coming up forty years of age,*" he said.
      "*You've no wife.*
        You've no home.
          You've no family.
            You've nothing.
40   *What have you got to show for yourself,*
      for all your years walking on the road?

      People," he says, "*got jobs.*
      They've homes and houses.
      You've nothing.
45   *My old mother,*" he said, "*would be ashamed of you.*" [laughter]

      He says, "What can I do about myself then?" [laughter]
      "Well," he says, "*it's your own fault.*"
      "Ah," he said, "I'll change it though.
      I'll change it."
50   "Well," he said, "*You should change it.*
      You're better if you can."
      He's talking to himself, you know?

So.
He said, "Look.
55 *You walked all day, didn't you?* [laughter]
You came over hills and down dales,
and you walked all along,
and you have nothing to show for it.

You are hungry, aren't you?" /
60 "Oh," he said, "I'm hungry." [laughter]

"And you're poor, not a penny in your pocket?" /
"Oh," he said, "not a penny, not a penny." [Duncan's words are swallowed by laughter]

"Well," he says, "*take a look at yourself.*"
"I'm looking at myself," he says. [laughter]
65 "I'm looking at myself," he said.
"So I am," he said, "I'm looking at myself."

"Well," he says, "*look.*
You'll have to start a new life."
"Och, where am I going to start it?"

70 And then he stopped.
Because he'd stopped beside a green field, ladies and gentlemen.
And sitting in the field was a big—brown—hare.
Sitting with its two lugs up like that [mimes hare's ears by wiggling index and middle finger] [laughter]
Sitting, picking at the grass, eating away.

75 And he looked across and he said,
"Ha, ha, ha," he said, "Hahahahaha," he said,
"You have, you, you called me a fool, didn't you?"
"Well," he said, "*I did.*"
I'm telling you he's talking to himself. /
80 He said, "Talking to a fool." /
He said, "*I called you a fool.*"
"You think," he said, "I spent my all my life," he said,
"wasting my life all these years?"
"*Course you did,*" he said.
85 "*You're forty years of age,*" he said.
　"*You've no home,*
　　no wife,
　　　no nothing."

Storytelling, Identity, and Worldview 129

"Ah, but," he says, "it's changed it right now," he says.
90 "This minute it's changed."
"*What do you think,*" he says, "*why are you going to change it?*"
He says, "Look, out there sit a big brown hare."
Two lugs, [mimes hare's ears again]—cropping the grass.

"Hahaha pal," he says, "this is where my life goes when I start."
95 He says, "I want no more talk from you."
"*Okay,*" he said, "*no more talk from you.* [laughter]
No more (?)."
"Because," he says, "out there in that field there sits a brown hare. [laughter continues]
And," he said, "that hare is going to make me my fortune. [laughter]
100 Because, you see," he said,
"I'm going out there to catch that hare,
and I'm going to take that hare to the butcher's,
and I'm going to sell that hare for two-and-six, half a croon.
Hahaha. But," he says, "I'm not going to spend it in drink!
105 You think I'm going to spend it in drink!"
"*I never said so,*" he said, said the voice. [loud laughter covers several words]
He said, "No way!
I'm no spending it in drink.

I'm going to go down to the market," he said,
110 "and I'm going to buy—myself—a piglet for two-and-six. [deliberately spaced words]
That's all they're worth, two-and-six."
"*Okay,*" he says,
"*go buy a piglet for two and six,*" said the voice. You see? [laughter]
"*Buy yourself a piglet.*
115 *But what are you going to do with it?*"
"Oho," he says, "what do you mean what am I going to do with it?
I'm going to bring it up," he said, "I'll rear it up
a sow piglet, not a male, a female." [laughter]
"*Okay,*" said the voice, "*you do it.*"

120 [AD] It would be a boring story otherwise. [laughter and some boos]
[DW] It's not a boring story. [laughter]

So.
He says, "*Okay, go ahead get yourself a piglet.*"

So.
125 There sat the hare eating away—crumping, his two ears going, in the field.
[mimes hare's ears] [laughter]

130 *Storytelling, Identity, and Worldview*

"And," he says, "after I get the hare, I'm going to sell it for two-and-six."
"*Okay, so you've got yourself the two-and-six.
What are you going to do next?*"
"Buy a piglet.
130   And I'm gonna rear it up."
"*Okay, you're going to rear it up.*"
"I'm gonna, I'm gonna cover it, and I'm gonna (?) a lot of little piglets.
And I'll sell all the piglets."
"*Okay,*" said the voice, he said, "*you do that.*" [laughter]
135   "Well," he says, "that's what I'm gonna do."

So, there sat the hare in the field, going away—
cropping with his ears going like that, cropping away. [mimes hare's ears]

"*Now,*" he says, "*what are you going to do next?*"
"Oho," he says, "what are you going to do next?" he said,
140   "What do you think I'm going to do next?" he says.
"I'm going to rear them up,
   make them fat,
      and sell them.
And then I'm going to get more money,
145   and I'm going to buy more piglets.
And," he says, "I'm going to buy myself a little farm
with the money I got from them.
And then I'm gonnae start and be a pig breeder and have all many pigs."
And the voice said, "*Well, I hope you manage.*"
150   And the wee hare sat there with his ears going. [mimes hare's ears]
   [laughter]

"*And then,*" he said, "*what are you going to do next?*"
"Oh, what do you mean am I going to do next?
I am going to get a wife," he said, "and marry her,
and start a piggery." [laughter]
155   "*Okay,*" said the voice, "*go ahead.*" [laughter]
And the hare sat with his two ears,
sitting like that [mimes hare's ears] in the field going,
and the hare never paid any attention to him.

And the voice said, "*What are you going to do next?*"
160   And he said, "What do you think I am going to do next?
I am going to marry, and I am going to have two baby sons."
"*Oh, two sons, oh, two boys, oh.*"
"Yes, I am going to have two boys.
And, by God," he said, "they'll no be as lazy as me!

165 And they'll no be as lazy as me! [laughter]
   They'll never be as lazy as I was.
   I've wasted my life, but they'll never waste their life.
   They'll get up every morning,
      and they'll go to work,
170   and they'll feed the pigs.

   Boys! [loudly]
   GET UP! [shouted]
   IT'S TIME TO FEED THE PIGS!" [shouted]
   And the wee hare got such a fright,
175 it went off. [explosion of laughter]
   Loppity, loppity, loppity, lop.
   And he watched it disappear in the distance. [laughter]
   And the hare disappeared and was gone. [laughter]
   And he turned round and the voice said,
180 "*Well, are you pleased, are you pleased?*" /
   "Well," he said, "it could have happened." [laughter and applause]

   [WM] It could have happened. /
   [DW] Well, it could've, couldn't it? /
   [AD] I couldn't resist that joke, Duncan.
185 [DW] Aha, okay. It's all right, Andrew.
   I, I'll forgive you.
   Anyway, whose troch is empty? (TS88004)

While this performance clearly parallels the structure of the story I presented earlier, it is also very different in a number of ways. Here, I highlight only the differences that are particularly relevant to understanding the creativity of Duncan's performance.

The first line of the transcription can be seen as the second half of Duncan's framing of Betsy's ballad (please sing, she is a good singer // wasn't she a good singer). This comment derives from Duncan's role as master of ceremonies, but it also establishes Duncan's control of the ceilidh speech. The "Okay" of line 2 is transitional, leading to the "So" of line 3, which acts as an initial marker (cf. D. Hymes 1981, 318), orienting listeners to the first segment of Duncan's story. As the initial framing of a storytelling performance, lines 2 and 3 implicitly announce that Duncan will assume accountability for a display of communicative competence that is open to the evaluation of the audience members. Note that this is a bold claim, since many people in the audience are competent performers themselves and can therefore be assumed to be competent judges of performance.

In line 4 Duncan begins the story and closely follows his normal pattern of performance in lines 4–9. But then things go wrong. Duncan makes an infelicitous slip. He garbles what I guess should have been "his feet were coming through the soles of his shoes" with lines 10–12: "His shoes were coming through— / his soles were coming through the shoes of his feet / toes was coming through." The audience responds to this slip with loud laughter that can be interpreted as a challenge to Duncan's competency as a storyteller. This laughter might also be termed a challenge to Duncan's "face," thereby invoking Goffman's insights on social value and the dynamics of self-image in social interaction (1967). Needless to say, this is a serious challenge. Duncan has based much of his private and public image on his competency as a storyteller. Among Travellers Duncan is noted as a good storyteller. At the time of this recording, Duncan's skill as a storyteller had also gained him an international reputation among non-Travellers. Further, Traveller stories are viewed not only as a form of entertainment but also as a vehicle for the memory of friends and family (see chapter 3). In this sense, Duncan's performance will create one strand of the memory that represents him when he is gone (TS87001). It is therefore very important to Duncan to respond to this challenge to his competency.

Duncan elegantly responds to this challenge to his competency without ever having to publicly acknowledge that there is any problem. He has two general strategies in this process. First, as he unfolds the story, Duncan blurs the distinction between the narrative event and narrated event by using the ambiguities of direct speech. The events and speech in the narrated event thus become resources that Duncan can use to covertly respond to the criticism he has endured in the narrative event. Second, he intensifies his performance of the story in ways that show off his virtuosity as a performer. In doing this, he re-establishes his face by a display of communicative competence that transcends all expectation. The skill with which Duncan uses the resources in the narrated event to respond to criticism (strategy 1) might be interpreted as part of this display of

Storytelling, Identity, and Worldview 133

communicative competence, and, in this sense, it complements his second strategy. Full awareness of this strategy, however, is dependent on a listener's familiarity with the "normal" performance of the story and on his or her understanding of formal patterning in story structure.

Duncan's first strategy in responding to audience criticism is to make use of the resources available to him in the narrated event. The first line after Duncan regains the focused attention of the audience is line 15, "He says to himself." This line sets the frame for the Traveller's reflexive criticism that begins in line 16: "Something must be done about you chap." As I argued about the 1987 performance, there is an ambiguity as to whether the object of this criticism is the hero of the story or Duncan himself. In this performance Duncan "plays" this ambiguity to create a channel through which he can respond to the audience criticism. He frames his direct speech as the reflexive thinking of the Traveller in the narrated event through the metanarrative comment in line 21, "talking to his self." Yet he also intimates the possibility that these words may be his own by not only asking questions but answering them as well. Further clarification of the object of this criticism comes in lines 22–25.

>He said, "Who do you think you are talking to?" /
>He says, "*I'm talking to you.*" [laughter]
>"Me?" he said. "You are talking to me?"
>25   He said, "*Oh, I'm talking to you.*"

The emphasis Duncan places on the word "me" in line 24 allows Duncan to point directly to himself and thereby suggest that he, as performer in the narrative event, may be the target of the voice's criticism.

If the target of the criticism is Duncan, the identity of the critic is left somewhat in limbo. This voice may represent Duncan himself in a self-deprecatory reflexive referencing. But the exchange from lines 104–108 opens another possibility. In this sequence, the Traveller has just projected selling the hare for two-and-six.

>"Hahaha. But," he says, "I'm not going to spend it in drink!
>105   You think I'm going to spend it in drink!"
>"*I never said so,*" he said, said the voice. [loud laughter covers several words]

134   *Storytelling, Identity, and Worldview*

> He said, "No way,
> I'm no spending it in drink."

Here the Traveller triumphantly rejects the critic's unstated, but expected, comment that this money will be immediately used to buy drink. Line 106, *"I never said so,"* sarcastically affirms that this was indeed the critic's assumption. Given the implicit criticism of Duncan's drinking and the ambiguity between narrated and narrative event, these lines can be interpreted as Duncan's direct response to the audience criticism that he has had too much to drink. This interpretation is supported by Duncan's portrayal of the critic as a disembodied "voice" in line 113, and frequently thereafter (lines 119, 134, 149, and 159). In the same way that Duncan uses this voice to give form to the unspoken criticisms of the Traveller in the narrated event, he uses this voice to give form to the audience's unspoken criticisms of his competency. Like the critic, the audience "never said so" but still holds their assumptions about Duncan's state of mind—as evinced by their laughter.

Through his use of the ambiguities of direct speech, Duncan has therefore offered an additional interpretive frame the audience can use in comprehending the meaning of the performance. This might be termed a *metanarrative frame* in that it brings Duncan's life and the dynamics of the performance event into the interpretive domain of the performance interaction. Within this frame, Duncan contingently accepts the audience criticism. He makes a parallel between himself and the Traveller in the narrated event, suggesting that, like this man, he has accepted the premise that changing his identity and trying to "better" himself is the solution to his problems. As the unfolding logic of the story vindicates the identity and behavior of the Traveller in the narrated event, as I suggested in my analysis of the previous performance, it simultaneously vindicates Duncan's identity and choices in the real world. The worldview that informed the choices of both men, prior to their misguided attempt to embrace non-Traveller values, is revealed to be sound. By his use of this additional interpretive frame, Duncan has therefore managed to transmute the logic of his story and use it as an answer to the criticism laid before him in the performance event—without ever publicly acknowledging the critique itself.

Duncan's second strategy for answering the audience's challenge to his competency is to intensify his performance of the story and unambiguously reassert his skill as a storyteller through direct example. As I have already noted, the performance frame highlights communicative competence by calling attention to how a communication is carried out and inviting audience evaluation of this communicative artistry. It is my suggestion that the increased length of the 1988 performance, 179 lines compared to 65 lines for the 1987 performance, is a direct product of Duncan's intensification of the artistry of his performance.

The most obvious change in this regard is that Duncan has the Traveller not only ask himself questions but also answer them as well. As I have argued, this change gives rise to an additional interpretive frame Duncan uses to respond to audience criticism. This change also opens an additional degree of expressive freedom that allows Duncan to generate dramatic tension and humor as he demonstrates the full degree of his performance artistry.

Evidence that the audience is aware of Duncan's heightened performance can be found in the timing of laughter during the two performances. In the 1987 performance, the audience laughs during Duncan's descriptions of the hare calmly eating grass while paying no attention to the Traveller or his fabrication. The audience also laughs when the fabrication collapses with the Traveller's shout. In the 1988 performance, the audience laughs not only at these places but also throughout the exchange between the Traveller and himself. Although the exact cause of this laughter is beyond the scope of my analysis, and although audience composition no doubt plays a role in the differing responses, the pattern of laughter does suggest that the audience is aware of and responding positively to Duncan's enhanced performance.

Yet Duncan's intensification of his performance reaches far beyond the addition of a reflexive dialog. An increased poetic marking can be found throughout the 1988 performance. In order to demonstrate how this poetic marking contributes to the intensification of performance, I focus attention on elements of prosody—intonation, loudness, and timing—since these resources play a crucial role in listeners' full comprehension of speech (Gumperz 1982, 107). In the transcriptions that follow, I present pitch contours above the phrases. An upward movement of this line indicates a rising pitch; a downward movement indicates a falling pitch. Note that the contours reflect the tonal pattern within a tone group but that the amplitude of pitch change is only roughly comparable with other groups. Stress is crudely indicated by use of bold type for stressed words.

Here is a segment of the 1987 performance that includes the Traveller's criticism of himself:

5   And one day he was far away in the West Highlands
    when he took a thought to himself,
    and he said to himself,
    "You know, I'm getting old.
    And I've travelled far.
10   And I've seen many things.
    But what have I got for it?
    Nothing!"
    He said, "I'll have to do something.
    I can't go on like this."

15 And he's walking on talking to himself.
    He said, "You're terrible.
    You haven't a penny to your name.
    All you have is the clothes that stand on your back.
    And you're hungry."
20 Talking away to himself.

As with the rest of the 1987 performance this segment is presented in a fairly even, relaxed tone of voice. There is very little variation in either

Storytelling, Identity, and Worldview   137

pacing or loudness except for some additional emphasis in line 12—"nothing."

Intonation is mainly used to highlight words central to referential meaning in the story. For example, there is intonational closure on all lines except 17 and 19. Line 17 leads into the further criticism of line 18, where the intonational closure takes place. Line 17 on the other hand is not resolved. The criticism breaks off in what is prosodically marked as the middle of a sentence, but the metanarrative comment in line 20 carries an implication that the criticism continues in the Traveller's mind as the narrator moves to discuss other aspects of the immediate situation.

Similarly, timing is used to create parallel structures that highlight particular meanings. For instance, in lines 8–12, the sequence of short lines creates a contrast between getting old, traveling far, and seeing many things and having nothing in the end. Pauses between these lines further clarify the parallel structure by breaking the story into thought-sized pieces that are easy to comprehend.

In contrast, the 1988 performance makes extensive use of intonation, timing, loudness, and vocal quality to not only guide listeners to meaning but also to provide an interpretive context for particular utterances. Here is an excerpt from the analogous section of the 1988 performance:

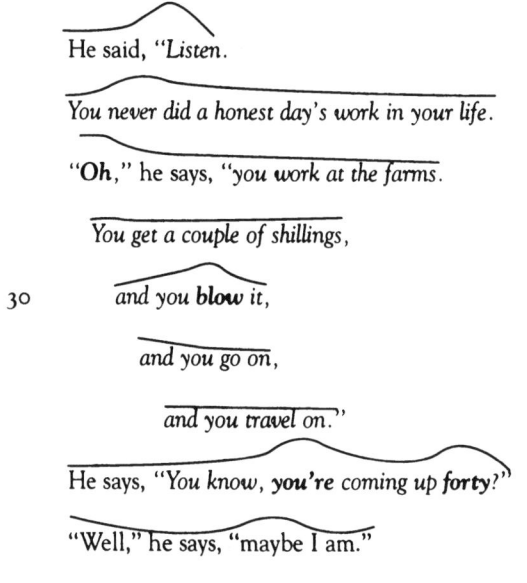

He said, "*Listen*.

You never did a honest day's work in your life.

"**Oh**," he says, "*you work at the farms*.

You get a couple of shillings,

30   *and you **blow** it,*

and you go on,

and you travel on."

He says, "You know, **you're** coming up **forty**?"

"Well," he says, "maybe I am."

35 "*You're coming up forty years of age,*" he said.

"***You've** no **wife**.*

* **You've** no **home**.*

*   **You've** no **family**.*

*   **You've** **nothing**.*

40 ***What** have you got to **show** for **yourself**,*

*for all your years **walking** on the road?*

***People**,* he says, *"got **jobs**.*

They've homes and houses.

*You've **nothing**.*

45 *My old **mother**,"* he said, *"**would be ashamed** of **you**."* [laughter]

In this performance prosodic and paralinguistic features serve to animate the argument the Traveller has with himself about his failure as a human being. For example, loudness, intonation and timing are allied in lines 26–33, to represent the "unquestionably correct" accusatory comments of the critic. Similarly, in line 34 ("Well," he says, "maybe I am"), and in the responses in lines 60 and 62, a rushed, meek, and quavering delivery is used to give life to the pathetic, tired, and hungry Traveller. As in the 1987 performance, parallelism is used to clarify and tighten the critic's argument. This is illustrated in lines 36–39, where the parallelism in unresolved intonational contour equates the terms "no wife," "no home," and "no family" with the term on which the intonational sequence resolves—"nothing" (see Jakobson 1960, 368). A similar parallelism is used in lines 42–44 to add the Traveller's lack of a job to the list of his failures.

Voice quality, loudness and timing are also used to generate humor through how the story is developed. Lines 48–69 embody a carefully orchestrated building of tension that relies not on an increased speed of narrative development but an intensification of conflict that actually slows narrative development and delays the expected resolution. This is a very conscious strategy that Duncan often employs (TS87013). The questions of lines 59 and 61, "You are hungry, aren't you?" and "And you're poor, not a penny in your pocket?" receive immediate and pathetic answers—the immediacy implying certainty of meaning. This quick exchange vividly symbolizes the absurd events and generates a good deal of laughter. Similarly, the reflexive frame in the story is reinforced by the intonationally framed demand of line 63:

"*Well*," he says, "*take a look at yourself.*"

"I'm looking at myself," he says. [laughter]

65 "I'm looking at myself," he said.

"So I am," he said, "I'm looking at myself."

In lines 64 and 65 the Traveller acknowledges that he is indeed looking at himself. But, intonationally, these lines have the form of questions—implying that he is looking but finding only more questions and not answers. Again, the audience finds this portrayal to be amusing.

In both the 1987 and 1988 performances, Duncan uses elements of prosody to clearly delineate voices, to clarify the meaning of speech, and to engage listeners in the story by providing interpretive clues as to the feelings and state of mind of the Traveller; however, his use of prosody is dramatically heightened in the 1988 performance. This heightened use of prosody is one facet of Duncan's overall intensification of his performance. Through this intensification he has simultaneously generated a complex performance that can be enjoyed for its intrinsic qualities, created an additional interpretive frame he uses to indirectly respond to audience criticism, and reaffirmed his competence as a performer.

Duncan's intensification of the 1988 performance is largely motivated by his need to respond to criticism that arises in the course of the narrative event. As such, this performance serves as one example of how the function and meaning of a given storytelling may emerge out of the dynamics of the performance interaction. Yet the functions and meanings I highlight here do not somehow replace the functions and meanings I discussed in my previous analysis of this story. The 1988 performance text embodies similar structures of meaning as those I found in the 1987 text.

What this suggests is that the answer to the question "What is going on here?" (see Goffman 1974, 8) cannot be answered simply, except with a fairly general response such as: "Meaningful communication is taking place." If a more specific answer is desired, the possible responses proliferate: entertaining storytelling, challenge and vindication of competency, challenge and vindication of lifestyle, cultural education, presentation of identity. There is no one correct answer. Nor is there one correct answer for a given individual. Duncan's virtuosity as a performer has insured that the performance embodies a polyphony of potential functions and meanings that may be accessible to listeners depending on their awareness of relevant background knowledge. Listeners may therefore be aware of one or more layers in this complexity as they follow and come to an understanding of the performance.

Lives and Stories

Thus far I have argued that storytelling is a potent communicative medium because of the creativity inherent in the act of performance and because the act of following a performance is experiential in that it parallels the interpretive process that takes place with lived experience. I have also demonstrated how tellers can creatively adapt traditional stories to the needs of the performance event. For these reasons, storytelling performances are powerful symbolic experiences that can be used to challenge and shape an individual's sense of worldview and identity. In other words, stories and lives intersect in significant ways.

Yet the relationship between stories and lives must be understood as an ongoing process of mutual influence. As I argued earlier, worldviews and identities are formed over time through the unfolding of individual experience with the world in relation to community interaction. In formulating worldview, individuals must integrate diverse lived experiences into a useful sense of how the world works. New experiences continue to feed this process. I have suggested that stories, as an experiential medium, can have an important influence on worldview. Yet a single storytelling performance must be understood as but one moment in this ongoing process. As children grow up, for example, they do not formulate their worldviews based on a single storytelling event. They hear many stories over the course of time. They may hear a given story many times in many versions. They also interact with others within their community. They interact with outsiders. Potentially, all of these experiences are integrated into their emerging constructs of worldview and identity. As the children grow and have new experiences, their constructs of worldview and identity will grow with them.

When I talk about stories being used to negotiate worldview and identity, I therefore envision this sense of ongoing, emerging exchange to be at the heart of the process. Although many of the analyses I present in this study explore how individual storytelling performances reflect or embody expressions of identity and worldview, it is important to recognize that these performances are often part of long-term exchanges. Because of space limitations, my transcriptions of these performances are sometimes stripped of ongoing interactions that extend well beyond the specific words I transcribe. Sometimes a story emerges out of the progression of ideas that runs through a long interview or conversation. Other times a story may provoke a series of responses that take place over days, weeks, or months. My interactions with Travellers such as Duncan and Jimmy Williamson and Nancy MacDonald extend over many years. A specific storytelling performance may therefore be one move in an ongoing dialog that builds on our previous exchanges and understandings as much as it does on the dynamics of the current performance event.

Individual storytelling performances can also elicit this kind of ongoing exchange in response to thoughts that arise long after the performance event has ended. Stories persist in memory as wholes that can be replayed and rethought many times. As I write this chapter, for example, I reflect upon the stories I was told during fieldwork encounters. These stories retain their persuasiveness and experiential quality as I now try and understand Traveller life, worldview, and identity. It is as if the story characters are alive in my head speaking to me, even arguing with me as I reach for understanding.

Given the potency of stories in negotiating worldview and identity and therefore for shaping the beliefs, interpretations, and meanings that orient individuals to the world in which they live, it is all the more important to understand the role played by the agency and artistry of the participants in the performance interaction. Whereas some performances embody statements or affirmations of worldview, other performances may incorporate transformations or strategic presentations of worldview intended for outsiders. If, however, the agency and artistry of performance and the influence of multiple performances are taken into account, the study of storytelling can yield deep insights into the way individuals and communities conceptualize, play with, and shape their understanding of both the world and themselves through the stories they choose to remember and retell.

3. "I Never Met My Grandfather, But I Heard Stories about Him"

Storytelling and Community

The more time I spent with Travellers, the more I became aware that social interactions are centrally important to the organization of Traveller lives. Testimonials to the importance of these interactions came most vividly from older Travellers lamenting the changes they have observed in their lifetimes. Bryce Whyte, a Traveller in his 80s, talked of how Travellers on the road looked forward to the company of other Travellers. He commented that in the old days:

> You were sure to always meet somebody . . . on your travels.
> And every camp you went tae,
> if you didn't get anybody,
> "Oh, oh, what's wrang?
> Naebody here?
> Well, we'll have to go farther afield."
> Maybe a couple mile on the road, or three mile,
> then you come to a place where it was full of Travelling People.
> Then you had a . . . good time to yourself
> maybe for two or three days.
> And then went farther on again.
> Some of them used to come with you. (TS93007)

When visiting, Bryce said people were always welcome: "At one time, if they saw you coming and they were working, everything was putten

Bryce Whyte and Duncan Williamson visiting together in 1992

down. Tools, tools was putten down and they come greeting with open arms" (TS93031).

Bryce worries that younger generations of Travellers no longer view these interactions as centrally important in their lives. When he recently went to visit friends and family at the daffodil harvest, he says no one would stop their work to talk with him. He also points to the television, which he says has replaced visiting as Travellers' central form of entertainment. He concludes, "There's no Travellers nowadays. No the same as it used to be" (TS93031).

Willie MacPhee, 83 at the time I recorded him, expressed a similar feeling: "It used to be that you'd meet other Travellers on the road and you'd sit and crack for hours." But nowadays, "if you go to any place to crack to some other body, they have no time to crack to you or to laugh or make fun or joke or nothing" (TS93027).

These depictions of the sad state of affairs among younger generations are perhaps the result of the rapid and extensive changes in Traveller life. Traveller life does not play out in the same patterns it did even a short

Storytelling and Community 145

time ago. Yet younger Travellers still point to the significance of social interactions in their lives. For example, Betty Townsley, a Traveller in her early forties, said what she enjoyed most about Traveller life was "meeting different people, hearing different stories, hearing different things about their life" (TS92025). When I asked what she would miss most if she had to give up life on the road, she continued, "Meeting up with other Travellers. . . . I mean we've got a great bond with the ones that we meet when we travel about. And I would miss them. I would miss that" (TS92025). Edie and Willie MacPhee, also in their forties, are contemplating return to the road full time—leaving a house they bought to escape harassment over illegal camping—because few Travellers come to visit them and they feel too isolated. Edie said, "I feel like I am missing something. . . . We feel like you've got to be with other Travellers and we are the only Travellers here" (TS93025). Edie contrasted this isolation with images of life on the road. She talked about the potato harvest they work every year, and how "there is always a fire. And there's always people sitting round about it and chatting" (TS93026). Or how, when families met at a road turn-out or lay-by, they would "stand and chat for hours" (TS93026).

I believe these interactions are not only important in Traveller social lives but also central to Traveller conceptions of identity and community. In *Passing the Time in Ballymenone*, a study of an Irish community, Henry Glassie sought to undertake research in a place where he would not be misled by labels of community but where he could "study people as they grouped themselves through action" (1982, 13). In my own research with the Travellers there is little to mislead me in trying to understand how Travellers group themselves into community. Because many Travellers are nomadic, community cannot be defined in terms of the relative proximity of individuals or physical living arrangements. Even where Travellers have settled on government sites or in private houses, these situations are often temporary (see Gentleman 1993, 20–21). Traveller communities cannot be fully defined by some generalized contrast to the "settled folk" who coexist within a given region with the Travellers. Nor can Traveller community be defined in terms of an ongoing economic interdependence. At times individuals, and especially extended families, will pool labor on jobs, but these interactions tend to take place on a fairly spontaneous basis.

For Travellers, community is a fluid construct that is rooted in the dynamics of the face-to-face encounters between individuals that take place whenever and wherever they meet. These encounters are informed by past experience, memory, and underlying family relationships. They provide a place where an individual's experience with the world can be displayed and compared with that of other individuals, where individual constructions of worldview, identity, and difference can be shared, negotiated, and attuned. I believe that these interactions, and especially the perceptions of identity that take place in these interactions, can provide a foundation for a sense of community. But a sense of community involves more than just a recognition of shared identity. Community implies the recognition of a deeper interconnection—an awareness of relationship that transcends individual encounters to include a continuity of interaction over time and the expectation and desire for interaction in the future.

Because Traveller stories and Traveller lives are so deeply intertwined, I believe storytelling performances that emphasize aspects of relationship and identity or that embody the essence of Traveller worldview can be used to create and refresh the links that interconnect individuals within the web of community. These performances may also serve to highlight the depth of interconnection between individuals over time and to suggest the expectation and desire for interaction in the future. In this sense, storytelling performances can traditionalize the ongoing relationships that are essential to a sense of community.

In this chapter I explore the relationships between Traveller storytelling and community in four interrelated sections. In the first section I look at a double performance—Duncan Williamson telling "The Crow and the Cheese" and Jimmy Williamson singing a song he composed to commemorate his father's storytelling—in order to demonstrate how storytelling performances create and maintain links between tellers and listeners. In a second section, I generalize the insights that arise from this analysis and suggest that these links play an important role in forming, commemorating, and traditionalizing links between people that are essential for perceptions of community.

In the third section, I investigate how tellers replay events through stories to expand the boundaries of face-to-face performance interactions and include individuals who are not physically present. In this way, storytelling performances play a key role in maintaining the continuity of interaction over time that is central to perceptions of community.

In a final section, I examine Duncan Williamson's performance of a Traveller version of "Cinderella" to show how performers can adopt and transform the content of fictional stories to embody Traveller identity, worldview, and style—even when the stories have their origin in a very different cultural tradition. I argue that these performances strengthen bonds in Traveller communities by giving listeners an experience of the coherency of their own identity and worldview.

Storytelling and the Meaning of Connection

In order to provide a context for developing my understanding of how stories can create and maintain the links that interconnect individuals in the web of community, I begin with a transcript of a performance that took place late in the evening on 20 October 1992. Earlier that evening Duncan Williamson was a featured performer at the Edinburgh Storytelling Festival at the Netherbow Theater. Jimmy Williamson (JW—Duncan's eldest son from his first marriage), Nancy MacDonald (NM—Jimmy's wife), and their son Jimmy attended this performance and then came to spend the night at Duncan's house in Peat Inn, Fife, before returning to their caravan site in Dumbartonshire, near Glasgow. Also present at this spontaneous ceilidh were Linda Williamson (LW—Duncan's wife), Thomas Burton (TB—a visiting folklorist who was staying with Duncan), Sue Grizzell (my wife), and myself (Sue and I were also staying with Duncan). We gathered in the living room, warmed by a wood fire. The evening was filled with songs, jokes, and stories performed by various participants. At the beginning of this session, Jimmy sang "Gin I Were A Lad Agin," a song he wrote for his father that nostalgically reflects on his father's childhood experience.[1] Duncan then requested "his favorite song" from Jimmy. Complying with this request, Jimmy sang "A

Jimmy Williamson, 1998

River of Blood"—a protest song he wrote about Northern Ireland.[2] These exchanges, focusing on the relationship between father and son, set the tone for the performance that immediately followed:

JW   [spoken to DW] I'll tell you what.
       You tell me the story of the—
       You ken, the "Crow with the Cheese"?
       And I'll sing a song.
DW   Eh?
LW   Oh, really? I've been working on that one too.
JW   You ken the "Crow with the Cheese"?
LW   The "Crow with the Cheese"?
DW   Yeah.
JW   You tell the story,
       and I'll sing a song about it (when you're done?).
LW   Oh, lovely!
       There's a song to go with it.
       Fantastic.
       I've been trying to get this story.

DW   The old fox was hunted and persecuted by the farmer.
       He had stole a chicken that morning.

Storytelling and Community

And for his reward,
he was hunted
   by the huntsmen
      and the farmers.

They chased him and hunted him.
He had not a chance to get a bite all day long.
And he crawled into a group of rocks.

The sun was warm and hot.

And as he lay under these rocks in the sun,
he thought to himself,
"Why are these human beings doing this to me?
What have I done?
I am only looking for something to eat."

He was hungry.
He was thirsty.

He said, "I shall die in here under the heat of these rocks.
But if I go out there,
they'll find me.
They'll kill me.
What choice have I got?"

"Well," he says,
"It's one or the other."
And he crawled out from under these rocks.

And the sun was blazing hot.
The rocks was hot with the sun.

But when he came out there,
he sniffed the air.
There was nobody around.
Not a soul.
[Duncan makes a sniffing noise]
Old Foxy said, "They're gone.
They're gone.
They've left me in peace.

But I have to find something to eat."
He was starving.
Hungry.

"Maybe there's something in the forest.
Maybe I'll find something there."

So he made his way down through the forest.
It was an oak forest,
these great big branching oak trees.
He thought maybe he would find something lying there under the trees,
    maybe a rabbit or something,
        a pheasant that had died, you know?

He was a scavenger, old Mister Foxy,
but he was hungry.

But as he went under the tree,
he stopped.
For there he smelled
    a beautiful smell
        like nothing on this world.
[sniffing noise] Sniffed to the east.
[multiple sniffing noises]
Ohhh!

And then he looked up on that branch.
And there sat an old black crow.

That old black crow had something in his beak the fox really wanted.
A big lump of beautiful cheese.
Ohhh! [spoken on inhale]
The smell was delicious.

And he thought to himself,
"That fox [crow] has got something I would love to have.
I've never had cheese for long time.
Would I love that piece of cheese.
That would make a beautiful meal for me," thought old Mister Fox.

But you know a fox is very clever and very wise.
He was going to get that piece of cheese from that crow.
And he knew how he was going to get it.
He had planned it very carefully in his mind.

As he stopped under that tree (and?) looked up.
    And there sat the crow
        with a big lump of cheese.

He said, "In aaaall my life,
I have never saw such a beautiful bird."

The crow watched him.

"And look how your feathers are glinting in the sun,
    and your beautiful legs,
        and your wings are so beautiful.
And that beak of yours,
is a something I have never seen before.

I've saw many's a bird.
But never like you.
You are the most beautiful bird that ever I have seen.

I remember stories from my father,
when I was just a cub,
who used to tell me about these wonderful birds.
But you are the first one that I have ever seen.

You are so beautiful,
so wonderful.
    And your feathers are glinting with the sun.
        And your beak is so nice.
            And your legs are so wonderful."

And the crow is watching him,
shaking its head from side to side as it looks.

"Oh, beautiful bird," he said,
"Beautiful bird.
I've, I'm so pleased I've saw you at last.
I believe my father told me so,
    but I didna believe him.
But now that I see you,
you're such beautiful—
But the only sadness in my heart,
my father told me I will never, never hear you sing.

Now I must be off
    to my den
        to lie tonight,
            think about you,
but never heard you sing.

Oh,
would it do my heart good
   just to give me a little song
      before I leave you?
Please?
Beautiful bird.
Will you sing me one single song before I go on my way?"

And the crow could take no more.
Flattery is a terrible thing, you know?
And he opened up his beak,
and he said, "CAW CAAAAAW." [throaty and coarse]

And the big lump of cheese
fell right at the fox's feet.

He gobbled it up quickly.
He enjoyed that piece of cheese like nothing on Earth.
He'd worked hard for it.

And then he turned around and he said,
"You,
you silly old black crow.
You could not sing one single note.
But thank you for the cheese. [laughter]

TB That's good.
JW [sings with guitar accompaniment]
    I remember sitting on my daddy's knee—

No, wait a minute. I got the wrong key. I gotta get the right key.

I remember sitting on my daddy's knee, as the candle guttered in the breeze.
A good fire roared in the chimney pipe, and the pot was full of tea.
Not a lot of food in our food box, but we were quite content.
We said, "Daddy, tell us a story," and off to bed we went.

'Cause Daddy is a storyteller, Daddy is a singer of songs,
and each one has a message that he wants to pass along.

I remember a simple story about a fox with a piece of cheese.
How a sly old fox with flattery, won it for himself with ease.
"Now," Daddy said, "Son, life's a lot like that. You've got to listen to what I
   have to say.
And some day when you're older, it'll help you on your way."

Fox and Crow

♩ = 138 *1st Verse:*

I re-mem-ber sit-ting on my dad-dy's knee as the can-dle gut-tered in the breeze. A good fire roared in the chim-ney pipe and the pot was full of tea. Not a lot of food in our food box but we were quite con-tent. We said, "Dad-dy tell us a sto-ry," and off to bed we went. 'Cause

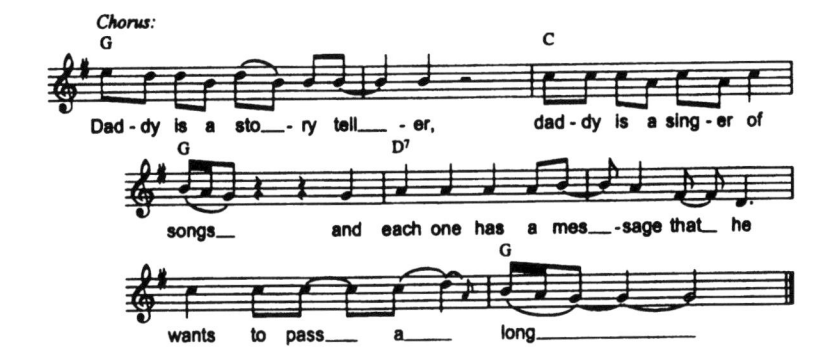

Chorus:

Dad-dy is a sto-ry tell-er, dad-dy is a sing-er of songs, and each one has a mes-sage that he wants to pass a-long.

154 *Storytelling and Community*

> 'Cause, Daddy is a storyteller, Daddy is a singer of songs,
> and each one has a message that he wants to pass along.
>
> [applause]

TB   Boy, that's really good for (your dissertation?).
DB   Yeah, well, that's lovely.
TB   That's very—

NM   Right, something to cheer it up. Come on.
TB   It's your turn.
NM   Cheer it up.
DB   A happy song (?).
NM   It's too sad.
TB   It's your turn, Nancy.
JW   [starts to play an instrumental piece on guitar]
LW   I heard that before, but not about the fox and the cheese.
NM   That's a wee bit added in.
LW   Huh?
NM   That's a wee bit added on.
LW   You added on?

DW   Come on then, Nancy, sing us a wee song. . . . (TS92026)

Duncan's performance of "The Crow and the Cheese" (a version of Aarne and Thompson type 57) forms one layer of this performance event. The narrated event replayed in this performance is an imagined encounter between a hungry fox and a crow—a clearly fictional event. Duncan's performance can, and does, stand as a whole unto itself. But Jimmy's request for Duncan to perform this story and his own singing that follows Duncan's performance function to create an interpretive frame that links these two performances together. This interpretive frame sets up Duncan's telling of "The Crow and the Cheese" as an ideal example that stands for many past storytelling events. Most importantly, however, this interpretive frame suggests that these performances are fundamentally about the importance of the relationship that exists between father and son. Because his memories of past storytelling events are meaningful to him, Jimmy has invested creative energy in composing this song and has chosen to perform it for his father during a session in which there is an explicit focus on their relationship—thereby publicly acknowledging the meaning of this connection to his father.

The link between storytelling and human relationship expressed in Jimmy's song provides an important dimension of meaning in Traveller storytelling traditions. Performing a story, hearing a story, or even thinking about a story can evoke meaning by eliciting a sense of connection between people. Jimmy's song, for example, implies that hearing Duncan's story performed, or perhaps remembering past performances of the story, has meaning for him because it evokes a memory that includes the story text, his perception of physical relationship to his father, and an awareness of the conditions surrounding the performance.[3] The depth of this meaning may be strengthened by other experiences of relationship that take place outside a specific performance event.

This dimension of meaning is often generated through the intimacy of the performance interaction. It may be tied to memories or associations that arise from direct social connection with others in the performance event. For instance, Jimmy's song explicitly states that the meaningfulness of his father's storytelling derives from his memory of their interaction in past storytelling sessions. A number of Travellers similarly commented that performing a story conjures up a vivid memory of the person from whom they heard the story (see also L. Williamson 1981). Betsy Whyte, for instance, spoke of this relationship between meaning, memory, and performance quite explicitly when she was asked by School of Scottish Studies archivist Alan Bruford how she remembers a story:

Well, ye're almost hearin yir mother tell it tae ye again, the whole thing, an when ye're sittin tellin these stories to yir ain bairns,* if yir mother's dead, the whole thing—the feeling even comes back o yir mother tellin ye the story an ye're full o emotion tellin your bairns the story. A found it like that wi me an lots o ither. ... travellin folk anyway, I don't know about anybody else, but ye sit there an the whole thing comes right back: instead o you tellin your mother [sc. bairns] the story, you're sittin there listenin tae yir mother tellin you the story, but the words are comin oot o your mouth. (quoted in Bruford 1979, 66)

In the same way Betty Townsley said the memory of her father that arises when she tells one of his stories is an important part of her experience in telling stories to her own children:

---

bairns = children

BT So I just sat them down and told them stories,
    the ones that Daddy always told me.
DB Unhuh. What, I mean,
    what sense do you have when you are telling those stories?
BT A good feeling actually.
    Yeah.
    It's just like you're just repeating what your daddy said
    because you actually, you can remember every—.
    And when you're telling the story,
    you're actually hearing it.
    Like he's telling me to tell them.
    You know what I mean?
DB So as you're, as you were telling it /
BT As you're telling it
    I can hear my daddy telling me the story.
DB Right, And so that brings back to you the /
BT The memory of my daddy sitting telling me the stories.
DB Right, and the feelings around that and /
BT Yeah.
    It felt really good sometimes when I do it . (TS92025)

When I asked if her grandmother had a similar feeling when she performed stories, Betty said:

Yeah.
Probably that's why she told the stories, isn't it?
She felt that.
And my daddy tells about his wee granny.
And he feels it too when he tells about his wee granny. (TS92025)

Note that Betty proposes that replaying these memories may, in fact, be one reason why her father and grandmother chose to tell stories.

Duncan Williamson was emphatic on this point. He said his memory of the teller is an essential part of the meaning for any story he tells. This came out when I asked Duncan if he ever made up his own stories. He answered:

No.
I would never make up a story, Donald.
Because you see,
if I made up a story,

Storytelling and Community   157

> I couldnae believe in it. . . .
> I wouldnae have no pictures or memory of the person who told it to me in my head. And it would be so empty.
> And so I mean it wouldnae have no meaning to me.
> So when I tell a story,
> not only of course for the sake of people to hear it,
> but it also gives me satisfaction
> that I am telling a story belonging to someone who is long gone
> and the tradition is still going on. (TS87013)

These comments from Betsy, Betty, and Duncan suggest that for Travellers, storytelling performances link performers and listeners in a vivid sense of connection or relationship. Although these meanings and stories are inextricably intertwined, the memories and associations that evoke them are not necessarily coded in the text of the story.

The meaning of the connection listeners feel might be enhanced by their understanding of what the performer does for them in telling the story. For example, storytelling performances may communicate important knowledge or beliefs between teller and listener. Jimmy acknowledges the educational value of Duncan's storytelling when he says in his song:

> "Now," Daddy said, "Son, life's a lot like that. You've got to listen to what I have to say.
> And some day when you're older, it'll help you on your way."

Similarly, a particularly moving or entertaining performance may add an emotional component to a listener's memory of a teller. This comes out in Jimmy's song when he alludes to this potency of Duncan's storytelling:

> Not a lot of food in our food box, but we were quite content.
> A good fire roared in the chimney pipe, and the pot was full of tea.
> We said, "Daddy tell us a story," and off to bed we went.

Implicit here is Jimmy's belief that his father's stories evoked contentment within the family despite the sparseness of food and the rigors of Traveller life. His song celebrates this quality of his relationship with his father. From this perspective, storytelling performances can evoke powerful memories because listeners are aware of not only their link to the teller but also the ways storytelling functions within their relationship with the performer.

An awareness of meaningful connection between storyteller and listeners may also derive from the content of the specific story or song that is performed. Stories such as personal experience narratives, family stories, and newsing stories that commemorate shared experiences or central values of Traveller life have the potential to evoke a sense of identification or connection between the storyteller and the other participants in the performance event. Jimmy's song, for example, is explicitly about his relationship with his father and therefore has meaning for Duncan because of this content that celebrates their relationship. Alternately, stories may evoke a sense of meaningful connection because they remind individuals that they share membership in a larger community. This sense of connection and cultural identity are closely linked. For example, because Jimmy's song commemorates aspects of Traveller life on the road—such as the warmth of a roaring fire, the possibility of food, the omnipresent pot of tea, the use of storytelling as a medium of relationship, and the importance of connection to family—it highlights the meaningful connection Duncan and Jimmy share by virtue of their identity and experience as Travellers. Awareness of meaningful connection might similarly be generated through story content that points up differences between settled people and Travellers (Jansen 1965; Bauman 1972). Stories that tell "who we are not" clarify by contrast "who we are" and therefore bring the outlines of community into sharper focus (see Basso 1979).

Multiple facets of connection might be evoked in a single performance. Jimmy's song serves as an excellent example of this process. One aspect of the song's meaning derives from the connection between Jimmy and Duncan. The song directly reaffirms their bonds of relationship. Another dimension of meaning arises from allusions to Traveller life and the experiences of the Williamson family. This commemoration of common experience, worldview, and identity is accessible in differing degrees to a number of those who are present. Finally, meaning is evoked through listeners' response to the performance. In this regard I find Nancy's comments at the end of the transcription to be revealing. She proposes that someone needs to sing a happy song to "cheer it up," presumably because of the emotional response evoked by the previous interaction.

Storytelling, Traditionalization, and Community

Because meanings evoked in storytelling performances link individuals to each other in a vivid sense of relationship, I believe that these meanings play an important role in motivating the choice to remember and perform that is at the heart of the process of tradition. Duncan Williamson makes this connection explicitly. In referring to a ballad he collected, he commented that his relationship to others in the Traveller community is a significant part of his sense of the traditionality of the ballad.

> Now when I sing that,
> I remember the old man.
> And I remember . . . how I searched for it,
> and how many people I met.
> And they are all probably gone and dead now.
> And when I sing,
> it brings me back memories of the old people who bring it to me.
> And I know in my heart,
> I'm passing on tradition
> because they sang it,
> and they kept it alive . . . after a hundred and eighty odd years.
> So that's what tradition means.
> Now if I had a wrote that myself,
> it wouldnae have any meaning to me
> except as a source of entertainment around a ceilidh or a club,
> just for fun for the night. (TS87013)

The link between his memory of a teller and the story is so strong for Duncan that he says he would never significantly change a story he heard, because he would lose his memory of the person who told it to him.

> [I] never change my own version for nobody.
> I keep to the first one I heard.
> That's the way, that's what true tradition is.
> You keep to the one [you] heard.

> If I changed to somebody else's one,
> right,
> then gone, lost is my thoughts of the first person who ever taught it to me.
> See what I mean? . . .
> Well, it's the same way with making a basket. . . .
> I sat with an old man who was a real professional.
> He was a non-Traveller . . .
> and I sat beside him and watched him making a basket. . . .
> I saw how he done it.
> But there is no way, if I was making a basket,
> would I copy that old man just because he was a professional.
> I would rather copy, listen to the teaching from my father.
> Because I have got memories of him.
> It's the same with the stories and song.
> It's the same thing. (TS87013)

This means that Duncan must remember all the versions he hears in order to remember all the tellers. This is what he in fact claims to do. In discussing one story, Duncan said:

> I have heard that story told from four or five different people,
> in different versions.
> And everyone had a different version.
> I might tell your version today.
> I might tell another man's version tomorrow.
> Do you see what I mean? . . .
> I don't build out a story from true fact.
> Only stories I tell that . . . it's a one-way story . . .
> is a story my father told me that nobody else had told me.
> Do you see what I mean?
> Then I have to keep to his way of telling it. . . .
> So, that's the way I'll tell.
> Well, you cannae just forget their memories
> just . . . because your father told you the same story. (TS87013)

Duncan also argues that the memories that are created during the storytelling process provide a very conscious motivation for performers, both so that they can keep alive the memory of their ancestors and so that they themselves will be remembered in future generations:

> They knew in their own mind that they were also leaving something
>   behind,

> a treasure that we could treasure their memory by.
> I mean Travelling People doesn't need to go and,
> when their old people dies,
> and buy a great granite tombstone
> and put it in a graveyard to remember them by. . . .
> They had the beautiful story told to them.
> And the moment they told that story over again,
> they could picture in their mind . . .
> > their father
> > > their mother
> > > > their granny
> > > > > their uncle
> who had told them the great story . . .
> The picture in their mind would never die
> as long as the stories remained with them.
> And that's what the old people left with them. (TS87001)

What emerges from these comments is a view of storytelling performance and tradition in which stories are remembered and performed not simply because they are old and have been passed down, but because the performance of these stories is intimately intertwined with connections to other people. The choice to remember and retell a story is consequently intertwined with the choice to remember and preserve both connections to others and a sense of the depth and continuity of these connections over time and space. Storytelling performances are therefore acts of traditionalization not only in the sense that they create and maintain the connections to a meaningful past that are essential for personal and social life (D. Hymes 1975a, 353–55) but also because they create and maintain the connections between individuals that form the basis of community.

The full extent of this network of connections comes into focus when storytelling is viewed as an ongoing process that involves multiple performance events. Each performance, while renewing existing connections, has the potential to create new ones. By way of illustration, the story "The Crow and the Cheese" has meaning for Duncan because he learned it from his grandmother (TS93012). When Duncan performed the story during Jimmy's childhood, these performances probably nurtured new meanings for Duncan that link him to his son. As his song suggests, these performances also nurtured meanings for Jimmy that celebrate his relationship with his father and may motivate Jimmy to want to hear the story again or to perform it for his own children. But "The Crow and the Cheese" is also a story that has a long history within Traveller communities. A performance of this story might conceivably evoke a sense of connection to a sequence of tellers who passed the story on. The knowledge that Duncan learned "The Crow and the Cheese" from Jimmy's great-grandmother, for example, probably adds to the meaning Jimmy finds in Duncan's performance. If Jimmy hears this story performed by someone other than Duncan, it will likely evoke memories and meanings for Jimmy that are associated both with the current performance and with his father's performances. Bryce Whyte said that this is the case for Travellers listening to someone sing a ballad that used to be sung by a now deceased parent or sibling. He said that listeners effectively hear both the current performance and their relative's voice "coming back to them" (SA77.202).

My point here is that storytelling performances are deeply implicated in the process of creating and maintaining the web of relationships that link Travellers to each other in a sense of community. Through memory, association, or content, these performances provide a potent means of generating and refreshing connections between individuals. The choice to tell a particular story is therefore not only about remembering that story but also about forming, commemorating, and traditionalizing links between people as they are arranged through time and space. Additionally, by fostering meaningful connections between individuals that motivate listeners to remember and perform a story in the future, each performance can generate the desire for interaction in the future that is essential for perceptions of community. Although no single performance may do all these things, the pattern of performances over time will have a significant effect in creating and maintaining community.

Extending the Boundaries of Community: Storytelling as Experiential Displacement

The potency of storytelling in forming and maintaining the web of community relationships goes well beyond the associational dimension of meaning I have just described. Because stories are in essence a symbolic medium for replaying events that have happened at another time and place, they also provide a means for expanding the boundaries of the face-to-face interactions that play an important role in forming and maintaining communities. Where a story replays events that include the words and actions of those who are not present, for example, listeners can follow and re-experience these events and can use this symbolic interaction as a way of formulating and attuning perceptions of worldview and identity. These interactions therefore serve as a way of refreshing and maintaining the continuity in relationships that is central to perceptions of community.

In this section I examine how narrative re-creations can function to expand the boundaries of community by analyzing performances of several stories. Consider, for example, the following story that Duncan Williamson recounts about his grandfather. As a preface to this telling, Duncan described Jock as a big, rough, raw-boned man:

> My [mother and] father was sitting
> and they had a, two tents—
>   bow tents,
>   you know these bow tents?—
> between each other in the summertime,
> and had a fire between the tents.
>
> And old Jeck had a, old Jock, my grandfather, had a wee tent away at the back.
> And he come back drunk one night,
>   put his pipes in the tent,
>   and he come, walked over to between my mother and father's tent—
>   and somebody was with him—
> He catched the whole fire in his two hands,
>   and he carried it over
>   and put it sitting in front of his own tent. [laughter]
>
> His two big hands, he just put round the fire like that
> and lifted it—
>   the whole fire—
>   sticks,
>   burning sticks,
>   and walked over
>   and put it—

"There, Belle," he said,
"there a fire to you." [laughter]

Left them without a fire.

And he carried it from here to the, to the tree out there
in his two hands.
The hale fire.
Because Granny was sitting she had nae fire.
He had just put his tent up. (TS93008)

When Duncan performs this story in Traveller circles, it might evoke particularly strong meanings for those who are related to Jock. But Duncan's performance accomplishes something more. Duncan's purpose in telling this story to me is to give me insight into his grandfather's character, and perhaps into the character of Travellers in general. Because of the nature of the process of following, Duncan's performance expresses key elements of who Jock is in a way that evokes an experience of the man. By telling his story, Duncan animates Jock as a participant in the performance event with respect to whom perceptions of identification and difference may take place.

This is in fact what has taken place in terms of Duncan's own relationship with his grandfather. Although the vividness of description and reported speech in the story imply that Jock is a very real person with whom Duncan has formed his own sense of relationship and identity, Duncan never met his grandfather. Jock died before Duncan was born. Duncan knows his grandfather only through the stories he has been told by others. Yet through these performances, Jock, like other Travellers who may not be present at the performance event, remains a viable member of the community. Through stories, then, Travellers can extend their experience of community through time to include family members who may no longer be alive but who nevertheless play important roles in family and community identity.

Newsing stories about what has happened to friends, relations, and community members can also serve to maintain and update the connections between people who may not have been able to see each other for some time. This is the case for a story I recorded from Duncan Williamson

Willie and Bella MacPhee with their great granddaughter, 1998

on New Year's Day 1993. While this storytelling is fairly complex compared to some newsing interactions, this performance—coupled with a story Willie MacPhee tells about the same event—illustrates some subtle aspects of how stories may function in expanding the boundaries of community. Note that these texts should not be misinterpreted as suggesting that Willie MacPhee, Duncan Williamson, or any Traveller is particularly violent. The nature of Traveller life, morality, and legal redress requires that an individual be able to defend his or her rights (see Acton, Caffrey, and Mundy 1997). Duncan and Willie never sought out fights, but both have found it necessary to protect themselves or their families from belligerent outsiders and wayward Travellers. Willie and Bella termed the sort of person who enjoyed throwing his weight around or fighting a "hard case"—a category of person we all agreed might be found in all cultures and all classes of people. The following stories should be interpreted with these comments in mind.

Willie MacPhee, Bella MacPhee, and Willie's nephew Jimmy had come to visit Duncan. We all gathered in the kitchen of the house where

Duncan lived near Peat Inn, Scotland. Present also were Linda Williamson, Sue Grizzell, and myself. The exchange was spirited, and a variety of songs were sung. Throughout the session, Duncan and Willie verbally sparred with each other. This intense joking is normal in their relationship. Commenting on a time when he and Duncan were down in London, Willie said:

> We used to carry on and argue,
> and the folks thought we were daft, you ken?
> Think we were going to come to blows sometime.
> We were just carrying on.
> Not serious.
> But not a smile. [laughs] (TS93028)

I believe that the intensity of the joking between Duncan and Willie is in fact a testament to the duration and strength of their friendship (cf. Basso 1979, 67–75).

During the course of their joking, the following exchange and storytelling performance took place:

WM   I want to fight.
        I want to fight.
        Can you fight? [said to Duncan] [BM laughs]
        Can you fight?
DW   I'll get Archie ——— to you. Right?
        He'll give you a sore mouth. [BM laughs]
        He'll give you a sore mouth. Right?
WM   [laughs] You (?)?
DW   Aye. He's a good one, eh?
        Aye, he's a good one.
        He'll never live that one down.
        He'll never live that one down.
BM   (?) a sore mouth (?) [WM laughs]
DW   "Go on, Cocky," he says.
        "Go on.
        Drive on, Cocky," he says.
        "Drive on."

        Wee Archie ——— come to me in Muthill,* eh, Jimmy?
        He was drunk.

---

*Muthill is a town about 15 miles west of Perth.

Him and, God rest, eh, Willie ———.
He says, eh, "Cock," he said, eh,
"I'm looking for a sore mouth.
And I need a lift to Muthill."

I says, "Okay."
"But," I says, eh,
"I'll give you a lift to Muthill,
but I'll get you a sore mouth first,
before you get, before you get to Muthill."
He says, "Do you think you could dae it, Cock?"
"Oh, no me," I says,
"No!
I couldnae dae it. No!"
I could have hit the man.
I could have twisted his neck off.
BM   (?)
DW   But I didn't want to (speak?) to him, you know? [BM laughs]

DW   He said, "I'm dying for a sore mouth."
I says, "All right.
Get in the van."

I drove down the brae* by old (banes?)
and down o'er the brig, you know?
And come down to Hellsfire Corner,
there a railway cross the road on it.
JM   Yeah, aye.
DW   Sitting in the front is a big green gelly,†
and a chrome lum.‡ [WM, BM laugh]
DW   A chrome lum,
   a pure chrome lum,
     and reek§ coming from it.

Pulled the van up, an "LD" I had.
I said, "Archie."
I says, eh, "Are you looking for a sore mouth?"
He says, "Aye.
I'm looking for a sore mouth, Cocky," he said.

---

*brae = hill
†*gelly* = a kind of Traveller tent made from branches and covered with canvas
‡*lum* = chimney pipe or stove pipe
§*reek* = smoke

"I'm looking for a sore one.
I'll get a sore mouth the night."

I says, "Look,
you're no needing to get it the night.
You'll just get it right now." [WM laughs]
I said, "See that green gelly up there?"
   Two big green flaps covering the chrome lum.
"Go up there and," I says, "throw the door oot,
and command the man out there," I says.
"And he'll—"
"Do you think he could, Cocky?" he says.
"Do you think he could?"
"Wha is it onyway?"
I said, "Young Willie MacPhee."
"Drive on, Cock,
Drive on!" [all laugh]

And that's true (?).
That's true.

But God rest old Willie ———.
He never said a word.
No.
Willie never said a word.
Old Willie never said a word.
Old Willie ——— knew better, eh?
"Drive on, Cocky," he says.
"Drive on.
Take us into Muthill.
Take us into Muthill."

I never seen him after that.
It was the last time I seen him.
Wee Archie, aye.
God rest him. (TS93001)

At the moment the transcription begins, Willie proposes, from clearly within the joking frame, that he and Duncan should elevate their "disagreement" to a physical fight. Duncan's response appears to continue in this direction when he suggests that he will get Archie to give Willie a "sore mouth." But the mention of Archie and wanting a "sore mouth" are allusions that link Duncan and Willie to people and events in their

Storytelling and Community 169

shared past. Duncan evokes Willie's memories of this past and the meanings that link Duncan, Willie, and Archie by reproducing Archie's words during one event in their common past: " 'Go on, Cocky,' he says. / 'Go on. / Drive on, Cocky,' he says. / 'Drive on.' " These lines are in fact the denouement to the longer story that traditionalizes aspects of the relationship between Duncan and Willie. While reporting Archie's words is enough to evoke Willie's memory, Duncan tells the story of this incident so that Jimmy and the rest of those present can "participate" in this past interaction. This allows us to experience "what happened" and to draw our own conclusions about Duncan, Willie, and Archie and the relationships that exist among them. Through following the performance, listeners "experience" for themselves Archie's apparent transformation from arrogance to fear as the story unfolds. They interpret for themselves the implications of the actions in the narrated event and the significance they have for Duncan's relationship with Willie.

A second performance I recorded suggests that this same event is implicated in how Willie MacPhee traditionalizes aspects both of his own identity and of his relationship with Duncan. This performance took place during an interview with Willie that I recorded four months after Duncan's performance. Sue Grizzell and I were visiting Willie and Bella MacPhee in their trailer on the Perth caravan site. Our conversation ranged from talk about storytelling to politics to Traveller life and the changes that have taken place in recent years. At one point our attention became focused on Willie's reminiscences about his relationship with Duncan Williamson. Willie recounted a brief story about an interaction the two of them had with a man who was a "hard case." Willie then told the following story:

WM It was one of the, one of the ——'s that come to—
 Duncan was camped, stopped at Crieff,*
 was working at Crieff up there.
 And this fellow,
 he was a hard case tae.

 And he—
  I dinnae, I cannae mind if it was—

---

*Crieff is a town that is about 15 miles west of Perth in Scotland.

It must have been afore that I gin him a doing.
And of course he didna ken I was there.
And he, he come to Duncan,
and he's throwing about.
He says—
    and this used to be a regular word of his—
"I'm looking, I'm looking for a sore mouth."
That was someone to give him a punch in the mouth, you ken?
He was a hard case.

Duncan says, eh,
Duncan says, "You're wantin, you wantin,
are you really wantin a sore mouth?"
"Aye," he says. /
"Oh," Duncan says,
"You'll maybe get it before the night's over."

So Duncan took him to the, up to Muthill, to the hotel.
He was taking him up there onyway.

SG Up to Muthill?
WM Up to Muthill. Aye.

And, eh,
Duncan says, "Are you, are you still, you still wantin that sore mouth?"
"Oh," he says,
"Oh, I wouldna mind a sore mouth."
He says, "Well you see that tent there?" he says,
that big tent there with the green cover over it?"
He said, "Aye, aye."
"Well," he says, "just go up there," he says,
"And chap* at that door," he says,
"and challenge that man out that's in there," he says.
"And I think you'll maybe get a sore mouth you want." [laughter]

And he said to Duncan,
"And who, who's in that?
Who's in that place?
Who's in that camp?
He says, "Willie MacPhee, young Willie MacPhee."
"Oh, no," he says.
"Keep going!" [laughter] (TS93028)

---

*chap = knock

The narrated event in Willie's story is the same as the narrated event of Duncan's story. Willie's choice to perform this story while reminiscing about his relationship with Duncan argues that this past event is meaningful for him in terms of his relationship with Duncan. But, interestingly, Willie is a participant in the narrated event only by implication. He was not actually present and did not experience the event for himself. He could therefore only know about this event by being told what happened through a newsing story about himself. Consequently, the aspects of Willie's relationships to Duncan and Archie that are traditionalized through the story of this event and the meanings Willie associates with this interaction were not formed through direct face-to-face interaction. They were mediated by storytelling performance. Other interactions among Willie, Duncan, and Archie may provide a significant context for his interpretation of the narrated event, but it is through a storytelling performance that Willie effectively participated in this event and used this participatory experience as data in forming his sense of identity and relationship with the others who figure in the narrated event.

Fictional Stories and Community

Stories do not need to be experiential in content to generate experiences for listeners that can strengthen the bonds of community. Consider the performance of "The Crow and the Cheese" transcribed earlier. This story is a clearly fictional event that takes place between a fox and a crow. Yet, several Travellers I interviewed identified with the characters in the story and interpreted the event as a metaphorical encounter between a Traveller and a non-Traveller. The content of the story hints at this interpretation. The opening lines of the story portray the fox as living outside settled society and being persecuted by the established social system represented by farmers and hunters. This context, coupled with the fox's hunger, his wonderment at why he is being persecuted for living a "natural" life, and even the allusion to the stories the fox's father told him as a child, evoke a parallel between the fox's life and the lives of Travellers. His actions and wit suggest that he embodies essential attributes of Traveller identity and ability. This identity is contrasted with that of the affluent, vain, and slow-witted crow—who is understood to be a non-Traveller. Because the story embodies a metaphorical representation of Travellerness that does not reference specific individuals, it can evoke associations and identifications with abstract aspects of what it means to be a member of a Traveller community. In this sense, listeners can form and attune perceptions of identity and worldview with respect to the fictional characters in the story. Where similar stories are imbued with a coherency that builds on deeply held facets of Traveller worldview and belief, listening to these stories can deepen and attune these perceptions of worldview and belief and therefore significantly strengthen the bonds of community.

Yet "The Crow and the Cheese," like many of the folktales Travellers tell, is a version of an internationally known folktale. Variants of these stories are found throughout the world and are so recognizable they have been cataloged in tale-type and motif indexes. "The Crow and the Cheese," for instance, is a version of Aarne and Thompson type 57, "Raven with Cheese in his Mouth." In order to understand how such a well-known story can evoke such a strong identification with Traveller worldview and community, remember that oral storytelling traditions do not preserve fixed texts but build on a creative process that transforms stories over time. In an article where he responds to claims that Travellers have preserved what is really Scottish folklore, Traveller Willie Reid writes:

> Where the School of Scottish Studies and the Revival claim that Gypsies/Travellers were the custodians and tradition-bearers of a Scottish culture, I would wish to argue that such folklore belongs to the Gypsy/Traveller community. Folklore has the power to transcend national and cultural boundaries and makes a distinctive home where it is most cared for; the folklore found amongst the Scottish Gypsy/Travellers has been shaped by the values and preoccupations of that community. It is one more strand of identity that makes up the intricate web that forms the Scottish Gypsy/Traveller. (Reid 1997, 34)

It is through this process of being nurtured over time that stories come to embody the values, beliefs, and worldviews of their tellers. Understanding how this process works requires the realization that stories only exist in performance or as memories of previous performances. Since listeners follow, understand, and therefore remember performances from their own unique perspective, these memories will already embody transformations from earlier performances. These memories will be further transformed and adapted by performers when they retell the story in such a way that it makes sense to a given audience within a given performance event. As a consequence of this process, specific folktales may on the surface appear to be identical to stories told in other cultures, but they may have been adapted in subtle ways to embody aspects of worldview and belief that are firmly rooted in the culture of the teller. In this sense, stories that appear to be similar on the surface may be radically different in terms of their underlying logic, coherence, and meaning.

An archival recording of Duncan Williamson's performance of Cinderella (Aarne and Thompson type 510) provides a useful focus for exploring how stories come to reflect the worldview and beliefs of the culture where the story is nurtured in tradition. The performance I present here was recorded by Linda Headlee[4] on 23 November 1976. In the discussion after the performance, Duncan says that he was a young man when he heard this story from his father. Only later did he hear and read "the country folks' way" of telling this story. In commenting on his preference for the Traveller version, Duncan said, "The other way meant nothing to me because I wasna in the other life. That was for the country folk" (SA76.221). While it is difficult to discern how much Duncan's awareness of these other versions of Cinderella has influenced his memory of his father's telling, note how the following performance echoes aspects of the Perrault version of the story while simultaneously transforming the content and meaning of the story to fit squarely within Traveller life and worldview.

> I'm gonnae tell you a wee story, Linda.
> This is gonnae be the—
> This is the Traveller version o' Cinderella.
> See?
> And this is the way the Travellers tell it,
> and how it happened to the Travellers.
> I mean, things that happens in fairy stories to other folk,
> happens to the Travellers forbyes, you know?
> So this is the Traveller version.

Duncan Williamson telling a story during a session at the Whyte home in Montrose, 1970s (photograph by Linda Williamson)

    Mary's faither and mother was real Travellers.
    And they wandered the country.
    And they had bings of wee weans,*
    ohhh, wee steps and stairs.
    And her old Granny, their old Granny, stayed with them.
    You see?

    But when Mary was born,
    there was another ten or twelve wee weans on the go.
    So old Granny, being staying beside them,
    she said, eh—to her dochter, Mary's mother—she said, eh,
    "You've too many wee weans," she says.
    And she says, "Seeing I bide myself," she says,
    "I'm only camped beside you," she said,
    "I'll take the youngest one," she says,
    "and rear her up just like my ain," she said.
    "It will give you a wee help."
    See?

**bings of wee weans* = lots of little children

Storytelling and Community

So the dochter—
She cried her Mary after herself, the old woman, the old Granny.
See?
And she reared Mary up to a good young woman.

But they wandered here and there.
And in wintertime,
they used to always come to this estate in a place, to this big estate.
And they used to get camping from the old laird.
And the old laird used to let them stay as long as they wanted.
And old Granny used to wander on the roads
   and read fortunes
      and sell scrubbers and baskets,
         whatever she could, you see?
But Mary was never far away fra her.
She was the bonniest wee lassie you ever seen.

But this winter they come to this,
back to this same camping place for the wintertime.
And this place where they stayed was at a crossroads.
And up by the crossroads was the big bene kane,*
where all the bene hantle† used to bing.‡
See?

But it was late at night when they come.
And the man and woman says,
"We'll have to," she says, "get settled down for the wintertime," she said.
She says to the man, you see?
"Oh, aye," he said.
"We'll go back to where we usually bide," he said.
"The old laird," he said, "he's up in years and he doesn't bother us,
and we can stay there as long as we like."
"And," he said, "It is fine and close to the town," he said,
"for old Granny to wander in to the hooses."
You see?

But anyway,
they pitched their camp for the wintertime. See?
And the man put up his camp for all his family.
And old Granny put up her own wee camp

---

*bene kane (pronounced BEAN KAYN) = rich man's house
†bene hantle = gentry, well to do people
‡bing = come, go

a good wee bit fra the rest of them. See?
And Mary stayed with her in her camp.
See?

But it was about—just before Christmas. See?
When they are sitting at their outside fire, around their campfire,
when they seen all these coaches passing. See?
"In the name of God," said the man, he says,
"Whar is all these coaches and horses going to?" See?
He said, "I've never seen so many bonnie horses in my life and so many
   bene hantle."
He said, "I'm going up the morning
  to play to them with my pipes,
    to the bene kane." See?
The woman says, "Look," she said,
"Dinnae bing up about the bene kane," she says.
"You'll get us shifted."
She said, "That's all bene hantle going up there," she says.
"To the laird's son is coming in twenty-one years the morn.
And they're having a great big birthday party for him," she said.
"And if you go up there with your pipes," she said,
"as low as my faither," she says,
"you'll get us shifted." [laughter]

Granny says, "I'm going up," she says,
"in the morning among them all," she said, "to read hands."
"No," says the woman.
"I'm telling you," she said.
"Leave the bene hantle alane," she said.
"You ken," she said, "the old laird doesna bother us as long as we stay here.
But," she said, "let the been hantle," she says—
"Don't pay attention to them," she says.
"Just keep the dogs and weans off the road till the carriages passes by."

But anyway.
It was about three o'clock in the afternoon.
The old woman made a drop of tea for her and Mary.
Her and Mary made their own meat,* you see?
Mary was about eighteen years of age
and the bonniest wee lassie you ever seen in your life.
She stayed with her Granny.
Granny reared her up.

**made their own meat* = made their own food, ate together

She says, "Granny."
"What, dochter?" she said.
"What is it?"
She said, "Can you tell me something?"
"Well," she said, "I'll tell—
I learned you an awful lot," she said.
"If there is anything else you want to ken,
I'd be willing to tell you now."
She says, "Granny,
whar is all these bonnie bene hantle going to that passes by there?"
"Well," she said, "did your father and mother no tell you where they are going to?"
"No, Granny," she said, "they never telled me."
"Well," she said, "I'll tell you where they are going."
She says, "The young bene cowl* up in the big bene kane is having a party.
And he's invited all the young maidens and guries† round all the country
to come to his twenty-one coming of age party.
And he's going to pick hisself a wife."

"Oh, Granny, dear," she said,
"I could a dae going up there." [laughter]
See?
"Oh," she says,
"What would you do up there?"
"Well," she said,
"I'm a young lassie, too," she said.
She said, "You ken they dinnae take Travellers up in the grand bene kanes."
See?
She says, "Never, Mary.
You couldnae gang up there."
"Oh, Granny," she says, "I wish I could."
She said, "If only I had the claes," she says, "and the way of going,
I would go in a minute."
See?

But anyway,
who wandered into the fire when Granny was cracking but—
Mother and father came in to crack to old Granny for a while, you ken?
And the faither heard her.
He said, "What's this fuss?" he said.
"You silly notion into your head," he says.

---

* *bene cowl* = rich man
† *guries* = young maidens

178 *Storytelling and Community*

"You cannae go up there among the bene hantle."
She said, "I was only telling Granny," she said,
"I would like to go up there," she said, "and see what is going on.
There must be—
Folk must be enjoying theirselves up there," she said, "in that big bene kane.
And all the lovely claes," she said,
"and all the lovely meat to eat and everything up there," she said.
"It must be great."
"God," she said, "I'd have been born a young bene mort."*
See?

Granny says, "Look," she says,
"I looked after you to be—"
"I ken, Granny," she said.
"You're good to me.
But," she says, "I would like to see what, what goes on up there."
She says, "I've never been in a house in my life."
"And," she says, "I'd like to have been up into that bene kane," she says,
"among all these young geds and guries† and gang to the dance."
"God bless us," says the man.
"That's a funny thing for a lassie of your age," he said.
"Better you think of a young Traveller man to yourself," he said,
"instead of speaking about a laird's son.
You'll never get any laird's son."
"You never know," says old Granny,
"What she may get yet," she says, "before she's off of the world."

But anyway,
they sit and cracked for a long while,
and the man and woman wandered away to their ain camp, you see?
And Mary's sitting with her head hanging down.
See?
And old Granny went away back into the tent, her ain self.
And she's mumbling away to her ain self at the back of the camp, you see?
Mary says, "Granny, who are you speaking to at the back of the—"
"I'm no speaking to naebody, lassie," she said.
And old Granny come out.
And she had a hankie tied on her head.
   And she had all her fancy earrings on
      and all her fancy jewelry on.
         She had it all hanging about her.

---
*bene mort = lady
†geds and guries = lads and lassies

"Granny, dear," she says,
"what are you all dressed up for?"
She said, "You're no going to the party, eh?"
"Oh, no me, Mary," she says.
"I'm no going to the party.
But," she says, "I'll tell you."
She says, "Dinnae tell your naiscowl* or your naismort,†
but," she says, "you're going to the party."

"What!" says Mary, "I cannae—"
"Wait," she says.
She says, "Don't tell them a thing.
But," she says, "I'll tell you.
   You wait.
      And you dae what I tell you."
         "And," she says, "you'll get to the party all right.
But," she says, "listen!
Remember one thing," she said.
"The party starts," she said, "tonight.
But," she says, "at twelve o'clock'—
keep your ee‡ out (??) the room window," she said—
and when you see the moon full, the night, make sure," she says—
"that party will go on till hours in the morning—
but," she says, "you make sure that you be back before the moon starts to drop."
"But, Granny," she says, "I'm no awa yet.
How can I, I cannae go (to a party).
Look at me!
I'm a bundle of rags."
She said, "The folk would chase me for my life if I went up there like that."
"Dinnae you worry," says Granny.
"Just you wait."

Away Granny goes to a wee pond at the back of the camp.
And she gets a crooked stick, an old staff she had,
and she cleeks§ two puddocks# out.
See?
And she ties them in a hankie.

---

*naiscowl = father
†naismort = mother
‡ee = eye
§cleeks = hooks
#puddocks = frogs

And she takes them back. See?
And she goes round to the back of the camp where she was cutting
 vegetables.
And she gets a great big monster cabbage leaf.
She brings that back with her.
And what—
Mary is sitting watching her.
"Granny, Granny," she says, "what are you going to do with that?"
"Never mind, lassie," she said.
"Mary, get thon," she says, "to me."
"What is it?" she said.
She said, "Do you see thon white butterfly?
Catch him to me."
The white butterfly is stotten, stotten, stotten around the camp, you ken,
 in the gloaming.
It is just coming on evening.
Mary's after—snap—catched the white butterfly and brung it back.

"Now, Mary," she says.
She says, "Whatever you see happening,
never mention it."
Old Granny took out this wee thing like a long stick
with a bunch of stars on it like that.
And she touched this cabbage leaf.
And before you could say a word,
it was the bonniest gleaming glass coach you ever seen in your life.
And she touched the two puddocks.
And the two puddocks—
No, I'll tell you what she done first.
She pulled the hairs out of her head, long hairs out of her hair.
And she made harness, putting it on the puddocks for harness.
She touched the hairs of her head,
and they were lovely silver mounted harness.
And she catched the butterfly.
And she touched the butterfly.
And there he was dressed,
   snow-white footman,
      dressed in snow white and a big tile hat,
         sitting in front of the carriage.
She done the same to Mary.
And she turned Mary into a grand bene mort.
[LW—what did the puddocks turn into?]
The puddocks turned into two white horses, I'm telling you, to the coach.

And Granny's mumbling away to herself.
Mary's in the coach now, sitting.

Storytelling and Community   181

Who comes over but her faither and mother.
Now the coach is lying across the old woman's camp.
And when Mary's faither and mother seen this,
she said, "Shannes,* shannes, we're quodit,"† she said.
"The bene hantle, the bene hantle must have went off the road," she said,
"and that old woman is sprachin them for luer."‡
"Mother," she says,
"you're going to get us quodit," she said.
"It's the bene hantle.
What did you stop the bene hantle's coach for?
I warned you not to be reading hands," she said, "the bene hantle's hands."
   [laughter]

The footman he's sitting on—
   white dickey on his neck,
      white bow on his neck,
         and he's not saying a word.
And these two beautiful white horses—
And this grand young bene mort is lying back in this coach.
"Right," says Granny to the footman.
"Drive on."
Away goes the coach.

"But, Mother," says the dochter, to the old Granny, she says,
"What were you mangin§ to the bene hantle?
Are you wanting to get us shifted?" she said.
She says, "I wasna mangin.
The coach went off the road," she says.
"And I didna ken—
They wanted to ken the road to the bene kane,
and I telled them to gang straicht on."
See?
She never said a word.

Anyway.
By this time the footman drove Mary's coach up.
It was the last coach up to the castle.
In the big square the coaches was sitting in dozens.
And the folk was just about to go in to the party,

---

shannes = [an expletive indicating the badness or shame of the situation]
†*we're quodit* = we are in trouble, we are going to be jailed
‡*sprachin them for luer* = asking or begging for money
§*mangin* = saying

when in comes this coach.
There never was a coach in the country like it.
And there weren't a matched pair of horses and their silver harnesses ever seen in the county.
And this footman, this footman is standing,
six foot he was,
and dressed in white, sitting on the coach.
And then he stepped down.
   He opened the door.
      And this lassie come out.
The folks' breath was tooken away when they seen this lassie coming out.
She was just like an angel.
And even her very shoes was made of glass, on her feet.
And they were that tiny.

Oh, everybody, folk bowed when they seed her coming.
They thought she was some queen or some princess away from some foreign land.
She was the last coach in.
And the young laird, his ain self, he ran out.
And he met her and invited her into the great big parlor.
And he took her into this place.
There were dozens of lords and ladies all sitting round, you ken,
drinking and carrying on.
Mary was just like an angel.
See?

Come in, and, oh, they made the best for him.
Put her sitting down and gave her everything.
The young laird couldna take his een* off of her.
Couldna take his een off of her at a'.
And all the guries is trying to get in close to him.
But nah, it was no use.
But he wouldna have nothing to do with them.
And he danced with Mary, and she was a licht as a butterfly.
Old Granny made an enchantment to her that made her (?) could dance like a butterfly.
And the laird was that happy, he didna see the time passing.
And he's waltzing round this great big room.

And Mary looked out.
And she looked out through (?)—out through the window.

---
*een = eyes

And she seen the moon was as full as could be,
right above the sky.

She excused herself,
and out through the hall door.
And just as she goed out,
    the first step,
        she slipped and one of the shoes fell ahind her.
But she never stopped.
She kept going.
And by the time she reached the foot of the step,
she was back to her ain self—
    two bare feet,
        long black hair hanging down her back,
            ragged dress on her.
Gone was the coach.
Gone was the footman.
Gone was the lot.

And one of the guards standing at the gate looked at her passing by.
The prince is out, no the prince, the laird is out.
And he's down the steps.
And he seen the shoe lying,
and he lifted it.
He says to one of the guards who was at the door, he says,
"Did you see the beautifullest girl in the world passing,
    lady in the world passing by here?"
"No me," says the guard, he said.
He said to the laird, he said,
"There nae one passed here," he said,
"but some of these Gypsy brats from the tinkers' camp down there," he said.
He said, "I seen her running down that road with her bare feet."
"Impossible," says the laird.
He says, "It's impossible."
He said, "There are no Gypsy brats here," he said.
"My lady was here," he said.
"She's gone.
Where did she disappear to?
Where is her coach?
Why did you not stop them?" he said.
"Why did you not stop the coach until I came out?"
"My Lord," he said, "I never saw any coach."
"Well, you are asleep, man," he said.

He said, "Look, there her shoe.
And," he said, "Her glass coach was here and her footman was here.
He was waiting on her.
You must have seen them."
He says, "I'll deal with you in the morning."

He goes back in.
But ach nae—
His night was finished.
His heart was broken.
See?
His heart was broken.
Didn't know what to do.
All the folk packed up, they seen that it was finished.
And he never spoke to the—
oh, hundreds of guries he never spoke to at all.

He was sitting, his old father came in to him.
"What's wrong with you, laddie?" he said to him.
"My son," he said, "what's wrong with you?"
"Well, father," he said, "it's (?)," he said.
"The loveliest thing in the world," he said, "came to me last night at my party.
And she danced with me all night," he said.
"And," he said, "she mysteriously disappeared out of my life," he said.
"And she's driving me crazy.
And I don't know what's wrong with me," he said.

"Well," says the father, he said, "there's only one thing for it."
He said, "Tomorrow morning," he said—
"I've got plenty horses and plenty men," he said, "on the estate,
and," he said, "we'll find her again for you."
He said, "Have you something that you'll know her by?
Do you know her name?"
"No me," he said, "I don't know her name."
"Why didn't you find her name?"
He said, "I never asked her name."
"Where did she come fae?
What was her footman like?
What kind of coach did she have?"
The young lad telled his father that.

The next day,
and for three days after that,

the young laird sent men all over the country,
searching for this coach and this young lady.
But nae, it was impossible.
See?

Old Granny, she was up the back door of the big hoose.
And she read all the fortunes—the cook,
   and the cook's fortune,
      read the cook's hand.
And she got stuff at the back door.
And they are all telling her this story about the lovely maiden that come to the (?).
Granny, old Granny never said a word, see?
Back down.

The man says,
   her faither, her son-in-law, it was Mary's mother's,
   Mary's father says to old Granny,
he says, "They tell me there was a wild carry on," he says, "up at the big house," he said, "the other night."
"Aye," she said, "There a wild carry on," she says.
"Some kind of carry on," she said.
"Some kind of lassie that come to the party.
And," she said, "the laird's going off his head, cannae get her."
And she says, "she disappeared."
"God bless me," says the man.

So they bide there for about three days.
And there are all riders passing by,
but they never looked at the Travellers' camp.

So one day the laird is sitting.
His faither come to him.
He says, "What's wrong, son?"
"Well," he says, "father, to tell you the truth," he says,
"I'm completely heartbroken.
I can't go on any longer."
"What way," he said, "you can't go on any longer?"
"Well," he says, "I've search men all over the country," he said.
"And," he said, "the coach couldn't get no further away," he said,
  "in three days," he said,
    "as a fast horseman could go.
And," he said, "they can't be gotten in the district.
She never was sawn.

She completely vanished off the face of the earth."
Father said, "I doubt, son," he said,
"there's some enchantment attached to this."
"Enchantment, my—" he said.
"Daddy, you know there is no such a thing."
He says, "Have you nothing that you would know her by?"
"Yes, father," he says, "I've got one thing."
"What is it?"
He said, "One of her shoes."
"Well," he says, "it is simple to do, isn't it?"
He said, "Just go tomorrow," he said, "and take some men with you," he said,
"and," he says, "search the country.
And every woman you come to, try the shoe on her foot.
And the foot that fits that will be—
   enchantment or no enchantment—
that will be the body."
He said, "If that shoe is special made"—
   old man looked at it,
      made of glass, pure crystal glass—
he said, "it will not fit another foot but the foot it was meant to fit."
"Father," he said, "You're right."
He said, "I'll dae that."

He called all his men to him the next morning,
   picked five of the best ones,
      five fast horses.
         And the young laird goes with them.
And away they go,
and around the country.
Round and round and round the country, all the fearing day.
Nope.
Trying everybody.
Lassies tried to crush their feet into it,
but nae, it was nae use.
Some of them even tried to get their toe into it,
and it's killing their feet trying to get it into this glass shoe.
Once or twice the laird thought it was going to fit on somebody's foot.
Nae, na, never, and then he was sick.
See?

But on the road back he come up the road going to the castle.
He hears the laughing and giggling and carrying on, you see?
This was the wee weans blethering.

Storytelling and Community

He stops his horse.
See?
He said, "What's that over there?"
"Oh, my Lord," he says, "that's nothing concerning you."
He said, "What do you mean it's nothing concerning me?"
"Oh," he says, "That's a tinker's encampment."
"Well," he said, "if it's a tinker's encampment," he said,
"what difference does it make?" he said.
"They'll have women there or girls," he said. [laughter]
"Oh my Lord," he said, "no, no, no," he said.
  "These girls, these are people," he said,
    "these are tinker people of the road," he said,
      "Travellers, tinkers, Gypsies."
"It makes no difference to me," he said,
"if they are Gypsies or what they are," he said,
"if there are young girls in them," he said.
"How do you know what's there?"
He says, "Come over with me."
See?

The bene cowl rode over to the Travellers' camp, the old man and woman, and his six men with him.
And the old man manged to his woman, you know?
"Oh shannes, shannes," he said.
"That's us shifted now," he said.
"That's us quodit.
I manged," he said, "about your naismort bingen sprachin* to the bene kane.
"I jan,† I jan, I jan, we're going to be shifted."
"That was your mother," he said,
"your old mother up reading fortunes at the back of the bene kane." You see?
"That's the bene gadgie‡ down now (?)," he said.
"That's the road for us the morn."
See?

Man come out, you ken.
"Well, my Lord," he said, "what is it?" he said.
"What are you here about?"
"Well, to tell you the truth, my man," bene cowl says, he said,

---

bingen sprachin = going begging
†*jan* = know
‡*bene gadgie* = gentleman

"I'm not here," he says, "about nothing."
He said, eh, "We're not doing any harm?"
"No, no," he said, "we're not here to shift you or do any harm," he said.
"We're just," he said, "making an inquiry."
"Oh," he said, "You're making an inquiry."
"Mhmm."
"What kind of inquiry?" he said.
"Well," he says, "I'll tell you."
He said, "Three nights ago," he said,
"there was—I gave a party," and he said, "for my twenty-oneth birthday."
And the man explained the story to him, you know?
The Traveller man says, "Yes," he said.
"And," he said, "The last to arrive," he said, "was a coach, crystal coach and," he says, "one footman, and one young maiden."
"You're right enough," says the Traveller man.
    "You're right enough," he said.
    "They were stopped here."
"What?" says the laird.
He said, "They were stopped at this very bit."
"Cahhh, good enough," says the laird.
"At last," he said, "at last I've got some word of them."
He said, "Did you talk to them?"
"No me," he said.
"Oh, it's a pity."
"Ah, but wait a minute."
He said, "It's a pity you didna talk to them
    and find out something about them," says the laird.
And, oh, he began to shake with excitement.
"Ah, but wait a minute," he said.
"My wife's old mother," he said, "in the next camp here,
she was cracking to them." [laughter]
He said, "I mind her cracking to the bene mort," he said, "in the coach.
Ah," he said, "I think she read her hand or telled her fortune or
    something."

Bene cowl says, "Here, old lady, come here."
"What is it?" she said.
He said, "Come here, old lady."
He said, "Don't be afraid," he said, "don't be afraid."
"I'll make it worth your while," he said, "if you can help me.
"What is it," she said, "my Lord."
He telled her the story.
"Oh, aye," she said, "the coach," she said.
"Oh, but," she says, "I couldn't help you," she said.

"Well," he says, "I've searched the country high and low."
"Oh," she said, "They stopped here," she said,
"and asked me," she says, "two or three questions.
And," she said, "I directed them up to the castle.
That's all I ken about them."
Anyway he says, "I'm sorry," he said.
And he put his hand in his pocket and he plunked the woman a gold sovereign.
"That will help you," he said, "old Granny," he says to the old woman.
"Thank you, sir," she said.

And just like that,
as he begin to walk awa,
who come out but Mary.
And the laird lookit.
He says, "Who's the girl?"
She said, "That's my granddaughter."
"Is it?" he said.
He said, "Come here, my girl."
"Shannes, shannes," says the lassie's mother, she said.
"We're quodit."
"What you quodit for says the (?)." [laughter]
And this foreman of this head bene cowl says,
"My Lord," he says, "that's a tinker."
He says, "I don't care," he says, "suppose it's Satan," he said.
"She's got a foot, doesn't she?"
"Oh, yes," he said, "and two lovely feet she has got."
"Well," he said, "get the shoe and try it on her foot," he said.
"She's as good as anybody else."

Bene cowl flung his leg off the horse and down he comes,
red riding britches on him.
He says, "Come here, my young woman."
Mary wandered over, you ken?
Oh young ged about twenty, twenty-one he was.
And she's about eighteen, you see, bonnie lassie.
She had her bare feet.
Bonnie wee tiny feet she had.
He says, "Put your foot on my knee."
"No me, sir," she said, "I'm no putting (?)—"
He says, "Put your foot on my knee."
She says, "What for?
Why?
Why should I put my foot on your knee?"

He says, "I want to try a shoe on your foot."
She says, "I never wear shoes.
I go in my bare feet."
"Well," he said, "look, I have been round all the country," he said.
And he said, "Probably you have heard the story.
And," he said, "if this shoe fits your foot, you're what I'm looking for."
Now she jant.* See?
Mary kent.
She held her foot out.

Slip.
   On her foot,
      just fitted neat.
"You're her," says the laird.
"You're my queen," he said, "my princess."
"Aye," says the old woman.
He says, "That's her."
She says, "That's her."
"Well," he says, "she must go—"
"No, no," says the old woman.
"No, no," she says, "you can't take her."
She says, "You can't take her," she said.
"Oh, but," says the laird, "I'm taking her," he said.
"She's mine," he said.
"I, I got her."
"No, no," she said, "she's my granddaughter."
"But," he said, "I must have her."

The man and her mother comes over.
"What's wrong, Granny," he says.
She says, "That man wants to take your wee lassie awa." [laughter]
He says to the laird, "What do you mean?" he says.
"She never done any harm," he said.
"Was she up at your castle stealing or something?"
"No, no, no, no, no," he said.
He says, "That's the girl."
"Nahhh," says the old man, "that's not the girl," he said.
"There's some mistake somewhere."
He says, "there no mistake," he said.
"There is not another foot in the world that that shoe will fit, but one."
"And," he said, "she's it.
"And" he said, "I must have her."

---

*jant = knew

Storytelling and Community   191

"Well," says the old woman, she says,
"If it must be, it must be."
She says, "I'll take Mary up to you later on in the day."

[LW—Okay, can I turn it [the tape] over here? / DW—Aye.]

"Right," says old Granny, she says,
"I'll take Mary up to youse," she says.
"Mary's her name," she says.
"I'll take her, deliver her to you in the afternoon."
"Well," says the laird, he said, "If you don't," he says, "I'll be back."
She said, her father and mother said, "Look, she's really a tinker, a Traveller."
He said, "It makes no difference to me," he said, "what she is."
He said, "She's mine and I want her."
"Well," says the father, "if you want her," he says,
"you better be good to her."
"Oh, I'll be good to her," he said, "don't worry.
I'll look after her," he said, "I'll be good to her."

He says to her, "Keep the shoe."
"But," he says, "remember—
Tonight," he said, "there going to be a bigger party.
And I'll be expecting you there tonight."

So.
The King, eh, the laird rode up to the castle
and sent word to—
sent all the men he had right through all the country telling everybody to come.
Tonight was—the laird had found his princess,
and he was going to have a bigger party tonight.
See?
Largest party in the country.
He telled his faither that he'd found his princess.
He never said where he got her, you ken.

So.
Away goes the laird.
Over comes Mary's faither and mother to the old Granny.
He says, "Granny, what were you mangin to the bene cowl?"
He says, "That lassie's no any princess," he said, "no any—
You're going to get us banished," he said.
"We're going to be quodit.
If you send her," he said,

192 *Storytelling and Community*

"in that bundle of rags up there at two o'clock," he said,
 "to the big party," he said,
  "we'll be jailt," he said,
   "and the rest of the weans will be taken off of us."
He said, "I'm shifting.
I'm binging avrie."*
"No, no," she said.
She says, "Everything's all right."
She says, "Everything's all right."
She said, "I'm a witch," she said,
"I ken."

He said, "I ken witches, with you working your witchcraft," he said.
"I ken all about you."
He said, "Many's the things, the trouble you got us in afore," he said,
"with your spells and your witchcraft."
"I ken all about you," he said.
"But," he said, "I'm shifting."
"No," she says, "you're no shifting."
She says, "You stay where you are and everything will be all right."

So.
She said, "Mary is going to marry the young laird," she said.
She said, "It'll be the best thing that ever happened."
She said, "Look," she said,
  "your dochter married to the laird, you can come here and camp and—
    all the days of your life," she said,
    "and nobody will ever bother you.
You'll be well off forever."
He said, "You're going to get me banished."
"No," she said, "you'll no be banished."
She said, "Leave it to me."
"All right, witch," he said, "we'll leave it to you."
And he went away to his own camp. [laughter]
See?

Two o'clock in the day comes again.
Back goes old Granny,
  another two puddocks,
    another cabbage leaf,
      half-a-dozen hairs out of her head,
        pulls them out,

---

*binging avrie = running away

Storytelling and Community 193

> harness the two puddocks,
> > harness the two puddocks,
> > > makes Mary catch another butterfly,
>
> same coach back over again,
> puts Mary back the same way she was.

"All right, footman, drive on."
Footman drove away, up to the castle.
Mary come out.
The young laird ran out,
kissed her and cuddled her.
Arms round her neck and took her into the parlor.
He said to his father—
"Come and meet my daddy," he said.
Took her and showed her to his father.
He said, "Father," he said,
"at last, I've found my princess.
"And," he says, "I'll be happy forever more," he said.

"Oh," he says, "by the way," he said to a man,
> "go out," he says, "to the door," he says,
> > "and fetch in the footman," he said,
> > > "and give him something to drink," he said,
> > > > "and get my sweetheart's horses stabled for her at once."

Out he goes.
His man goes out.
Nothing.
Two big puddocks away hopping along the road.
And a wee cabbage leaf (withered?), blowing away with the wind.
Nothing.
All was gone.

And Mary married the young laird.
And lived happy ever after and had a big family.
And the old Traveller man camped there all the days of his life,
every winter until his family was reared up.
And that is the last of my wee story.

[laughter]
And that's the Travellers' version of Cinderella. (SA76.221)

Duncan's performance of this story has a distinct Traveller flavor because he uses Traveller language and speech patterns and has set the story within

194   *Storytelling and Community*

the context of Traveller daily life. Yet, in large part, this performance follows the outline of the familiar variant of the Cinderella story that was published by Charles Perrault.[5]

Here is the tale-type outline of the Cinderella tale type (Aarne and Thompson type 510), edited to focus on the sequence of motifs that fit the Perrault version of the story:

> I. *The Persecuted Heroine.* (a) The heroine is abused by her stepmother and stepsisters and (a1) stays on the hearth or in the ashes and, (a2) is dressed in rough clothing. . . .
> II. *Magic Help.* While she is acting as a servant (at home or among strangers) she is advised, provided for, and fed by . . . (c) a supernatural being. . . .
> III. *Meeting the Prince.* (a) She dances in beautiful clothing several times with the prince, who seeks in vain to keep her. . . .
> IV. *Proof of Identity.* (a) She is discovered through the slipper-test. . . .
> V. *Marriage with the Prince.* . . . (Aarne and Thompson 1961, 175)

Although the two stories are quite similar, a closer analysis reveals some differences. The Perrault version of the story opens with Cinderella as a young woman who is abused by her new stepmother and stepsisters (point I in the outline above). This persecution sets up her physical and psychological needs that are resolved through supernatural help and marriage to the prince. In Duncan's version of the story, however, Mary is not abused by her family. Travellers care deeply for their children and will do anything for them. The abusive stepmother motif may therefore be missing in Duncan's performance because this abuse does not make sense within Traveller culture. Instead, the story describes a situation where Mary is raised by her grandmother and continues to live in close proximity to the rest of her loving family.

Because of the family relationships developed in the opening scene, it makes sense that the supernatural help and advice that Mary receives (point II in the outline) comes not from her godmother as it does in the Perrault version but from her grandmother, a figure in the story who embodies nurturing, wisdom, and possibility. While the grandmother-as-witch motif fits the logic of the story, keep in mind that this is a folktale. Attributing magical powers to the grandmother in the story does not necessarily imply that Travellers believe they have magical powers. Notwithstanding this change in character, Mary's grandmother, like the godmother, uses her powers to transform animals and vegetables into the carriage and servants that take Mary to the party.

From this point on the stories parallel each other in terms of plot, although Duncan's version is much richer in detail. The laird falls in love with Mary as quickly as the prince does with Cinderella (point III in the outline). Mary has no sisters who compete with her, but there are many other potential brides who fulfill this function in the story. The clock chiming midnight of the Perrault version is replaced by the movement of the moon, but Mary runs from the party and loses her slipper just as Cinderella does, and is finally discovered by means of the slipper test (point IV). Like Cinderella, Mary marries the laird and they live happily ever after (point V).

The changes in the story seem to be fairly superficial since they deal with minor elements of style and characterization. Yet these subtle differences give rise to significant changes in the meaning of the story. Central to this transformation is the realization that unlike Cinderella, Mary is not persecuted by her family. She is happy in her life and in her relationships with her parents and her grandmother. Further, even after Mary is married and presumably wealthy, her parents and grandmother choose to continue their nomadic way of life, returning each winter to camp on the laird's estate. Consequently, the story cannot be interpreted as a rags-to-riches success story or as embodying a tension in social structure that is resolved when Mary moves from a life of misery and low status to a life of wealth and high status (cf. Pace 1982). Granny does say to her son-in-law that Mary's marriage to the laird will be "the best thing that ever happened" and that they will be "well off forever," but what she means is that the family:

> ". . . can come here and camp and—
> all the days of your life," she said,
> "and nobody will ever bother you."

In this sense, Duncan's performance embodies the claim that success does not lie in social status and wealth but in the freedom to live your life as you wish. For Travellers this appears to mean continuing to live by Traveller beliefs and practices.

What then of Mary's choice to marry the laird? It is curiosity, not misery, that motivates Mary's desire to go to the bene hantle's party. She wants to find out what non-Traveller life is like. At one point she says to her grandmother "You're good to me. But . . . I would like to see what goes on up there." Her grandmother helps her and supports her in this quest by providing the transportation and outward appearance that allows Mary to attend the party. She even supports Mary's choice to marry the laird and pursue a path that appears to lead away from the traditions of Traveller life. But these actions are not necessarily antithetical to Traveller worldview. Researcher Farnham Rehfisch notes, for example, that Travellers are free to choose their own spouses and that marriages between Travellers and settled folks are not uncommon (1961). Mary's choices also exemplify the fundamental Traveller belief in the freedom to live one's life as one wishes—to make choices and explore their consequences for oneself. Note, however, that Mary's choice in this regard is somewhat problematic. After the laird discovers her in the Travellers' camp and expresses his desire to take her away, Granny objects. The laird responds by saying, "I'm taking her. . . . She's mine. . . . I must have her"—statements that imply ownership and the apparent end to Mary's autonomy. I find this element of the tale puzzling. It may serve as a warning about differences in Traveller and settled beliefs and therefore about the problems of mixed relationships and the concessions that will be needed from both individuals to make such a marriage work. It may be intended as a way of highlighting the intensity of the laird's feelings in the scene where he at long last discovers that Mary is his beloved. Alternatively, this dialog may simply express the male belief that wives are the property of their husbands.

Yet, whatever the ultimate meaning of her marriage to the laird, Mary's curiosity about non-Travellers and her consequent engagement with the non-Traveller world sets up an interpretive frame that focuses attention on the contrast between Traveller and non-Traveller cultures. This interpretive frame highlights the nature of the relationship between the groups and especially the discrimination against Travellers that provides one of the driving tensions of the story.

This pattern of discrimination is most visible in the words and actions of the laird's men. When the guard is questioned as to whether he saw a beautiful woman run out of the party, for instance, he responds, "Nae one passed here . . . but some of these Gypsy brats from the tinkers' camp down there." Similarly, when the laird's men are ordered to search for the princess, they do not even think of looking in the Traveller camp that is on the laird's estate. When the young laird sees the camp and wonders what it is, his servant responds, "Oh, no, my lord . . . that's nothing concerning you." But when the laird wonders if the young woman he seeks might be in this camp, his foreman replies:

> "Oh, my Lord," he said, "no, no, no," he said.
> "These girls, these are people," he said,
> "these are tinker people of the road," he said,
> "Travellers, tinkers, Gypsies."

These comments suggest that non-Travellers view Travellers as being somehow inferior, perhaps even subhuman.

Mary's mother and father are clearly aware of this worldview and the discrimination it can foster, as their responses to interactions with non-Travellers indicate. For example, when they see the coach at granny's camp, Mary's mother worries that they will be shifted or jailed for interfering. Similarly, when the young laird comes to the camp with the glass slipper, Mary's mother and father worry about what they might have done to anger the laird and bring about his visit.

Duncan's story challenges this discriminatory worldview and the insecurity it generates by questioning the inherent assumption that Travellers are inferior to non-Travellers. The challenge comes chiefly from the words and actions of the young laird. Despite the efforts of his foreman to convince him that he should not even consider looking in the Traveller camp, the laird responds "It makes no difference to me . . . if they are Gypsies or what they are." His attitude comes out even more explicitly when he responds to repeated attempts by his men to dissuade him from trying the slipper on Mary's foot:

> And this foreman of this head bene cowl says,
> "My Lord," he says, "that's a tinker."
> He says, "I don't care," he says, "suppose it's Satan," he said.
> "She's got a foot, doesn't she?"
> "Oh, yes," he said, "and two lovely feet she has got."
> "Well," he said, "get the shoe and try it on her foot," he said.
> "She's as good as anybody else."

The laird's words explicitly challenge ethnocentric views of the Travellers and validate the belief that Travellers are as human as anyone else, regardless of cultural differences. It may seem puzzling that Duncan puts the criticism of ethnocentric views of Travellers into the laird's mouth. Perhaps this is a way of pointing out that not all settled folk are equally prejudiced. It may also be a strategic choice in that non-Traveller listeners might more readily accept a non-Traveller's evaluation of the validity of Traveller identity than they will a Traveller evaluation of their own identity.

This egalitarian view of cultural differences is also supported by the character of Mary's grandmother. It is Granny who directly supports Mary's desire to go to the laird's party and who consistently speaks with a voice of knowledge about the relationship between Travellers and non-Travellers. For example, in response to Mary's father's concern over Mary's desire to go the party, Granny responds, "You never know . . . what she might get yet, . . . before she's off this world." It is also Granny who reassures her family as to how events will unfold after contact with the non-Travellers. Where Mary's parents are pessimistic and expect the worst in all situations involving contact with non-Travellers, Granny and the laird prove them wrong. In this sense, her character complements that of the laird by suggesting that Travellers might be as prejudiced as non-Travellers and that non-Travellers may be as human as Travellers.

Yet the figures of the laird and Granny are not entirely analogous. Where the laird expresses acceptance of Travellers as human beings, his perspective appears to have developed in ignorance of the pervasive settled beliefs about the inferiority of Travellers. This innocence allows him to see beyond stereotypes and see Mary as a human being. Granny, however, seems to accept that non-Travellers can be good human beings based on her enhanced knowledge of both Traveller and non-Traveller worlds. As she herself suggests, she "kens" things. Because the story centers around Mary's curiosity about the non-Traveller world, a pattern emerges, suggesting that a great deal of the discrimination and misunderstanding between the cultures arises from a lack of knowledge about the other culture. It is Mary's curiosity about the non-Travellers that leads her to the laird's party. Through meeting the laird face-to-face, the influence of a great deal of misunderstanding and stereotyping is eliminated. This point is supported symbolically through Mary's transformation. As a Traveller, Mary is ignored by the laird's men. When she is transformed by Granny's magic into an "angel" with the outward appearance of a non-Traveller, she is noticed and admired by all. Yet the Mary the laird meets and falls in love with is the same Mary he meets in the Traveller camp. Her inner self remains unchanged despite the transformation in her appearance that takes place through Granny's magic.

Because of this focus on issues of cultural difference and discrimination, Duncan's performance communicates not only about Mary's transformation in personal identity but also about the relationship between Travellers and non-Travellers at the level of cultural identity. Although the story does not imply that one way of life is better than the other, it does support the validity of Traveller identity and worldview and suggests that both Travellers and non-Travellers are equally human.

Given this underlying framework of meaning, listeners might come away from Duncan's story understanding that individual freedom is an essential component of Traveller worldview. They might better comprehend what it means to be a Traveller living in a world that is rife with discrimination. They might even gain a deeper sense of the process of discrimination and the inherent value of all human beings. One key point here is that the world of fictional storytelling is therefore not simply an entertaining diversion. Listeners may identify with fictional characters in just the same way they might identify with a real character in an experiential story. In some cases fictional stories may be understood as metaphorical commentaries on important aspects of Traveller life. Listeners may also understand the play with beliefs, relationships, or interpretive strategies that takes place in performing a fictional story as being relevant to ongoing attempts to make sense of the world of lived experience (see chapter 5). In this sense, performances of fictional stories are a powerful way of creating imaginative worlds that can evoke experiences that are directly relevant to constructions of worldview and identity. Performers can use these experiences as a way of expanding conceptions of community in abstract ways, thereby strengthening the ties that link Travellers in a meaningful web of community.

Throughout the examples in this chapter, I have focused on the interconnections between Traveller stories and Traveller lives. I have argued that stories are inextricably entwined with a meaningful sense of relationship whenever an individual performs, hears, or even thinks about a particular story. I have also suggested that storytelling performances can be used to expand the boundaries of face-to-face encounters over space to include people who are not physically present and through time to include people who may no longer be alive but who continue to influence perceptions of community. Finally, I have illustrated how fictional stories may be used to creatively explore issues or representations of community.

In these ways stories can be used to create, traditionalize, and transform aspects of relationship and connection between human beings that are essential to perceptions of identity and community. They can also strengthen Travellers' sense of community by projecting the expectation and desire for interaction into the future. Stories may similarly be used to define the boundaries of Traveller communities by exploring the differences between Travellers and outsiders. It is to this use of stories that I now direct attention.

4. "You'll Have to Change Your Ways"

The Negotiation of Identity in Storytelling Performance

Given the importance of storytelling in Traveller life and given the virtuosity with which Travellers deal with stories, it is not surprising that Travellers use stories not only as vehicles for shaping belief and identity within their communities but also for negotiating issues of identity and worldview in interactions with outsiders. During my interviews, for example, when I asked questions about Traveller lives and beliefs, I was often answered by stories that replayed past events as a way of teaching me about Traveller identity and worldview. A similar process can take place whenever there is some mediation of the barrier between Travellers and outsiders—in work relationships, during meetings with sympathetic outsiders, or where friendships have formed. Similarly, public performances intended for non-Travellers, often made possible through the interests of the folk revival, put the performer on display and highlight his or her unique identity and worldview. These events therefore provide opportunities for Travellers to challenge misinformed images or stereotypes of their identity that may be held by audience members.

In this chapter I examine one kind of Traveller story that is particularly effective in dealing with issues of identity and worldview. I term these stories *interaction stories* because they narrate interactions between Travellers and non-Travellers. By focusing on observable events in the "real world," these stories engage identity and worldview in pragmatic terms—as they are actually expressed through the words and actions of individuals, not as they are conceptualized in some abstract or ideal world. This anchor in the "real world" additionally suggests these narrative representations have objective validity.

Understanding how these stories work across cultural boundaries requires careful attention to not only story content but also to the choices narrators make in the selection and presentation of "what happened" in the narrated event. These choices may build on diverse communicative strategies that present Traveller identity and argue for its validity or that contrast Traveller and settled identities. They may also involve the creation of formal or stylistic patterns that influence how listeners experience and understand the performance.

In this chapter I explore five strategies Travellers use in performing interaction stories during events when non-Travellers are present. These strategies include: (1) reporting words or actions that embody key facets of identity, (2) replaying events as a focus for evaluations and interpretations of identity in the performance event, (3) reporting evaluations of identity from participants in the narrated event, (4) suggesting conceptions of identity as listeners follow the interactions of fictional characters, and (5) presenting metaphorical commentaries on differential identity. In any given performance, these strategies are often combined.

The cracks I use in illustrating these strategies were recorded in response to my questions about Traveller life and experience or emerged during informal conversations when the tape recorder was left running. The folktales in sections IV and V were recorded during public performances. Since my focus in this chapter is on identity and worldview, I make no attempt to fully address other aspects of the function and meaning of the performances, trusting that comments in other chapters can suggest strategies for more complete analyses. Nor do I directly address the stereotypes Travellers hold of non-Travellers that may implicitly or explicitly inform the stories they use to challenge outsider views. I end the chapter with some thoughts on how narrative negotiations of identity can transcend face-to face interactions. In particular I will comment on the effect of media presentations of Traveller stories.

I. Reported Speech and Action

One key to the potency of interaction stories in engaging issues of identity and worldview derives from their use by performers to re-create past events or interactions. As I argued in chapter 3, storytelling can function to give listeners experiences of the narrated events and therefore to expand the "data" that are available within these interactions for individuals to use in creating their senses of worldview and identity. In cross-cultural interactions this use of stories becomes particularly relevant, for it allows a performer to give non-Travellers experiences they might never have in any other way. This allows non-Travellers insight into how and why Travellers view the world the way they do.

In response to my questions about relations between the groups, Travellers often told me stories that reported the words and actions of non-Travellers. One illustration of this strategy came during a discussion with Jimmy Williamson about problems with the camping sites constructed under the direction of the Secretary of State's Advisory Committee on Scotland's Travelling People.[1] Jimmy told me how he and other Travellers were angered because the Lochgilphead Traveller site was hidden away in a bog, presumably to hide Travellers from public view. I commented that Duncan, Jimmy's father, had been a consultant to the committee at one time, but that the committee ignored all of his advice—an action that made me suspicious the committee ever wanted his advice in the first place. In the following story fragment, Jimmy confirms my suspicion by relating an event that took place during a public meeting with the Secretary of State's Committee:

> No, they didn't want it.
> They just—
> It's a token.
> They wanted someone there as a token,
> to say that there was a Traveller there,
> as a token person being there.
>
> I mean, that cousin I was telling you . . . [about]. . ?
> Well, he—
> He stood up and said—

He was going to speak.
And one of them says,
"Sit!
I know more about Travellers than you do.
I have been studying for ten years." (TS92035)

Through reporting this event, Jimmy demonstrates the committee's lack of interest in Traveller input. Jimmy's re-creation lets me participate in the meeting and draw my own conclusions by inferring the worldview that informs the committee member's suggestion that ten years of academic study is more important than a lifetime of experience. As I follow the story, I therefore gain insight into Traveller frustration with government policy.

A story that similarly reports the words and actions of a non-Traveller was told by Betty Townsley during a recording session that included Betty, Thomas Burton, Sue Grizzell, and myself. Our conversation centered on Traveller life and occupation. I asked a question about the Traveller practice of moving in groups in response to harassment from non-Travellers. Betty commented: "So if you've got safety in numbers it's okay. You live with it. You've got to live with this sort of fear as well. You—there's a fear there as well" (TS92025). The following exchange came shortly after Betty's comment:

DB Do you get a lot of problems with that,
    when you go door to door selling things,
    that people are very upset with you?
BT Mhmm.
TB Have you had any bad experiences yourself?
BT Mhmm.

    One woman chased me down the driveway with a knife. [laughs]
    (All the way?)
    I went up.
    And she says,
    "I'm sick fed up with people coming to my door.
    I'm fed up with tarmackers.*
    I'm fed up."

---

*tarmackers = people who lay tarmac or blacktop for a living

Negotiation of Identity in Storytelling Performance   205

I said,
"I only come to ask you the time," You know?
  I wasn't really.
  I was going to sell her some peat.
I said,
"All I want to do is ask you the time."

Well, down the road—
She had this big knife,
and she's chasing me down the drive. (TS92025)

I can imagine this story being told among Travellers as a warning about how crazy the settled folk can be. In the interview context, however, Betty's re-creation serves as graphic evidence of settled worldview and the irrationality of their response to Travellers. Tom Burton's question prompts Betty to shift from talking abstractly about the kinds of harassment Travellers might endure to talking concretely about an injustice that she did endure. But Betty does not just tell us she feels uneasy around settled people. She shows us why she feels this way. Her story re-creates the interaction in a way that allows all present in the performance event to formulate their own understanding of what happened and why. By following Betty's performance, I can experience what it must be like to be suddenly chased down the drive with a knife while knowing I need to keep ringing doorbells to survive economically. By putting myself in Betty's position, I can also empathize with her about the ongoing hostility Travellers must deal with throughout their lives.

In these two performances, Jimmy and Betty use stories that focus on non-Travellers to show events, actions, or words from the past. These events are selected because they speak for themselves. In this sense, they are not so much presentations of Traveller identity as they are presentations of the context within which Traveller identity is formed and maintained. This is an important foundation for understanding Traveller identity. If outsiders can understand the fears and prejudices that permeate non-Traveller interactions with Travellers, they can better understand how Travellers understand and respond to the world.

A complementary group of stories presents an image of Traveller identity through the narration of Traveller words and actions. One such story was told by Duncan Williamson during an interview on 6 February 1993 that focused on aspects of his genealogy. As he talked about Maggie MacLaren, a distant relation, Duncan commented that she was a good storyteller. He then told the following story as an example of the kinds of stories she liked to tell.[2]

      She was telling me another story.
      Auld Sandy Cameron, she said,
      her man's faither, Old San—, Old Chief,
      he was a great fisherman. He liked to fish.
5   And he was fishing in some private loch, see?
         She was a great story[teller],
         she could tell you stories about anything.
      And she says, Old Sandy, God rest his soul—
         And she'd swear . . . life away
10   trying to make you believe it was true.
      Maybe it was.

      And, she said, Old Chief was fishing, she said,
      with a bit stick and a line.
      And she said, he was casting on a
15   some kind of private river somewhere.
      Some estate out in Perthshire.

      On—
      Along came a big gentleman, you know?
         Gentleman.
20   Big waders, you know?
         And the basket on his back,
           and the (landing?) net, you know?
      Real gentleman.
      And he's casting away and casting away.

25   And Old Sandy pulled in a big sea trout [gesture miming pulling in fish]
      about that size. [gesture to indicate size]
      And the gentleman was watching him.

      He hooked it off
      and threw it back.
30   Gentleman's staring at him.

         He's casting away with a cast of flies.
         Old Sandy's casting the worms he had.

And he's (?) cast again, see?
He knew he was in trouble, you see?
35　Cast again.
The gentleman's watching him.

Because he, he thought it was the laird, you see?
He could have done with a fish but—

And he hooked another ane* about this size. [gesture to indicate size]
40　And the gentleman's watching him again.
It was close together.

He's hooked it off.
"Away you go, you fishie."
And he put it back again.
45　And the gentleman come up.

"Excuse me, sir," he says.
Why are you fishing here?"
And he said, "I'm fishing in the river," he said.

"Don't you know," he said, "you are on private property?"
50　"I didn't know it was private property," he said.
　　"I'm one of the Travelling folk," he said.
　　"I'm just trying to get a fish."

"But what's the sense of—
You see, I've been here for an hour,
55　and I can't catch anything.
What's the secret?"
"Well," he said,
"just a handful of worms, mister," he said to him. [brusque voice]
　You know the way the Travellers speak?
60　　kind of rough.
"A handful of worms." [brusque voice]

"Well," he says, "I saw you putting two nice fish back, didn't you?"
He says, "Why did you put them back?"
He says, "I'll tell you why I put them back."
65　"Why did you put them back then?"
He says, "My pan's only that size." [indicates a size smaller than the two fish he caught] [laughter]

---

*ane = one (pronounced YIN)

>   And he pulled in his line and walked away.
>   Gentleman watched him.
>   Never said a word. [laughter]
>
> 70   That's the only way he could get out of it, you know?
>   He was going to charge him for fishing.
>
>   He said, "My, my, my wee frying pan, mister,
>   is only that size," he says.
>   "And they're too big for my pan,
> 75   so I'll no bother mair the day."
>   And he walked away.
>   The gentleman looked at him,
>   the laird,
>   fishing the stream, private river. (TS93005)

While Duncan's performance of this story is complex and multifaceted, I limit my comments to aspects of the performance that function to communicate about Traveller identity. In lines 1–16 Duncan contextualizes his performance as a replaying of Maggie MacLaren's own performance from some previous performance event. By quoting Maggie's words, and by commenting on her performance style, Duncan maintains our focus on genealogical issues. Additionally, the protagonist in the narrated event is Maggie's father-in-law, another of Duncan's relations. Duncan's narration therefore communicates about the identities of specific family members and perhaps about more general aspects of family identity.

Duncan's contextualization of this story also points to a second possible interpretation. In lines 9 and 10, "And she'd swear . . . life away / trying to make you believe it was true," Duncan raises the possibility that many of Maggie's stories are fabrications. Consequently, this story about Old Chief may be apocryphal—not to be understood as actually having happened. Duncan intentionally leaves the truth status of the story open by commenting in line 11, "Maybe it was [true]."

Duncan's framing of the story is therefore ambiguous. The story is indeed a story that Maggie told about her father-in-law. But whether it actually happened to Sandy or is a creative fabrication, attention to Duncan's formal patterning of the story reveals a carefully crafted presentation of Traveller identity. Within this performance, the ambiguity in truth status implies that Old Chief's words and actions should be understood as both reflective of Old Chief's personal identity and as representative of facets of identity shared by Travellers as a group.

In lines 2–16 Duncan's narration is effectively a replaying of Maggie's earlier narration. By line 18, however, Duncan assumes accountability for the performance of the story himself. After setting the scene with the image of Sandy, Old Chief, fishing with "a bit stick and a line," lines 18–23 introduce the "gentleman," who embodies the privilege and power of the non-Traveller world. Duncan then sets up a pattern of expectation through the formal features of his performance. A series of syntactically keyed narrative segments contrast Old Chief's actions with the gentleman's response. For example, in lines 25–27, Sandy pulls in a big sea trout and "the gentleman was watching him." This pattern is repeated in 28–30, 33–36, 39–40, 42–45, 67–69, and 76–77. Each time the narrative segment ends with a close variant of "the gentleman was watching him" (lines 27, 30, 36, 40, 45, 68, and 77)—an apparently passive response to Sandy's illegal fishing.[3] With each repetition of the pattern Duncan builds the tension by indicating that Sandy knows he is in trouble. This pattern also builds expectation for the gentleman's response. Yet in lines 25–44 the gentleman continues to watch as Sandy catches fish after fish—apparently releasing them because they are caught illegally.

This pattern of expectation reaches a climax in line 45 where the gentleman does not passively watch but ". . . the gentleman come up." This break in the pattern emphasizes the gentleman's action and marks a key shift in the story. The gentleman moves from passively watching to actively asserting his legal claim to the water and the fish it contains. Line 45 also marks a shift in the story from a focus on action to a focus on speech.

In lines 46–66 it is Sandy who responds to the gentleman's questions—a reversal of the pattern of action and response that takes place in lines 25–45. Sandy's responses are straightforward, as in lines 50–52: "I didn't know it was private property / I'm, one of the Travelling folk, . . . / I'm just trying to get a fish." In lines 54–55 it becomes clear that the gentleman is not just upset about the illegal fishing, he is puzzled by Sandy's success in contrast to his own failure, despite his superior fishing equipment. Again Sandy's response is direct. He is fishing with no more than "a handful of worms."

In lines 62–66, the gentleman's control of the situation changes subtly. In lines 62–63 the gentleman asks why Sandy has put the fish back. Sandy's response in line 64, ". . . I'll tell you why I put them back," does not directly answer the gentleman's question. This answer seizes the initiative, forcing the gentleman to ask "why did you put them back then?" in response to Sandy's comment. This shift in initiative foreshadows the shift in power that takes place through the punch line "My pan's only that size," in line 66. Sandy's words leave the gentleman speechless, and Sandy walks away a free man. He has bested the gentleman in spheres of both action, through his competent fishing, and speech, through the wit of his words. Lines 67–69 also present the return of the earlier pattern of action and response in which Sandy's actions are met by the gentleman's silent watching. Through the transformation accomplished by the punch line, this pattern is retroactively revealed to embody not only a powerful gentleman observing a Traveller's illegal poaching, but also the competent and witty behavior of a Traveller in eluding the consequences of his actions.

The repeated line, "And the gentleman was watching him," serves another function in the performance as well. It repeatedly focuses audience attention, in the narrative event, on the words and actions of Old Chief. In a parallel to how the gentleman tries to make sense of Sandy's actions, the audience is invited to make sense out of these same actions with respect to issues of Traveller identity. In the narrated event, Sandy masterfully plays on the prevailing stereotype of Travellers as ignorant and potentially irrational. He reveals himself to be quick thinking and witty in his verbal exchange. Sandy's actions in the narrated event demonstrate the ability of Travellers to make skillful use of whatever resources they have. Here Sandy manages to catch two fish with a "bit stick and a line" and a "handful of worms," while the gentleman with all his fancy gear can't catch anything. But it is the formal patterning of the storytelling performance that provides a guiding framework that leads me to understand the value and validity of these elements of Traveller identity. In following Sandy's actions in the narrated event and in following Duncan's

Negotiation of Identity in Storytelling Performance 211

presentation of these actions, I learn something about how Travellers have managed to survive in a hostile world and therefore about central elements of Traveller identity.

II. Evaluations of Narrated Action

In other performances, Travellers use stories not only to replay events but also to provide a context for their interpretations and evaluations of Traveller and non-Traveller identities. This was the case in a performance I recorded that was done by Betty Townsley. Worried by a government proposal to change the Caravan Sites Act of 1968 (Department of the Environment 1992), Betty, Sue Grizzell, and I were talking about problems Travellers encounter during life on the road. Betty said Travellers endure constant abuse from locals and police despite the "non-harassment policy" that is in force in many parts of Scotland.[4] Her illustrations of this practice revealed that much of the Traveller/non-Traveller conflict grows out of ingrained stereotypes held by non-Travellers about Traveller behavior. Following a comment by Sue about the belief that all Travellers and Gypsies are thieves, Betty said she has to keep receipts for everything she owns so that the police will not confiscate her possessions under suspicion of theft. She then narrated the following experience:

> Well, I mind that we were,
> they nearly took our trailer from us,
> more or less about,
> maybe about two year ago.
>
> 5 They come in a Landrover
> and about—ten—detectives.
> Just because one man on the motorway passed by
> and thought it was his.
>   Thought it was his.
> 10   It looked like his.
>
> Now, how many cars look alike?
> You can't just go and point,
>   "That, that's my trailer.

That's it.
15   I want it."

Now this trailer was only,
    what, months old.
And he come down with this
    big Landrover
and just reversed it in.

And Willie said, "What are
    you doing?"
20 He said, "We got a report that
    this trailer is stolen."
And he said, "What proof have
    you got?"
He said, "Well, we've got some
    numbers here."
"Well," Willie said, "There's
    my number there."
He said, "Check it."

Betty Townsley, 1998

25 Right.
One letter was the same.
One!
It was a eight.
    I remember eight was the same.
30   One eight.

Right.
He says, "Well, eh,"—
Now this young boy, he was really cheeky—
"I think we should take it away to go through it proper."

35 And (?) the one who was above him said, "No."
"No," he says,
"It's okay," he says.

And then the boy, it was supposed to be his trailer that was stolen,
he says, "Well,"
40 "I've got reflectors."
You know how you've got orange reflectors along the big sides?
He said, "the middle one,"
he said, "I had a hole in it."
He said, "And I filled it with paste,"
45 he said, "and put the reflector on it."

Negotiation of Identity in Storytelling Performance   213

"Oh, that's okay," the policeman said.
"Okay."
RRRIP.
   Ripped it off.
50   Broke it off.
There was nothing behind it because it was new.

And he said, "I don't think it was that one, I think it was that one."
So he ripped that one off.

And we're standing. [laughs]
55 And (he?) said, "Just tear it in."
I'm watching this.

So I went down to the phone,
and I phoned a lawyer.
Because we've got a lawyer in the thingummy. [referencing a booklet on legal rights published for Travellers].

60 And they followed me to the phone.
Knocked on the [Betty knocks on the table] phone,
and I pulled the door open.
"You don't have to phone your lawyer.
We decided we are not going to do it.
65 We'll come back in the morning.
We won't take it away."
Followed me to the phone. [laughs]

Hmm?

That was horrible, that. (TS92031)

Betty's performance brings her experience into the narrative event and anchors it with respect to Sue's and my emerging understanding of Traveller identity and the "Traveller problem" in Scotland. She tells us what happened so we can experience what Traveller life is like. She also actively evaluates what happened from a Traveller perspective, giving us insight into the underlying conflicts in identity and worldview that inform this event. Betty accomplishes this evaluation through her commentary on what happens in the narrated event and through her choices in terms of how she tells the story (see Labov 1972). In lines 7–8, for example, Betty suggests that the whole interaction is motivated by one man's conclusion that she and her husband must be in possession of his stolen trailer because he "thought it was his." Betty emphasizes the absurdity of this conclusion through her repetition "Thought it was his. / It looked like his," in lines 9–10; her question "Now, how many cars look alike?" in line 11; and her reenactment of frivolous claims of ownership in lines 12–15. Yet the flimsiest suggestion of theft is apparently believed by the police, who arrive with no fewer than "ten detectives" ready to haul the trailer away without any further evidence. Even the fact that only one number of the serial number matches the stolen trailer—a point Betty again emphasizes through repetition in lines 26–30—is not sufficient to awaken the authorities to the thought they may have made a mistake. One supervisor notes that they might have made a mistake, in lines 35–37, but the detectives continue to assume that the trailer must be stolen and tear off parts of the trailer to prove the theft.

By telling the story in this way, Betty puts front and center the conception of Traveller identity that is implicit in the police actions. They are so sure that all Travellers are liars and thieves that evidence to the contrary does not register with them. They have trusted the word of a non-Traveller as to theft but entirely ignore the Travellers' (assumed) comments that the trailer in fact belongs to them. Also implicit in the police action is the belief that all Travellers are lazy and never work. All money or expensive possessions, such as the trailer, must therefore be the product of theft. I should note that many Traveller trailers I have seen are quite elaborate, spotlessly clean, and surely expensive. This fact probably plays into the police assumption that no Traveller could legitimately afford such a costly trailer.

In contrast to the actions of the police, Betty portrays the Travellers as incredulous but sane participants in the event. Upon being told that the police suspect their trailer is stolen, Betty's husband sensibly proposes they check the serial number before hauling it away (lines 19–24). Since the trailer is not stolen, the serial numbers do not match. When parts of their nearly new trailer are torn off to prove the theft, Betty and her husband do not go wild but stand and watch in civilized horror (see lines 54–56). Where any other citizen might call the police to prevent these outrageous acts, Betty cannot—since it is the police themselves who are committing the acts. Instead, Betty goes to the phone to call her lawyer. This action awakens the detectives to the fact that they are not dealing with what they have assumed is an unintelligent, passive thief. Betty is well aware of the law and her rights under the law. She is also aware that she is responding to police action in a manner that is meaningful from the perspective of settled worldview. Perhaps the courts will even overlook any prejudice against Travellers and understand the absurdity and injustice of the police actions. It is therefore not the rights of the Travellers that force the detectives to back off, but the fear of the potential consequences of legal action.

Through her creative presentation of this story, then, Betty not only replays a past event but also evaluates and interprets what happened in such a way that we, as outsiders, can understand the motivations and beliefs that inform participant words and actions. In following Betty's performance, Sue and I therefore gain insight into the underlying contrast between Traveller and non-Traveller worldviews and identities.

The effective use of interaction stories as a focus for evaluations of worldview and identity requires careful selection of the event to be narrated. One factor that makes Betty's story so effective is that the narrated event recounts a troubling interaction, even when viewed from an outsider perspective. While Betty's evaluative comments certainly influence how listeners perceive the event, it is difficult to imagine how this event might be narrated differently in order to validate the police actions. It is, in fact, doubtful that any of the non-Travellers present at the time would choose to narrate this event.

Another reason Betty's story works so effectively is that it invokes concepts—such as truth, justice, and home—that play meaningful roles in non-Traveller lives. These concepts engage listeners and invite them to experience the narrated event and understand how these symbols are interpreted within the context of Traveller lives.

A story that similarly uses contrasting interpretations of symbols to focus attention on differences in worldview and identity emerged during a 1988 interview with Duncan Williamson. Duncan and I were discussing "The Hawker's Lament," a song he composed in the 1960s to address the interrelated problems of police harassment and finding legal camping sites. Duncan has performed this song frequently for both Traveller and non-Traveller audiences. Here is a transcription of this song from a performance I recorded during my first visit with Duncan in 1985:

The Hawker's Lament

Oh, come all you hawkers, you men of the road,
You hawkers who wander around,
For my story it is sad, it will sadden your heart,
For they're closing our camping grounds down.

Though we fought for our country and we fought for our king,
And some gave their life for this land,
It's out there in Dunkirk it's many we fell
With our blood mixed up with the sand.

But what did we fight for and why did we die?
For freedom to wander around.
But where can we wander we have no place to go,
For they're closing our camping grounds down.

They say we are not wanted, just keep moving on,
Though it be rain or be snow.
But where can we move to when we move along?
For we have got nowhere to go.

So listen my friends, if another war it comes,
Just you keep moving around.
You have nothing to fight for, you have no house nor home,
And they've closed all your camping grounds down.

But maybe some day, when we are gone from this world,
And we're buried deep down in the ground.
Will God make us welcome, will he give us a home,
Or will he tell us to keep moving on? (TS85005)

During our 1988 interview, Duncan told me that the BBC heard of his song, recorded it from him, and broadcast it over the radio. But Duncan said the broadcast cut out the third verse, the one that questions why Travellers gave their lives in World War II, because BBC officials felt it was "too political." Here is the verse as Duncan sang it to me in 1988:

The Hawker's Lament

1st Verse:
Oh come all you hawkers you men of the road, you hawkers who wander around For my story it is sad, it will sadden your heart, for they're clo-sing our campin' grounds down.

2nd Verse:
Though we fought for our country and we fought for our king, and some gave their life for this land It's out there in Dunkirk it's many we fell, with our blood mixed up with the sand.

Sung with flexible, somewhat free meter; rhythm follows text closely so it differs considerably from verse to verse.

⌢ indicates elongation of note (not extended hold).

218   *Negotiation of Identity in Storytelling Performance*

> *Oh, what did we fight for and why did we die?*
> *For freedom to wander around.*
> *But where can we wander? We have no place to go,*
> *For they've closed all our camping grounds down.* (TS88006)

This song invokes associations with World War II—an experience that is deeply imbedded in the lives and identities of people throughout Scotland. In the song, Duncan suggests that the sacrifices Travellers made fighting for freedom in World War II have been forgotten, as evinced by the current treatment of Travellers. But from the perspective of settled worldview, the connections made through the song's logic between sacrifice and freedom may be difficult to accept. While everyone might agree that the war was fought for freedom, the concept of freedom is inevitably defined ethnocentrically—from each group's point of view. Yet, it is this apparent contradiction between Traveller and settled interpretations of freedom that is key to the potency of Duncan's song. If settled listeners follow the song's logic and accept the Traveller definition of freedom, and if conceptions of justice are sufficiently similar for both groups, they will be forced to recognize the injustice that has taken place and therefore to rethink the ideological assumptions implicit in policies of assimilation. Ultimately this experience may lead to a more reasonable approach to the "Traveller problem."

Not surprisingly, Duncan was furious at the BBC's omission of the verse during their broadcast. He commented to me that the song "had nothing political in it"—that the song was simply "telling the actual truth" (TS88006). In support of his argument, Duncan told me of the number of family members who had given their lives in wars fighting for freedom. He then told the following story that relates the experience of his uncle Sandy in the 1914 war.

> I'll tell you a story, Donald,
> a true story.
> My mother had a brother called Sandy.
> Now Sandy was in the 1914 war, all through the 1914 war.
> For five years, 1914 war, and never got a scratch.
> Right?
>
> Now.
> Down in Dumbarton, near a place called Hellensburgh—

you passed through Dumbarton, you came over Dumbarton—
there was a camping place by the shore side
where all the Travellers used to spend their days in Dumbarton city.
And at nighttime, they would push their handcarts or ponies down to the beach.
And then they would put their tents for the night
and stay a night, maybe two nights, maybe three nights,
on the beach shore, on the shorefront.
Which was hurting nobody.

My Uncle Sandy came back from France in 1915 in his kilt.
And his wife met him at the station.
She says, "Look, I'm down on the beach.
We'll walk down to the beach," she says, "where I'm tented."
And the man was wanting to come back with his wife.
He'd been away for over a year.

He came back to the beach.
He'd only been there—
She was making him a little cup of tea,
when in comes the police.
He says, "You'll have to shift from here.
You're not allowed to stay here."
Sandy says, "Why?"
He said, "You're on private property.
This is the beach," he says.
"It's private property."

Sandy says, "Look,
do you understand, young man," he says, "I'm only back from France?"
He says, "I don't care if you're back from France or Germany,
but you're not going to stay here for the night."
Well, Sandy says, "Look, I'm only come—
I've been in the trenches," he says, "in France for five years."
"And," he said, "my kilt is full of lice.
Can I have ten minutes to kill the lice in my kilt before I shift?"
He said, "NO!"
And that's a true story.

And he went back—
He had to shift that night.
And my Uncle Sandy—
If you were down tomorrow, I could take you to Furnace.
I'd take you to the monument,

and there's his name, and his brother Charles, on the stone.
That—
He stayed two weeks with his wife.
He had to shift that night.
He went back to France.
And he got a blast, a bomb to his self and he never was heard of.
That was his last time.

My mother's brother,
Charlie, Sandy Townsley.
That's true. . . .

So you see why I had to write this.
I had to write this song.

So.
As far as I was concerned, Donald
that, it wasnae political at all.
I was only—
To me I was only telling the truth. (TS88006)

During our interview Duncan's storytelling performance serves a number of functions: It strengthens my understanding of his motivation for writing "The Hawker's Lament," it clarifies why Duncan believes that his song is not political but simply tells the truth, and it deepens my understanding of the role played by ethnocentrism in the conflict between Travellers and non-Travellers. Like Betty's story, Duncan's performance accomplishes these functions through bringing a past event into the performance event as a focus for interpretation and analysis. By selecting a story that focuses on sacrifice and freedom, Duncan elicits any associations I might have with these terms as a way of engaging me in the contrast in worldview that informs the interaction between Sandy and the police. Sandy is risking his life to defend freedom for Travellers, non-Travellers, and perhaps the entire world. Yet the police, as representatives of non-Traveller authority, ignore Sandy's contribution in the service of freedom and deny Sandy a camping site in which to rest—let alone a cup of tea, or even ten minutes in which to kill the lice in his kilt. The power of Duncan's story lies in the realization that the potentially minor act of shifting Sandy and his wife from the beach disrupts their last meeting before Sandy goes back to France and is killed fighting for freedom as he understands it—including his freedom to live his life as a Traveller. As Duncan says, "he got a blast, a bomb to his self and he never was heard of."

While Duncan frames this story as a true incident that can be verified by finding Sandy's name on the war memorial in the town of Furnace, he also uses his Uncle Sandy's experience in World War I to represent the underlying worldview and identity of both non-Traveller and Traveller participants as representatives of their respective cultural groups. Sandy gives his life fighting for a freedom that he never sees. The policeman's actions are offered as representative of the ongoing denial of Traveller worldview and identity that permeates the settled response to Travellers. This story and Duncan's song "The Hawker's Lament" are therefore complementary. Both use differences in understanding the concepts of sacrifice and freedom as a way of evaluating and challenging outsider understanding of Traveller worldview and identity. Together these stories present a mosaic of experience that functions to negotiate issues of identity and worldview.

A performer's choices as to how to present and evaluate participant actions as a story unfolds will influence listener understanding of the narrated event. In this sense, a single story can be reshaped to serve specific functions within a given performance. This point is nicely illustrated with respect to a second version of Duncan's story about his Uncle Sandy that I recorded in 1992. During this performance, Duncan uses the story to exemplify how police "were very hard on the Travellers" (TS92033). This intent changes how Duncan shapes the telling of the story. Consider, for example, Duncan's emphasis in the exchange between the policeman and Sandy:

> ... Down comes the police.
> The police said, "Come on, you cannae stay here.
> You've got to move on."
> He said, "Look, I'm only here for forty-eight hours to meet my wife."
> He, "You're going.
> You're moving.
> Get says, "I don't care if, care if you're only here for three hours."
> He said that tent down and that fire out."

> And Big Sandy said, "Look," he says,
> "can you give me twenty minutes to clean the lice from my kilt?"
>
> He says, "You'll move on and take your lice with you."
> And he kicked out the fire.
>
> And that policeman wouldn't let him,
> he wouldn't let him stay five minutes there after he come back from the war. (TS92033)

In this story Duncan's focus is on the identity of the specific policeman as opposed to official policy as it is in the previous performance. Here the policeman is portrayed as aggressive and nasty, whereas in the previous version he takes a more passive role, citing regulations he must enforce. The narrated event does not change significantly between the two stories, but Duncan's purpose in telling the story and therefore his evaluation of the narrated event does change. The final lines of this second story confirm Duncan's focus: "And that policeman wouldn't let him, he wouldn't let him stay five minutes there after he come back from the war" (TS92033).

III. Reported Evaluations of Identity

A third strategy used in interaction stories involves replaying narrated events in which non-Travellers themselves evaluate the identity of the Traveller participants in the event. This approach is exemplified in a story I recorded that was told by Bryce Whyte at his home in Montrose on 25 October 1992. Also present during this recording were Sue Grizzell and Thomas Burton. During an exchange that focused on Bryce's memories of Traveller life on the road, he talked about the Travellers' need for independence, and contrasted this with the experience some Travellers had in the British Army during World War II. He then narrated an incident that took place during his own training in the army. Bryce said he and his unit were taken on a survival exercise up into the hills around Aberdeen on a very cold and snowy day. Each soldier was given matches, water, meat, and vegetables, and was told to pair up and cook their food. Bryce teamed up with another Traveller, and the two of them first built a shelter similar to a Traveller bow tent out of bent sticks and army ground sheets. Once they got the fire lit and the food in the pot, Bryce took a look around at how the others were getting on:

So.
I lookit,
I stood up and [laughs] and lookit oot at some o' the rest them,
the un-Travellers, you ken?
The boys that come frae, maybe the like o' Glasgow, Edinburgh, and these big places.
You know what?
They were running, running looking for stones,
for tae build a wee fire, tae make the fireplace.
I says, "Poor buggers." [laughs]
I says, "They'll never make it."
I says, "They'll never make it."
I said, "They'll have tae want meat the day."

So.
This officer said, "The first one that's got their grub made," he says,
"I've got tae come up," he says, "and sample it."
So we wis there a good while afore they got it boiled . . .

So.
I says tae, I says tae, tae Hughie,
that was his name, Hughie MacAllister.
[Bryce acts out dipping finger into pot, putting it into his mouth, and smacking his lips.]
Tasted it.
I says, "I think it's ready."
And we tasted a wee bit o' the beef,
   a wee bitty,
      we just sampled it.

So.
I stood up and I said tae—
"Excuse me, sir," I says,
"I think, eh, I think we're ready for you."
He says, "Already?
You're what?!" he said.
"Are youse, are youse ready for, for me?"
I said, "Yeah."

So.
He was a great big, big man.
He was in the 1914 war, you ken?
He was an old-timer.
Stood over this thing that we had made, you ken?
And he lookit doon like that.
[Sniffs as if smelling the cooking odor] "Mmmm,"

He said, eh, "Very nice, very nice," he said, "Very nice."
And, eh, I [sic] says—
"How dae you get intae this?"
And I says, "Oh, just pull the flap over like that."
And he had a kilt on and his two bare knees, you ken?
Down on the, down on the ground like that. [Bryce kneels, demonstrating]
I says, "Come in, if you can manage tae get in."
He just got in a wee bit and
says, eh, "Gimme your spoon."
Tasted it.
He said, he looked at the two of us he says,
"You know," he says, "You know what I'm going tae tell you?"
He says "I could sit here," he says,
"And muck in wi' you two fellas," he says, "fine."

So.
Uh, that was okay.
And I says tae him, "God help the rest o' them."
He says, "You know," he says,
"I would like," he said, "all my company," he said,
"the whole lot," he says "that's here," he says,
"I would them tae be like youse."

And, eh,
he kenned we was Travellers.
He kenned we was Travellers.
"It's not the first time," he says, "youse has done this."
I says, "And I hope the hell it," I said, "it'll no be the last either!' [laughter]
I said tae him, I says, "I hope tae hell it'll no be the last either!" . . .

[When they get back to base, the Captain calls them into his office]

We went intae the office.
And he says tae, says, eh, "Youse two," he says—
"That, eh," he says, "that was a lovely grub," he says, "youse made," he says.
He says, "Youse has done that," he says, "quite a few times."

Negotiation of Identity in Storytelling Performance   225

I says, "Well—"
He says, "Are you Travellers?"
He says, (are you?) "What we call tinkers?" he said.
I says, "Yes sir, and proud o' it."
He says, "And so am I."
He said, "I wish to hell," he says, "all my company was tinkers," he says.
He says, "I remember," he says, "in the 1914 war," he says,
"I had three or four of them in my company."
And he says, "They were just like youse."
He said, "All the rest o' them (you see?) were starving," he says.
"And they survived."
Says, "They survived."

So.
That was a good thing for us. (TS92030)

Bryce's story is crafted as a statement about Traveller identity, but the evaluation of identity in this story does not come from a Traveller. It is reported from someone that a non-Traveller would consider a respected member of society—an army captain. Bryce's narration also re-creates the event that provides the captain's motivation for making his evaluation. The captain is responsible for training soldiers to fight to defend the freedom of all British citizens. He fought in the 1914 war and knows what it will take to survive and successfully defend the country. The captain is therefore a competent judge in these matters. These evaluations are also made with regard to abilities that profoundly affect all who are touched by World War II. By selecting and presenting his experience as he does, Bryce invites us to draw on our knowledge and experience to interpret the narrated event for ourselves. But he also reports the captain's words, thereby suggesting that in following the actions of the narrated event, we should reach the same conclusion as does the captain.

I recorded a similarly argued but more complexly structured story from Duncan Williamson on 1 February 1993. The story deals with the non-Traveller belief that Travellers never work. Farnham Rehfisch (1958) argues this perception is a self fulfilling—people never see Travellers working because anyone they see working is, by definition, not a Traveller (quoted in Douglas 1985, 99). Travellers I met could not understand how non-Travellers could believe this, saying that from their perspective Travellers "are never idle" (TS93018). Duncan has made the point that Travellers had to prove themselves reliable and hard working or they would not be invited back to work for farmers during the winter months and therefore might have no long-term place to stay (TS93003). In supporting this contention, Duncan told me he asked one farmer how he could stand to have so many Travellers staying on his land. The farmer responded: " 'I'll tell you something,' he says, 'They may be Travellers to a lot of folk, but they're my workers and there's some bloody good men among them' " (TS93003).

Duncan's story addresses the stereotype of Traveller work habits by focusing on the actions of his brother Jimmy as being typical of Travellers. Duncan first told this story during an unrecorded conversation that I had with him at his kitchen table (field notes 1/9/93). During our interview in February 1993, I asked Duncan to tell the story again so I could record it.

> Let's record this for you before you run out of tape.
> As I told you, when my brother and I—
> we lived in, in Fife.
> We always, we always sure . . . to get a job for the wintertime.
>
> But,
> this time, horses were getting kind of, beginning to fade out.
> And I had already passed my test.
> And my brother says to me, he says, "I want to go to the school of motoring.
> And," he said, "I want to sell my horse and get a car.
> And," he says, "best thing I can do is go and look for a job."
> He says, "There's nae sense the two of us biding on one farm,
> because," he says, "we'll run out of work."
>
> So.
> He went up to Kennoway,* just here at Kennoway,
> and he fell in with two old brothers and a sister called the Shaws.
> Kingsdale, the name of the farm, Kingsdale.
> The Shaws of Kingsdale.
> And whatever kind of notion—
>   the two brothers had never married,

---

*Kennoway is a town just east of Glenrothes in Fife.

    the older, Jimmy, had married,
    and sister, old Maggie, she had a lame leg.
I visited him many times,
    visited him at his work,
        talked to the old Shaws.
Cally was the younger brother.
He was the kind of foreman,
and Jimmy was the boss.

And of course—
    I'll show you the very place where he put his tent, where he had his tent.
    Someday I'll take you 'round that way,
    and I'll show you where Jimmy,
    and I'll show you Kingsdale forbyes so you can have it in your (record?).
    And Jimmy worked with these Shaws all winter long.
        Then to the school of motoring
            and passed his test
                and bought himself a van.

But it so happened that—
It was during the winter months.
It must have been the month of January, Donald,
that he went down to see—
He always appeared in the stable every morning.
His big gelly* sitting, a big barricade, sitting in the, in the field,
oh, it, beside the road leading to the drive.
There a group of holly trees on one side
and a group of big trees on the other side, big beech trees on the other side.
Jimmy had (?) up nice comfortable place for his tent.

And of course, he'd always appear in the stable every morning
for to get to start his work with the rest of the men.

And of course, Jimmy's a good worker.
I mean he was only maybe twenty-three, twenty-four years old,
    six foot, six foot three,
        big tall man,
             all muscle, not a pinch of fat on him.
And of course he's younger than me by ten years.
And of course Cally had a great notion of Jimmy
because Jimmy was a great worker.

    But.
It so happened that he went down to the stable one morning.

---

*gelly and barricade are Traveller tents intended for long-term stay in the wintertime.

He said, "Jimmy," he said, "I have a problem."
Now they had a big sewerage blockage under the farm.
All the waste from the byres* and the reeds and all was carried in one big pipe.
And there was a big kind of, eh—
what you call these big dams down below where it was all collected,
kind of big, eh, sewage tank, where it was collected.
But there was a big block in between.
He says, "Jimmy, we'll have to get that blinking thing rid," he says.
"It's backing up inside the farmhouse.
It's backing up inside the byre."

And it was the month of January, Donald.
It was awfa', awfa' cold.
Wet and cold.
Sleet and snow.

So.
Jimmy says, "Let's go, then," he says.
"But, Jimmy, Christ, man," he said,
"I'm bloody sorry," he says.
"I dinnae have a bloody wellie in the place."
   Used to get big wellies up to your knees.
"I dinnae have a wellie in the place."
"And," he says, "it's bloody cold and wet down there," he says.
Jimmy says, "You got any plastic bags?"
   You ken these big plastic bags?
He said, "I'll put a couple plastic bags on my legs," he says,
"and tie them there and up to the thighs,
and it'll keep them, my legs dry.
Let's get the bloody drain cleaned out."
See?

But it so happened, that something happened to—
Jimmy had phoned Reekie Plant down here in Cupar.
   That's it where you see the tractors lying,
   Reekie Plant in Cupar.
This is a true story.
And he'd phoned Reekie Plant in Cupar,
and he sent out a, an engineer to see some of the machines on the farm
that was broken down or needing a new part, what was needed.

---
*byre = cowshed

So.
Old Jimmy had went off to Cupar.
It was a Tuesday morning.
Jimmy went to Cupar to the (?) to the market.
Cally and Jimmy, my brother Jimmy—
The two ploughmen was out ploughing,
Jock Rodgers was out ploughing,
and old Mary was in the kitchen hersel'
when the man came from Reekie Plant.
See?

He drove in with his car.
You see it was the first time he went to Kingsdale.
And he saw the big gelly sitting in the—
No smoke coming.
Jimmy probably went down in the morning and left his wife.
He didn't have any kids, it was my wee kids he had.
He left Edith sleeping in the tent in the morning, you see?
But he just got up
    and made himself a cup of tea
        and go off to his work.

So Jimmy got started digging down into the drain.
Dug the (?) drain.
Jimmy's up to the waist,
and the water begin to come in, sewage began to come in.
But it couldna, it wasn't coming above the plastic bags.
You would be quite dry with plastic bags.
It couldna come through.
It was as good as wellies.

And Jimmy's standing up to above his knees.
And he's down about, I would say, about five or six foot. See?
It wasn't a big hole, just enough to take a, take a person down in this hole.
When, eh, engineer came out from Reekie Plant.
"Good morning, Mr. Shaw."
"Oh, good morning."
He says, eh, "Your brother phoned."
"Oh, aye," he says," he did.
"Jimmy phoned before he left."

So.
Cally says to him, he says, eh, "It's such and such a machine on the farm."
    I don't know what machine it was, but it'll no matter.

He says, "One of the machines is broken down."
  Could be the milk machine or something.
He said, "You having a bit of problem with your drains?"
Cally says, "Hell of (?) man," he says.
"Whole thing's backing up," he says, "blocked," he says, "completely."
And he said, eh, "By God," he says, "it must be cold down there," he says, "and kind of wet."
He's standing—new suit collar and tie.

So they talk for a few minutes.
He says, "Mr. Shaw," he says, "Em, can you tell me something?"
"Aye," he says.
"What is it you want?" he says.
"I see a tent in your field up there.
It's a tinker's tent in your field."
"Aye," he says, "a tinker's tent in my field."
He says, "What in the name of God are you doing with these people?"
  Cally, Cally (?), he has a big nose, and it is full of blackheads, you know?
  Great, (?) great domino player.
  I played against him.

Cally said, "What did you say?"
He said, eh, "Who's living in the tent up there," he says, "in your field?
It's your property, your field?"
"Aye," Cally says,
"(He's been?) there," he says, eh, "been there for a few months," he said,
"In fact, he was there last year forbyes."
"But in the name of God," he says, "what are you doing with them?
What are you doing with these people in your field?" he says.
"They're still asleep, aren't they," he said, "in the tent?"
"And," he said, "there are you," he said, "and your man digging that bloody drain.
And these buggers is lying on your ground sound asleep," he says, "like a bug in a rug."
He said, "They're lazy good-for-nothing," he said.
"That's all they want," he said.

Cally said, "Is that right?"
He said, "Eh, [coughs] you work in an office," he said, "in, eh—
Do you work in an office?"
He says, "Aye. I'm a salesman."
"Oh, you're a salesman," he says.
"And," he says, "you've got a company car, haven't you?"
  Cally's, Cally's weel (?)—.

"Aye," he says, "of course.
We've all got a company car," he says.
And he said, eh—collar and tie—
"And," he says, "just wait for a phone call and go out," he says.

He said, "Would you go down in that drain,
   and dig that drain this morning,
     out at half past seven?"
  Must be about eight o'clock now.
"No," he says, "I don't think, that's not my kind of work."
"Well," he says, "do you know who's down there," he says,
   "to clean my drains so my beasts," he said, "can get a drink
     and my wife," no, he said, "my sister-in-law can get to the toilet?
THAT'S A TINKER," he said, "that you're talking about,
that you think are asleep in the tent.
That's a tinker down there," he says, "this morning at half past seven.
That you think they'll neither work nor want.
That's a tinker.
And," he says, "he's the best damned worker I've ever had."
"And," he said, "he will be HERE as long as he wants to stay ON my land."

Salesman said, "I'm sorry, young man," he said to Jimmy.
Jimmy got up, took some water.
Says, "It's okay," he said.
"Everyone treats us like that," he said.
"But," he said, "they'll learn the difference some day."
And, Donald, that is a true story. (TS93004)

The evaluation of Traveller identity in this story comes in the form of reported speech and action. Listeners hear Cally defend Traveller identity from the stereotyped criticism of the engineer from Reekie Plant. Jimmy's willingness to work—to dig the drain at 7:30 on an "awfa', awfa' cold" and wet winter morning, with sewage past his knees, and nothing but old plastic bags to protect him—provides a supporting context for Cally's evaluation of Traveller identity. But there is more here as well. Faced with Cally's arguments and Jimmy's actions, the engineer is forced to rethink his understanding of Travellers, their work habits, and therefore their identity. The engineer's admission that he would not do the work Jimmy is doing and his apology to Jimmy are themselves reported evaluations of Traveller identity.

As listeners, Sue Grizzell and I participate in the interactions of the narrated event. We follow the details of Cally's arguments and hear what he has to say about Jimmy as a worker. We also witness the response of the engineer from Reekie plant. This experience suggests that we, like the engineer, should use our interpretation of this event to rethink our own understandings of Traveller identity.

Duncan's performance is easy to follow since it is rich in detail. Duncan draws on his knowledge of his brother, his knowledge of Cally, his memory of the weather that January, his own use of plastic bags for wellies, and so on. He vividly describes the environment, words, and actions of all the participants in the event. In addition Duncan explicitly states: "This is a true story." Interestingly, Duncan was not actually present to witness this interaction. He heard about this incident only because Cally told him the story of what happened. While it is not possible to reconstruct Cally's story from Duncan's retelling, the fact that Duncan is reporting Cally's story adds additional weight to the story. It is Cally, a non-Traveller, who has recognized this event as being important enough to remember and retell. This implies that the primary coherence and continuity given to the event in the act of narration may have been influenced by settled and not Traveller worldview. Awareness of this origin of the story therefore adds credibility to the story as an objective rendering of Traveller identity and may, in fact, be an intentional component of Duncan's strategy in replaying this event.

IV. Fictional Portrayals of Interaction

From a performance-centered perspective, tellers have a great deal of freedom to choose how they replay a story within the performance event. With regard to issues of worldview and identity, this freedom of choice becomes a resource Travellers use to enhance the efficacy of communications with non-Travellers. While experience stories may restrict some of the creative choices tellers can make, there are few such limitations in the performance of fictional stories.

Within constraints of the plot, tellers of fictional stories have full license to create character personality, words, and actions as needed to depict Traveller and non-Traveller identity. This freedom of expression may result in an overt statement of identity through, for instance, casting a Traveller in the role of a wise character in the story. As the story hero demonstrates his or her wisdom with respect to some non-Traveller, the suggestion is made that these abilities parallel the lives of Travellers and non-Travellers in the real world.

An example of this strategy emerged during the 1993 National Storytelling Festival in Jonesborough, Tennessee. Traveller Stanley Robertson told his version of the King and the Abbot (Aarne and Thompson type 922), in which it is a poor Gypsy lad who wisely answers the Devil's questions and therefore saves the life of the "wise," settled person in the story. I later asked Stanley if he intended to communicate something about Gypsies to the audience:

DB Is there an intent on your part to communicate something about Gypsies to the audience there?
SR Exactly.
In Scotland I could say,
"You can learn from a poor Traveller."
DB Right.
SR It gets a wee dig back at the scaldie* for us, you ken?
It's quite coarse, but—.
Here it doesnae have the same effect
because they dinnae ken the Travellers and all.
So I use *Gypsy* because they are more international. (TS93053)

A second example of how fictional characters can be used to portray differences in identity came in a story I recorded from Duncan Williamson. Duncan says he learned the story "Archie's Besom" from Neil MacCallum, a non-Traveller stone mason in the West Highlands of Scotland (TS87013). I recorded the following performance on 8 October 1987 during a public concert for adults at the Caroll Reece Museum, at East Tennessee State University, in Johnson City. The story begins with an encounter between a Traveller besom† maker and a settled crofter, Archie. Here I reproduce only the opening episode of the story.[5]

---

scaldie = Traveller cant term for non-Traveller
†*besom* = broom (pronounced BEHzum)

Back on the west coast of Argyll there once lived two brothers.
And they had a small farm.
Which we call just a croft.
One brother was a little older than the other.
The one, oldest one's name was Donald.
And the youngest one's name was Archie.
Now because Archie was young, Donald overruled him.
He made him do most of the work on the farm.
And he paid him little money.
But they were quite happy.
But poor Archie was always the underdog.

But one day they were up on the hillside.
And they were building the stone dikes to keep the sheep frae getting on the road.
When at that moment, along comes one of the tinkers, Travelling folk, with his bundling on his back.
And he stops when he sees the two brothers working at the dike side.
And he begs them for a match.
And he said, "Would youse have a match on you?"
And Donald said, "Yes, I ha—, give you a match."
So he gave the tinker man a match.

And he lighted up his pipe.
He said, "Do you own the land around here?" said the tinker man.
And Donald said, "Yes, we own as far as you can see, that's our land."
And he said, "Well, you wouldn't mind me pulling some of the heather?"
Donald said, "What would you be wanting heather for?"
"Well," he said, "you see, I make besoms."
   Like you see in the museum up there, the witches' broom, these broomsticks.
   They were very popular in bygone times.
He says, "I make heather besoms.
And I sell them around the doors.
That's my trade."
And Donald said, "Help yourself.
Take as much heather as you want."
He said, "The sheep doesn't even eat it."

So the tinker man goes over the dike,
and he starts pulling and bundling up this bundle of heather.

Now.
Archie gets interested in this,

>   and he goes over, the younger brother,
>   and he watches.
> And he said to the tinker man, "What are you gonna do with all that stuff?"
> He said, "I'm going to make a besom with it.
> I told you, I make besoms, broomsticks."
> And Archie said, "How much do you get for them when you make them?"
> "Well," said the tinker man, "I probably get a shilling or a sixpence.
> Depends, how good I make them."

> Archie said, "How long does it take you to make one of these besoms?"
> He said, "Probably," he said, "about fifteen minutes, twenty minutes.
> Depends how good I make it."
> Archie says, "You mean to tell me now"— [Duncan speaks with a Highland accent]
>   he was very Highland—
> that you can make a shilling in twenty minutes?
> And here is me working and toiling to my brother,
> from morning till night,
>   milking the cows,
>   tidying the house,
>   making the food,
>   doing all the jobs,
>   cutting corn, hay,
>   feeding the cattle,
> and he only gives me a sixpence a week on pay?"
> "Well," said the tinker man,
> "it's nothing to do with me," he said.
> "That's your problem."

> Archie says, "Before you go, tell me something.
> Are they hard to make, these besoms?"
> Tinker man said, "Not really," he said.
> "They're not very hard to make."
> He said, "Just to get a bundle of heather,
>   get yourself a nice handle for a, a nice stick for a handle,
>   and tie it in with a piece of rope,
>   and make yoursel a nice broomstick.
> And you can sell it for a shilling or a sixpence."
> "It sounds easy," said Archie.

> So.
> The tinker man picked up his heather,
> went on his way,

gone tinker man.
No more tinker man.

But Archie walked over and Donald said,
"Archie, come and help me lift this big stone.
It's too much for me to put it on the dike."
Archie said, "Indeed, I will not!
I am not lifting any more stones to you.
I am not working to you any more.
I'll stay with you.
But I'll never do another hand's turn for you."
And Donald said, "How are you going to survive?
Where are you going to get your living?"
He said, "The farm's as much as mine as yours.
Father left it to us both."
He said, "I'm gonnae become a besom maker."

"But Archie, Archie brother," he said,
"how can you become a besom maker?"
He said, "The tinker man told me how to make them.
And if a tinker can make them, so can I."
He said, "Archie, these people are professionals.
They know what to do.
That's their job.
They do it all their life."
"Well," he says, "I can try, can't I?
I can make myself a besom just as good as he can."
"Come on, Archie," he says, "help me with this stone."
He says, "I told you,
no more work will you get from me,
not another hand's turn.
I am becoming a besom maker."

Like that, he walks over to the hill.
And he pulls hisself a great big bunch of heather,
more than the tinker man had picked up.
He carries it under his arm,
and he walks down to the little croft,
   goes behind the door,
      and takes one of the great staffs that they use for the sheep on the hill,
         cuts off the top,
           and makes hisself a besom.
The most ugliest looking besom you ever saw in your life. [laughter]
It was neither dressed nor it was neither tidy.

> It was as big as that, [laughter]
> and ugly,
>> ends sticking that way,
>>> and ends sticking that way,
>>>> and a handle sticking up.
> But it looked like a besom.
> But Archie was proud of it.
> He could barely keep his eyes off it.
> And he rubbed his hands in glee and he said,
> "She's (is?) a good one!
> Wait till Donald sees this when he comes back." (TS87006)

This story replays the words and actions of a Traveller besom maker as he interacts with two settled crofters. It also reports the evaluations of Traveller identity made by the crofters in the narrated event. Archie, for example, is so impressed by the Traveller's skill in making a living that he seeks to abandon his hard crofting life and imitate the Traveller. While Duncan's performance may draw on his real-world experience, his story presents purely fictional events that are a creation of his skill as a storyteller. The Traveller besom maker is portrayed as a competent figure, well able to earn a good living from materials that he gathers, processes, and sells. He is friendly, courteous in asking permission to pull heather, and generous in freely telling Archie the proper way to make a besom. Yet the apparent simplicity of the tinker's life is contrasted with Donald's comments that the tinkers are "professionals." Donald asserts Travellers have specialized skills and know their jobs—a point supported by Archie's subsequent failure at besom making.

The story logic does not demand this positive portrayal of the Traveller. Yet Duncan's choice to narrate this episode in this way allows him an opportunity to project a positive image of Traveller identity to his non-Traveller audience. By contrasting the skill and politeness of the Traveller with the limited visions of the crofters, Duncan argues against stereotyped assumptions that are often part of settled views of Traveller identity.

V. Metaphor and Identity in Fictional Stories

Another strategy used in interaction stories makes use of metaphor to comment on facets of differential identity. To illustrate this strategy, I transcribe a performance by Duncan Williamson that was recorded at the National Storytelling Festival in Jonesborough, Tennessee, on 9 October 1987. At this time, Duncan was in America as part of a storytelling tour I arranged for him. The audience was primarily adults who knew little about Traveller culture.

The Fox and the Dog

    And this story
    is about a little fox, too.

    For he had been hunted for many days
    with the gamekeeper and the farmers.
5   For he had stole a chicken the day before from a farm.

    And he lay there in his den in the rocks,
    and the sun was shining.
    It was very, very warm.
    And for two days he lay there
10   afraid and terrified to come out from his den.
    And the heat was terrible inside these rocks.

    And he said to himself,
    "You know,
    I must find something to eat
15   or something to drink
        or I'm going to die.
    I've only got two choices:
      stay here and die
      or go out and be shot." [laughter]

20   So finally,
    he crawled from his den hungry and thirsty.
    But there was no one around.
    And he traveled across the moors.
    All the streams had dried up with the sun.
25   He couldn't find himself a dead bird
      or a rabbit
        or nothing to eat.
    But he looked down there in the valley and he saw the farm.
    He said, "I would love to go down there," he said.
30   "But, if I do they might catch me this time."

"But," he said, "I've an old friend down there
whom I haven't saw for many years.
The old dog.
And he lies there behind the farm.
35 And he might have something in his dish
that he could spare for me."

So he crawled down the best way he could.
Trying to conceal himself among the bushes
and finally he came behind the farm.
40 There was nobody around.

There lay the old dog
  with his paws crossed,
    asleep in his barrel
      among the straw.
45 Before him stood a large dish of beautiful food,
scraps and bones and milk,
everything that was needed.

The fox crawled up,
and he said, "Cousin Dog?
50 Are you awake?"
The old dog got up,
  and he opened his eyes
    and gave himself a stretch.
And he says, "Of course, it's your old sel, ol Mister Foxy.
55 What are you doing here?"
He said, "I'm hungry."
He said, "You know what happens if the farmer finds you here."
He said, "You'll be shot."
"Well," he says, "It's either be shot or die with the hunger."

60 He says, "What do you want from me?"
He said, "Whed something from that dish."
The old dog says, "Help yourself.
  Take the lot.
    I'm not hungry," he said.

65 So quickly the old fox, Foxy, he gobbled up everything,
  licked his lips,
    and said,
"Doggy," he said, "I really enjoyed that."

And the dog said, "Foxy," he said, "Look,
70 you'll have to change your ways." [laughter]
He said, "You can't go around stealing from people," he said,
"And expecting to survive the way you do." [laughter]
He said, "Why don't you get a job for yourself?" [loud laughter]

He said, "A job?"
75 "Yeah," he says, "like me.
Be a, be a guard dog." [laughter]
He said, "Cousin, who would take a fox for a guard dog?" [laughter]
He said, "Have you ever tried?" [laughter]
"No," said old Foxy, "I never had the chance to try."

80 "Well, anyhow," he says, "Look what I've got, here."
Foxy says, "What have you got?"
He said, "I've got my barrel
and my straw.
And," he said, "I lie here all day in the sun."

85 Foxy said, "That sounds good. [laughter]
But," he said, "What else have you got?"

"Well," he said, "I have my chain, my collar."
Foxy said, "What did you say?" [laughter]
He said, "My chain and my collar, of course."
90 Foxy said, "What do you need a chain and a collar for?"
He said, "To tie me up."
Foxy says, "You mean to tell me that you get tied up all ti all day long?"
"Well," he says, "Sometimes my master lets me loose—
but not very often."

95 "Ah, well," old Foxy said,
"Look," he said,
"It wouldn't be for me."
Said, "You keep your barrel,
    and keep your straw,
100   and keep your dish.
And," he says, "I'll go on my way."
He said, "I might be hungry,
but I'll be free."
He said, "Freedom and hunger for me."
105 And then the old fox was gone.

The old dog lived for a long, long time on that farm.
But he never saw his old cousin Foxy again. [applause] (TS87008)

Negotiation of Identity in Storytelling Performance 241

Jimmy Williamson posing with a carved fox in Argyll, 1998

On the surface, this story is a version of the internationally known folktale "The Lean Dog Prefers Liberty to Abundant Food and a Chain" (Aarne and Thompson type 201).[6] Yet Duncan's version of the story is deeply saturated with Traveller beliefs and values. On several occasions, Duncan Williamson commented that this story is "a real Traveller story" (e.g., field notes 9/20/94; TS92034). Duncan says he first heard the story from his father (SA76.108) and has told this story many times to his own children. Two of his children, now in their 40s, remembered hearing this story as youngsters and associating their identity as Travellers with that of the fox in the story (TS93017, TS93025).

The connection between this story and Traveller culture emerges, in part, because Travellers see parallels between their own experience and the treatment of foxes. Duncan illustrated this point when he commented:

> The only animal I am really sorry for is the fox.
> Among all the animals that is protected,
> the fox is the one that is hunted for no reason at all.

What does he do?
He only hunts for a little to eat.
And once he has his belly full,
he will go off and sleep" (TS92034).

These comments correspond to Traveller feelings that they are similarly persecuted for no reason at all. They also echo Traveller beliefs that poaching a salmon or taking a few potatoes from a farmer's field is not really theft but a justifiable act, since it is based on the need to survive, not on greed.

Associations between foxes and Travellers also arise through the role of the fox in Traveller storytelling traditions. During our interview, Duncan said the character of the fox was like a "Jack among the animals" (TS92034). Jack is a common folktale hero and role model in Traveller stories. Duncan said that Traveller fathers often tell "Jack stories to their sons because, in a way, they would . . . probably want their sons to grow up like Jack" (TS92034). Since animal tales are common teaching stories for Traveller children, it can be inferred that stories about foxes may similarly model culturally appropriate behavior.

Given the associations Travellers have with foxes, it is therefore not surprising that this folktale is understood as a metaphorical commentary on differences between Travellers and settled folk. When I asked Duncan about why he felt this was a "real Traveller story," his answer made this point in great detail:

DW   Because it is the idea of someone wanting to be free.
I mean the Travellers don't have a nine-to-five job like the dog.
The dog had a nine-to-five job in that barrel.
And he was a guard dog in the barrel.
The Travellers regard themselves as the fox. You see what I mean?
The dog is a non-Traveller. See what I mean?
That's what the story means.
The dog, okay, the dog is nice, he's a non-Traveller—
The Travellers, mind, had many friends among the non-Travellers, like farmers and shepherds.
But as far as they concerned they would never do what he done.
They don't want this five-to-nine job.
They want this freedom. . . .
The fox was the Traveller, the free—

He'd come and beg a little food fra the—
We, we done it.
I begged a little bit of food from the people who gone to work from nine-to-five myself, when I was young.
But I didn't want their way of life.
I respected their wee bit of food they gave me,
    a piece at the door,
    a wee cup of tea,
but I would never have their way of life.
So that's what it means. The (?)—

DB So it's—and people who hear that understand that that's what's going on?
DW Understand the—Yes.
That is what that story means.
That's what's the idea of the Dog and the Fox.
That's why they called it a Traveller story.
Because they compared, the Travellers compared to the fox.
The free, who wanted free says,
"Freedom and Hunger for me."
The Travellers prefer freedom than have a nine-to-five job.
They would rather go hungry
than have a job that tied them down where they couldn't wander
and see what they wanted to see.
And this was their idea. You see?
That's why they compared themselves to the fox.
The idea of the fox played an important part in Travellers' lives
because the fox wanted to be free.
He would suffer, be hungry,
be wet, be cold,
but he would be free.
No one would tell him what to do.
You see what I mean?
He was a free spirit.
The dog was tied up wi' a chain and a barrel.
He was a dog right enough.
And he done his job,
and he had his food and he had his warm bed.
But what in the hell else did he have?
NOTHING!
Do you see what I mean?
So that's why it's called, classed as a Traveller story. (TS92038)

Direct parallels to this attitude can be found in the ways that other Travellers value their time. This view is expressed by Betsy Whyte in her autobiography when she refers to the departure of another family from a communal camping site: "Like all Travelling People they just had to keep moving. It is only with this sense of freedom that they can get any joy out of living and they are willing to bear discomfort, even hardships, to keep that freedom" (1990, 183).

For non-Traveller audience members, these deep cultural associations with foxes may not be available to key this dimension of the story's meaning. Yet this metaphorical meaning is also keyed by content and formal features of Duncan's performance. His use of reported speech presents some problems in interpretation. Foxes and dogs do not normally talk. In addition, the content of their talk does not seem very foxlike or very doglike. This becomes most evident beginning at line 69, where the conversation turns to issues of the relative benefits of different jobs and lifestyles. These problems in interpretation clearly suggest that the story embodies something more than an amusing conversation between a fox and a dog.

Further, while lines such as 13–19 and 29–36 are clearly framed as "what was said" in the narrated event—and the audience presumably follows this projection and hears the action "as if" it was an event that took place at some point in the past—the performance has a present-tense feeling that arises through the use of reported speech.[7] The ambiguity inherent in reported speech enables the possibility that the present-tense dialog may be anchored in the narrative event where a Traveller performer is speaking to an audience of non- Travellers. If these words belong to Duncan himself, then the expressions of identity in the story may be representative of a more general expression of Traveller identity. This suggests a parallel framing, in which the dialog should be interpreted both literally as part of a fictional event and metaphorically as part of an ongoing dialog that comments on the differential identity between Travellers and non-Travellers.

In the metaphorical frame, the fox and dog serve as symbolic representatives in an abstract encounter between Traveller and non-Traveller identities. The indirect referencing, however, allows the difference in identities to be developed without engaging stereotypes non-Traveller listeners may have about Travellers. This frame points to differences between

Travellers and non-Travellers by highlighting the contrast between the stable but constrained lifestyle of the dog—his gainful employment, his food dish, and his collar—and the uncertain but free lifestyle of the fox. This contrast is perhaps oversimplified, but it is also effective.

The metaphorical link between the two frames also enhances the richness of this contrast in identities. For example, an equation is made between the traditional cleverness of the fox—as conveyed in many other stories and in direct observation—with the creative abilities of the Traveller to exploit the "system" without being dominated by it. The use of metaphor additionally implies that Traveller identity and worldview are just as much in agreement with "nature" or the "natural way of things" as is the fox within the story.

But this story does not just summarize the differences between the lives of dogs and foxes; it communicates a far more subtle experience of contrasting worldviews and identities. The story allows listeners to experience this difference through the process of "following" the story. The story introduces listeners to the character of the fox in a manner that invites sympathy and identification with the fox's experience. Thus engaged, listeners follow the fox's search for food and survival. They understand the fear of the farm and yet share the driving hunger. The encounter with the dog takes place from the fox's perspective, and as the terms of the dog's employment unfold, they are revealed as absurdly unacceptable. Of course! No one wants a collar![8] The final statement: "Freedom and hunger for me," is an acceptable conclusion from the events as they unfold and are followed from a listener's, that is, the fox's, position.

It is in this sense that fictional stories can be used to negotiate worldview and identity. Through narrative re-creations, fictional characters that metaphorically stand for representatives of different cultural groups become participants in the performance interaction. In following the story, listeners interact with these characters and extract experiential meanings from their interactions. Performers and listeners can form and attune issues of identity and worldview with respect to these fictional events and characters. The experience a listener has will, of course, be different depending on his or her background. "The Fox and the Dog" may confirm deeply held values for a Traveller listener. For a non-Traveller listener, the same story may introduce the possibility that Travellers are not so crazy after all.

VI. Negotiating Identity through the Media

Throughout this chapter I focus on the negotiation of identity through stories told in face-to-face interactions—in what Erving Goffman (1983) has termed "the interaction order." But the influence of storytelling performances on perceptions of identity can transcend the confines of the performance event. This is true in the sense that following a storytelling performance is a process that can generate experiential resources for listeners that can be carried away from the performance and thought with and thought through in ongoing attempts to understand the world. When I contemplate questions of Traveller identity, I recall many of the storytelling performances I experienced during my field research. These experiences are resources that embody how Traveller identity is played out through interaction. They provide me with valuable and dynamic references for my own constructions of Traveller identity, and they have been incorporated into my own sense of worldview as it relates to the Travelling People.

The modern world provides other channels through which the influence of storytelling performances can transcend face-to-face situations. These channels include radio, television, film, and print media. Whether news stories that focus on problems of illegal camping or fictional stories that involve some Traveller characters, most of the stories about Travellers told through these media are the constructions of non-Travellers. These stories tend to be informed by non-Traveller beliefs and therefore to perpetuate non-Traveller conceptions of Traveller identity. Several Travellers I met commented on the inaccuracy of the portrayals of Travellers in the media. Willie MacPhee, for instance, complained that the BBC interviewed him for over an hour and that he "telled them a lot of things about the Travellers" (TS92023). In the broadcast he said they only used "three or four words" out of all he said. Willie commented "I was actually telling them the truth. But they werna broadcasting the truth." Edie MacPhee and Tracy Donaldson commented that the portrayals of Travellers they had seen on television were "always" inaccurate (TS93025). Two studies of the depiction of Gypsies and Travellers in children's literature confirm the pervasive use of stereotyped images (Binns 1984, Kenrick 1984). Beyond these studies little research has been undertaken to establish the content or effects of these non-Traveller constructions of Traveller identity.

There are occasions when Travellers get to tell their own stories through the media. A number of documentary films and videotapes on Traveller lives and folklore have been made and broadcast—though these tend to be conceived and edited by non-Travellers. Radio and television broadcasts have also provided some opportunities for Traveller commentary and the performance of ballads and stories. Published books and articles of Traveller storytelling provide another communicative medium (see S. Robertson 1988, 1989; D. Williamson 1983–1992; Douglas 1987). These mediated stories reach a wide audience and move discussions of identity from face-to-face encounters to a larger political arena.

It is my belief, however, that mediated communications dilute the efficacy of storytelling as a medium for negotiating identity. This dilution results from a number of factors. Most importantly, the interaction that takes place in mediated communication is indirect. There is little or no audience feedback. Performers cannot fully contextualize performances for an unknown audience. Consequently, mediated performances are typically characterized by a lack of involvement or engagement with the act of performance. Further, the audience may have a limited experience of the performance event. In the case of a story printed in a book, for example, listeners may only have access to the verbal text of the story. Important meanings encoded in channels such as prosody and gesture will therefore be lost.

Despite these limitations, some Travellers I interviewed believe mediated performances might have a positive effect by exposing non-Travellers to aspects of Traveller culture and belief. Willie MacPhee, for instance, said television programs such as Peggy Seeger and Ewan MacColl's 1982 broadcast "Go! Move! Shift!" might positively affect non-Travellers by telling part of the truth about the influence of settled policies on Traveller lives (TS92023). Others, however, worry that the compromises made by performers in addressing the media, and the non-Traveller world in general, might limit any potential gain in settled awareness of Travellers and thereby prevent these performances from having any real influence in solving problems of Traveller life on the road.

Understanding differences in how face-to-face and mediated storytelling performances function to negotiate identity, and assessing the possible effects of these performances, requires extensive field research that lies well beyond the scope of the present work. I hope that my models as to how experiential and fictional stories can function in face-to-face interactions might be of some use in addressing questions of mediated communication.

5. "Did It Happen or Did It Not?"

Creativity, Worldview, and Narrative Knowing

The relationship between Traveller stories and Traveller lives should not be oversimplified. Stories are the creative and flexible products of performance. This creativity not only enables performers to adapt stories to accomplish valuable functions within the performance event but also gives performers freedom to play with possibility, explore the relationship between coherence and worldview, and fabricate fictional accounts that may mirror the lived world but which may diverge from it in a number of different ways. Stories can therefore be used to suggest alternate beliefs, ideas, relationships, and interpretive strategies. It is because of this creative freedom that storytelling performances provide a potent medium within which worldviews can be created, attuned, affirmed, challenged, or transformed.

I investigate the creativity of Traveller storytelling traditions through one particularly interesting category of oral stories I encountered during my field research among the Travellers.[1] Duncan Williamson called these fictional stories *dream stories*. Dream stories are intriguing because they unfold complex and ambiguous temporal references that cannot be resolved into a coherent sequence of "what happened." They consequently defy the ability of listeners to "follow the story" and leave them wondering: "Did it actually happen or was the narrative protagonist dreaming?"

Using the distinction between performance event and narrated event,

---

An earlier version of this chapter appeared in Braid 1998a.

the questions I address in this chapter can be stated concisely. Why do Travellers tell stories that do not evoke a coherent narrated event? Are these stories, therefore, failures, or are they intentional artistic products? What functions and meanings do these stories serve for participants in the performance event? What insights do these stories offer for understanding how storytelling performances engage the world of lived experience and therefore how they function as a unique way of knowing?

In what follows, I explore the significance of dream stories on several levels. First, I focus on the dynamics of the performance interaction. I argue that dream stories are an artistically coherent genre of Traveller storytelling. In this sense, the confusion that the listener feels in trying to figure out "what happened" in the narrated event is an intentional product of the artistry of performing a dream story. I further argue that Travellers tell dream stories because the incoherency they embody makes dream story performances particularly engaging. This engaging quality allows dream stories to be used as effective entertainment that relieves the omnipresent worries of Traveller life. This engaging quality also enhances the retention of meanings encoded in storytelling performances. Next, I focus on the narrated events constituted through the formal features of performance. I argue that dream stories not only demonstrate Traveller virtuosity as storytellers but also function as an important commentary on the creative and interpretive nature of the storytelling process and therefore on the validity of narrative knowing—a crucial issue in a culture that relies heavily on stories as a medium of communication. In a final section, I examine parallels between dream stories and contemporary legends in order to take a closer look at how storytelling performances engage the world of lived experience. This analysis leads to an understanding of the dialectical relationship between experience and worldview that lies at the heart of the process of narrative knowing.

Dream Stories—Some Examples

During my research with the Travellers, I encountered a number of dream stories. I begin my discussion with a particularly good example

Bryce and Betsy Whyte in their Montrose home, 1970s (photograph by Linda Williamson)

of the genre, Betsy Whyte's performance of "The Black Laird and the Cattleman." This story is widely known among Traveller families (TS93005). It is alternately known as "The Bailer" or "The Man with No Story to Tell." The following performance was recorded by Peter Cooke and Linda Headlee in Betsy's home in Montrose, Scotland in 1975.[2]

The Black Laird and the Cattleman

> Aye, that [the previous story] was one o' my grandfather's too.
> My mother used to tell us it.
> To make us laugh she telled this one.
>
> But it was aboot this eh, black laird,* you see?
> He'd this big farm.

---

*laird = any owner of landed property or an estate

And every year they used to just have a meetin
   and a carry on
      and what we cry a ceilidh.
And they didna have much tae eat or drink,
   but whatever they had,
      they enjoyed it.
And everyone had to tell a story, you see?
And whoever told the best story,
they got a guinea from this black laird.
But it had to be the biggest lie, you see?
This story had to be the biggest lie.

So.
They were all gathered 'round into this farmhoose,
and they hed a great big pot o' sowans*...
So they were all sitten telling their stories,
   and telling their stories,
      and telling their stories.
And this cattleman—
   he was a bit saft, you ken?
   no very good,
   and just lived in a bothy,†
   and never had seen very much in aa his life—
he was there.

And they said, "Come on now.
It's your turn to tell us a story."
He says, "Ah, ye ken fine I cannae tell nae stories."
He says, "I dinnae ken nothin tae tell.
I've never seen nothin."
He says, "Jist—now you've got to tell us something."
He says, "You could tell as big a lie as well as anybody else."
"Well," he says, "I dinnae ken nothing."

So the black laird says tae him,
"Well," he said,
"if ye can tell nothing," he says,
"make yoursel useful somehow," he says.
"Go doon tae the river,
and clean my boat."

---

*sowans = a sour oat porridge
†bothy = bunkhouse or other accommodation for farm workers

He says, "It's been lying there fir ages.
And see that it's waterproof an that."

So down he goes,
down to the river.
And he started to—
He says, "This thing's lettin in water.
It's aa moss and fog* and everything.
    You ken, yon green stuff off o' the water?

So he goes intae it
and starts tae bail it oot.
But this boat,
it's off wi him.
It started away wi him,
    right across the water and—
        and across the water.
And he says, "I cannae stop this thing."
He says, "This is terrible."

But he looked doon
(and says, "What's this?")
Ye see, he hed on his auld corduroy moleskin troosers, ye ken?
And big guttery† boots wi dung and aa things sticking on them.
When he looked down,
and there's this dainty little shoes,
    and silk stockings
        and—
(?) and he was wearing them.
And he says, "Whits this?"

But anyway, he jist couldna dae anything aboot it.
And this boat's keepin goin wi him.
And he couldnae,
he had nothing,
nae paddles nor nothing,
and he couldna dae anything wi it anyway.

So anyhow,
he landed right away at the other side o' this river.
And when he got tae the other side o' this river,

---

*fog = grass, moss, or lichen
†*guttery* = muddy

he wis just aboot tae come oot o' the boat,
and boat was goin like this, ye ken, [rocking]
when a young man came down the bank
   and took, and took him by the hand,
      and took him oot o' the boat.
And says, "Oh, goodness,
what are you doing there,
   a nice lookin girl like you,
      all on your own?
You could get drowned, you know?" [laughter]

Anyway,
they got to know each other.
And he lived there for quite a while.
And eventually they got married
   and had two o' a family
      and are very happy.

But one day in the spring o' the year—
   oh, it must have been three years later.
   And they had these two bairns.
   And they [were] walking doon the banks o' the river again.
   And she says, "Oh, look, darling!" she says.
"That's the little boat I came in.
Oh, just look," she said.
"I must go down and see it.
I must go down."

So,
down she goes.
And she stepped intae it, you see?
But this boat's away with her again.
   Right away on,
      no stopping.
         And he's shouting and runnin in the water.
           But it was no use.
              He couldn't stop it.
It's away.

And halfway across the water—
   She was standing and almost capsizing the boat
   tae try and get back tae her husband you see?
But,
half-way across, she stopped,

and she looked down.
And this was this auld boots, all dung.
And troosers all coo shairn* and everything. [laughter]
And he put up his hand, felt the stubble o' a beard.
And, "Ohhhh,"
started to greetin and roarin†
and greetin and cairryin on.

But the boat took him right back to where he had come from, you see?

So he come out.
   But he was greeting
   and just breakin his hert.
And he came wanderin up.
But when he came up—
and they were aa just sittin the same way.
Sowans wis still on the fire.
and, eh—

"Come in!"
And the laird says tae him, "Well," he says,
"did ye see the boat?"
"Oh, aye," he says,
   "Oh, dinnae speak tae me," he says.
      "Leave me alane, would ye?"
He says, "Whits adae‡ wi ye?"
He says, "Dinnae (?) dinnae speak tae me," tears tripping him.
He says, "Come on in and tell us aboot it."

So he came in and he sat.
Between tears rolling down his cheeks,
he telt them aboot this man and his bairns.
And the laird says,
"Well, that's the best lie we've heard the nicht.
So ye'll get the, [laughter]
ye'll get the golden guinea." (SA75.10)

While this is a fascinating performance that deserves close analysis, I limit my comments here to the question of coherency. Betsy's perform-

---

*coo shairn = cow dung
†greetin and roaring = crying, weeping
‡whit's adae = what's the matter

ance does not yield a coherent account of what happened in the narrated event. The story does not resolve the contradiction between the twenty minutes the cattleman has been gone in the laird's experience and the three years he has been away raising children in the cattleman's experience. The listener is left to ponder a number of possibilities. Did the cattleman dream his experience of becoming a woman? Did he fabricate this experience as a lie? Was this some enchantment put on him by the black laird? Did the transformation actually happen? While any of these frames might provide a solution to the narrated events, the performance itself remains ambiguous on this point.

I should note that in a postperformance comment Betsy does suggest that the experience was somehow the product of the black laird's powers: "But it was really the black laird that—. . . . He thought he'd been away for three or four years, you see? But he'd only been away about . . . twenty minutes or so!" (SA75.10). Betsy's comment appears to present a possible resolution to the incoherency, but it really only substitutes one mystery for another. How is it possible for the black laird to impart years of vivid experience to the cattleman in the space of twenty minutes? Why does the cattleman accept his experience as reality? This interpretation, however, does raise interesting questions about the relationship between story coherence and the beliefs audience members must accept in order to follow the story. I return to this point at the end of the chapter.

Not all dream stories follow the same format. Some dream stories confound the coherence-making of the listener by providing tangible "evidence" that inhibits resolution during the process of following. This is the case in "The Boy and the Blacksmith," a story Duncan Williamson learned from his father. The following performance was recorded during a public concert that took place at Fort Warden, in Washington, during a Traditional Tellers Seminar that I helped organize for the Seattle Storytellers' Guild during Duncan's tour of the United States in 1987. Present at this performance were approximately sixty-five participants who had spent the weekend with Duncan and three other traditional storytellers. This concert was the final gathering and took place on the Sunday of this seminar.

The Boy and the Blacksmith

Now I'd like to tell you a story tonight, which I hope you'll enjoy.
It's called "The Boy and the Blacksmith."
A long time ago in the West Highlands of Scotland,
there lived an old blacksmith and his old wife.
And they had a small smiddy up there in the Highlands.
And they were very poor, but they did little work.
Just the local farmers brought in their horses to get shod, you know?
Because it was mostly all horses in these days.
And the old woman she was a very (knacky?) old woman.
She was all getting onto her old husband John
    to get out to the smiddy,
        and do some work,
             and not sit around the house.
He never got much peace from her.

So.
He'd usually escape into the smiddy.
And there, he would kindle up his fire,
and sit there by himself,
just to get away from her nagging tongue, as we say.

But one particular morning,
she hunted him out of the house again,
saying, "John, get out to the blacksmith's shop and do something.
There must be something you can find to do for yourself in the blacksmith's shop."
He says, "Woman, there havna been a horse come near the blacksmith's shop for days."
"Well," she says, "do something.
Get out of my sight." [laughter]

So old John walks up to the blacksmith's shop,
    and he kindles up the blacksmith's fire,
        does little jobs around,
           tidies up round the smiddy.
And then a knock comes to the smiddy door,
because he'd closed the door with the wind.
And he goes to the door,
and there stands a young man
    dressed in green,
        with a young lady on his back.
He said, "Are you the blacksmith?"

And he said, "Yes, I am the blacksmith."
He said, "What can I do for you?"
"Well," he says, "look blacksmith," he said,
"I'll pay you if you let me use your smiddy fire for a few moments."
And old John says, "Well, I'm not very busy," he said.
"Come on in."
And he brought the young woman in,
and he placed her on the anvil.

Now her head was back to front. [laughter]
And she was very still and quiet. [laughter]
She never moved, as if she was in some kind of a coma.

Now the young man says, "Look, blacksmith," he said,
"I'll tell you what I'm gonna do with you.
I'm gonna pay you."
"But," he says, "remember one thing.
Never you try and do what you see me or anyone else doing."
And the old smiddy man said,
"I hear you," he said.
"Well," he said, "just sit there quietly."
And he put his hand in his pocket,
and he gave the old blacksmith seven gold pieces.

And then the young boy blew up the smiddy fire til it was red hot.
He said to the old blacksmith,
"Can I borrow one of your knives you use for cutting the horses' hooves?"
The old blacksmith said, "There's plenty there and they are all sharp.
I've nothing else to do."

So the young man goes over and he cuts off the woman's head.
There was no blood from her neck or anything.
And then he puts her head in the fire.
And he puffs up
  and he blows
    and he blows
      and he blows,
'til he burned her head away until nothing but the bones was left.

And the old blacksmith,
  he's standing there,
    and he's watching this. [laughter]

And then he gathers the white, burnt bones, the young boy does,
  and he puts them on the anvil,
    and he beats them to a powder with a hammer.

Creativity, Worldview, and Narrative Knowing

And then he spits on them and he makes a paste,
   and he goes over to the girl who's lying there,
     and he puts it round her neck.

And then there is an amazing thing that happened.
All this blue smoke came up from the burning bones.
And . . . when the smoke faded,
there stood the head of the most beautiful young woman you ever saw.
   And her eyes opened,
     and she smiled.
       and she stood up,
         and she put her arms round the young man.
And the young man turned to the blacksmith,
and he said, "Now, old man, remember,
never try and do what you see me doing."
And they walked away. [laughter]

The old blacksmith stood there in amazement. [loud laughter]
He had never seen anything like this in his life before. [laughter]

And then he heard a knock on the door.
And in comes his old, bended wife with a cup of tea.
She said, "Are you there, you lazy old bachel?
I've brought in your tea."
   And *bachel* in Gaelic means *old man*.
He said, "Yes, I'm here."

And he thought to himself what a beautiful young woman had walked out
   the door.
And he takes a look at his old wife. [extended, loud laughter]
And he grabs her. [laughter]
She says, "Let me go, you old bachel."
But he held on to her.
He took her to the blacksmith's—, to the anvil,
and he cut off her head. [laughter]
And there her poor old body fell on the floor.
Blood all over the place.

He catched her head,
and he put it in the fire.
And he pumped up the fire,
and he burnt her head until it was white, nothing but the bone.
And then he done what the boy done:
   gathered all the bones,

put them on the anvil,
    tap, tap, til he made some dust.
And then he rubbed his hands in glee.
And he walked over to the old woman.
And he got all this dust,
and he spat on it and made a paste.
And he wrapped it round her neck.
But it fell off on the floor. [laughter]

He gathered it up again with some of the ashes from the floor,
and his fingers was shakin,
and he made another paste.
But still it fell off again.
There lay the old woman, no head.
"Oh, my God," he said.
"What have I done?"

So he quickly, he gathered the remains of the body of the old woman,
and he went to the bunker that held his coal.
And he buried her in the coal.
  Covered her up,
    swept up the smiddy,
      locked the door,
        goes into his little house,
          takes a few possessions with him,
            locks the little house door,
and off he goes.

He travels far and wide through the country.
His old wife, she's forgotten about.
And he travels for over a year doing little jobs around the country.
Til one day he was down and out and broke.
And he came to this large town.
And sitting by the roadside was an old man.

And he said to the old man,
"Have you a piece of tobacco you could spare me," said the old blacksmith,
"for my pipe?"
The old man said, "Yes," he said,
"I'll give you some tobacco for your pipe."
And he gave the old blacksmith a bit of tobacco.
And the old blacksmith [sic] said, "What do you do?"
He said, "I'm a blacksmith."
"Oh, well," he said, "you should find plenty of jobs in the town today

because there is a great fair and a great fete going on in town.
But he said, "Sad, sad, it's oh, so sad," said the old man.
And the blacksmith said, "What's so sad about it?"
"Och," he said, "the poor girl.
The king's daughter," he said, "the princess,
she'll never make it this year.
Something terrible happened to her."
"And what happened to her?" said the old blacksmith.
"Oh, well," he said, "something queer."
He said, "She cannot walk.
And her head is back to front." [laughter]
"Oh, dear," said the old blacksmith, "that's terrible."
And in his mind,
he remembers back what happened with his own self.
"And," he said, "the king has offering a large reward
to anyone who can help her." [laughter]
Now the old blacksmith says to himself, he says,
"Maybe it didn't work the first time—
maybe the second time—." [words drowned in laughter]

So he makes his way into the town,
and he makes his way up to the palace.
He was soon stopped with the guards with their crossed spears, you see?
He said, "Where are you going?"
He said, "I want to see the king."
And he said, "What would an old man want to see the king for?"
He said, "What are you?
Are you a quack of some kind?
Or a magician who's come to help the king's daughter, the princess?"
"No," he said, "I'm better than that."
He said, "I'm a blacksmith.
And," he said, "I think I can help the king's daughter."

Soon word was passed and he was led before the king.
And the king said, to the old blacksmith, he said,
"You've come up to help my daughter.
Well," he said, "if you can help my daughter, I'll make it worthwhile for you.
You'll never need to be a blacksmith again.
But," he said, "if anything else happens," he said,
"you'll never live five minutes later."
He said to the king, he said,
"Do you have a blacksmith's shop in the place."
The king said, "Yes, there is a blacksmith's shop," he says, "in the palace.

We need it," he said, "for shoeing the horses for the riders of the palace."
"Right," said the old blacksmith.
"Lead me to the blacksmith's shop."
"And," he says, "then bring down the princess.
See?

So.
The old blacksmith was led down to the beautiful blacksmith's shop.
and there was everything he needed.
He kindled up the blacksmith's fire as usual,
swept the anvil.
And then they came down carrying the princess.
Poor little princess lying still and quiet,
with her head back to front.
"Now," said the old blacksmith, he said,
"close the door and leave me in peace."
"How long will you need?" said the king.
"Oh," said the blacksmith, he said, "about ten, fifteen minutes.
Come back, and she'll be well."
This made the king very happy.

So they left the old blacksmith
with the princess lying there on the anvil.
He took off the princess's head with one of the knives, sharp knife,
and he put it in the fire as usual.
And he pumped it up.
And he blowed
  and he blowed
    and he blowed
until he burnt her head away to the white bone.
And then like what the boy done,
he put it on the anvil and he tapped, tap, tapped it again
and made some dust.
And then, he spat on the dust and made a paste.
And he went over to the princes' neck,
and he put it all round her neck,
and it fell off. [gentle laughter]
And he said, "I couldn't have done it right."

So he gathered it up from the floor again,
with some ashes mixed through it.
And he tried again.
It fell off.
Now the old blacksmith was in real trouble. [laughter]

The King was coming in another five minutes.
And he's really upset,
and he's shaking and he doesn't know what to do.
When slowly behind him, the door opened.
And then he got a skelp [loud slap noise] on the ear
that knocked him scattering across the blacksmith's shop.

And there stood the boy once more.
He said, "Didn't I tell you, old man, never to do what you saw me doing?
I WARNED you," he said.
"Now," he said, "SIT there and behave yourself."
"But," he says, "here, for the last time."
Seven gold pieces.

"Now," he said, "I'm going to save your life this time, but no more."
Quickly the boy gathered what was left of the remains of the dust.
And he just done that [holds hands out palm down] from the floor,
and it rose up to meet his hands.
And he put it on the anvil and he made a paste.
And he put it round the girl's neck.
And then the blue smoke began to come.
And then she took the form of a beautiful young woman.
The princess was as beautiful as ever before.
"Now, remember," said the boy.
"Never do what you see another person doing."
And they turned and walked through the door and was gone.

The old blacksmith sat there in a daze for a long, long time.
And then the door opened,
and he heard a voice saying, "Are you there, you old bachel?
I see a man coming down the road with a pair of horses,
and you've been sitting there asleep."

And the old blacksmith stood up.
And there was his old wife with a wee cup of tea.
She said, "John, here's tea for you."
And he was so happy,
  he ran to her,
    put his arms round her,
      and kissed her for the first time in fifty years. [loud laughter]

She said, "Let me go, you old bachel," she said.
"You know I'm so weak I can hardly stand up for the want of food."
"And," she said, "there is not a penny in the house."
He said, "Not a penny in the house?"

She said, "Get the horses shod; we need some food.
We need some money."
And the old blacksmith put his hand in his pocket.
And he took out seven gold pieces.
And he gave them to the old woman.
He says, "Buy as much food as you like for that."
"And," he says, "I'll get you some more
when the man comes with the horses."

[laughter and applause] (TS87021)

Since Duncan's performance is rather lengthy, here a summary of the key points of the story:[3]

I. A blacksmith rents his smithy to a young man dressed in green who "heals" a woman by cutting off her head, burning it to ashes, and magically reconstructing it.
II. The young man pays the blacksmith seven gold pieces and warns him not to try and repeat the procedure that he witnessed.
III. The blacksmith tries the procedure on his wife—hoping it will restore her beauty. The procedure fails and the wife is killed.
IV. The blacksmith flees and travels for a year. He then tries to repeat the healing procedure with the head of an ailing princess. He fails again.
V. The young man reappears, saves the princess, and reiterates his warning.
VI. He pays the blacksmith another seven gold pieces.
VII. The blacksmith finds himself back at home. His wife is still alive—as if all had been a dream.
VIII. The blacksmith finds seven gold pieces in his pocket.

As with Betsy's story, no clear sequence of events can be extracted from this performance. What really happened in the narrated event? Did the boy in green heal the young woman in the blacksmith's shop? Did the blacksmith decapitate his wife? Did he try to heal the princess? Was he saved by the young man in green and returned to his wife? Part of what prevents the resolution of the narrated event is the presence of the gold pieces that alternately are only a dream and also are quite real. Part VII reframes all or part of the preceding events as a potential dream sequence, but the money in his pocket in part VIII implies that the young man must somehow be real. A further complication comes in the fact that the blacksmith (presumably) only has seven gold pieces in his pocket, although the young man gave him a total of fourteen—though it might be argued that he spent the first seven during his time on the road. This does allow a potential resolution in which parts I and II are real and parts III-VII are purely dream—but the story does not provide a clear resolution of this point. Yet even this interpretation does not resolve all of the loose ends in the narrated event. If part II is real, the implication is that the young man did have the power to heal the first young woman by decapitating her and bringing her back to life. Who is the young man and where does his power come from? Does he additionally have the power to change reality and bring the blacksmith's wife back to life? How much, then, of the rest of this story is real and how much a dream?

Wondering What Really Happened

In both the stories just presented and in dream stories in general, no coherent narrated event is presented through performance. Instead, these performances stubbornly resist being followed. They remain a narrative "knot" that can be rethought but not unraveled. Yet, as I hope the two examples demonstrate, dream stories do not yield hopelessly chaotic or failed performances. Dream story performances are intentionally formed artistic wholes. A great deal of artistry goes into evoking the confusion listeners feel in trying to figure out "what happened" in the narrated event.

The artistry of dream story performance leaves traces in the text. For example, note the indirect descriptive language Betsy Whyte uses to mark the cattleman's transformation to a woman. Note also her masterful play with the pronouns "he" and "she" throughout the transformation episode of her story—especially the shift that takes place when the cattleman sees the boat down by the river in preparation for being carried off for the second time. Similarly, Duncan Williamson uses great care as he unfolds the events within his performance so as to maintain alternate possible interpretations. For instance, he highlights the payment of the gold pieces—an apparently superfluous detail but an important element of the dream story because it confounds easy resolution of the narrated event. He is also careful to mention the lack of blood when the boy cuts off the young woman's head and the presence of blood when the blacksmith cuts off his wife's head, and not to mention blood at all when the blacksmith cuts off the princess's head—thereby prolonging the listener's uncertainty about what has happened. When the blacksmith asks the king to shut the door when he leaves the palace smithy, this enables the door to be quietly opened behind him when the boy in green arrives to save him. The door also quietly opens when his wife enters, but now "the door" refers to the door to the blacksmith's own smithy. This overlap blurs the boundaries between interpretational frames and thereby heightens the listener's confusion in following the story.

But why intentionally inject incoherence into storytelling performances? What possible value can there be in intentionally confusing listeners? With respect to the dynamics of the performance event, I suggest that Travellers tell dream stories because they are particularly engaging. During an interview about Traveller storytelling, Duncan Williamson commented that Travellers loved dream stories because they left them with something puzzling to think about.

> Everybody told different types of stories...
> But the one who told the dream story,
>   to give somebody something to think about,
> it was: "Laddie, whar did you hear that?"
>   "Eh, that was an interesting thing," you know?
>   "It's got me puzzled."
>   "I cannae fathom it."
>   "I cannae think about it."
> Do you see what I mean?
> Well, this is what the idea was—
> that the dream stories were made to make you think,
> "Did it happen or did it not?" (TS92021)

This sense of engagement persists well beyond the performance event. As Duncan commented: "Now away in their mind, after the . . . storytelling

Creativity, Worldview, and Narrative Knowing   267

night was over, [was] the simple thought in their mind, 'I wonder what really happened' " (TS92021).

One consequence of this deeper engagement with dream stories is that their entertainment potential is enhanced. Duncan Williamson pointed out that dream stories effectively function to take listeners' minds off the omnipresent worries of Traveller life.

> They loved the dream stories because it gave them something to think about.
> It gave them something to puzzle in their mind, you know?
> Of course, they had their worries, you know, too, Donald.
> Travellers had their worries:
>   where their next bite was coming from,
>   where they would camp the next day,
>   or was the police coming to shift them, you know?
> And it give them—
> well, actually it took them away from their way of life.
> Do you know what I mean?
> Some (?), "That was a strange story."
> And then they'd discuss it and talk to you.
> And they'd ask questions among each other, like you and I [do]. (TS92021)

In this way, dream stories allow a pleasurable focus on puzzling but not life-threatening problems, a way of diverting unproductive worry from problems that may not have an immediate solution.

A second consequence of this deeper engagement with dream stories is an enhancement in the ability of dream stories to evoke meanings in an effective and memorable way. Despite their lack of coherence in one dimension, dream stories do communicate coherently in other dimensions. Betsy's story "The Black Laird" carries potential meanings about the importance of being able to entertain fellow Travellers. That Travellers might place value on the ability to entertain is not surprising, given that oral communication is a primary medium of interaction among Traveller groups. Remember also the premium placed on entertaining and witty crack in Traveller interactions, a point that is supported by the positive evaluation of wit in stories such as "The Laird and the Crane."

Similarly, "The Boy and the Blacksmith" embodies pragmatic meanings about Traveller life. Minimally, this story communicates the importance of autonomy by commenting on the morality and wisdom of copying the actions of others. This message is explicitly stated in the boy's warnings to the blacksmith, "Now, old man, remember, / never try and do what you see me doing." This story also implicitly comments on the value of being satisfied with what you have, rather than trying to recast things in another form (a point offered in literal terms with regard to the blacksmith's wife)—a meaning found in other Traveller stories, such as "The Traveller and the Hare," in chapter 2.

My point is that the confusion engendered in dream story performance motivates an ongoing interpretive process wherein individuals must work to make sense out of what happened in the narrated event. As listeners endeavor to disentangle the incoherent dimension of the story, their attention will engage other, more coherent messages encoded in the performance. This ongoing, focused attention not only makes these meanings stand out clearly, but also enhances their retention in memory.

The overall goal in performing a dream story, therefore, is not confusion for its own sake. Generating confusion serves the purpose of engaging listeners, thereby focusing interpretive attention on the performance. This engagement increases entertainment potential by drawing individuals into the story world and away from daily worries. This engagement also ensures that listeners will explore the story sufficiently to understand and remember the key meanings suggested by the narrator through the formal features of his or her performance.

The Validity of Narrative Knowing

Further insight into why Travellers tell dream stories emerges from a consideration of how stories work as a way of knowing. By "way of knowing" I mean that stories can be used as a unique way of understanding the world and communicating this understanding to others. This view of storytelling is not new. Courtney Cazden and Dell Hymes (1978), for example, write that narrative is a viable but often undervalued mode of thought. Similarly, philosopher of history Louis Mink claims that "narrative is a primary cognitive instrument—an instrument rivaled, in fact, only by theory and metaphor as irreducible ways of making the flux of experience comprehensible" (1978, 129).

Understanding how stories work as a way of knowing requires understanding how the qualities of sequence and coherence that stories embody (see chapter 2) are related to each other and to events in the real world. On the surface, this relationship appears to be fairly simple. In his *Poetics*, Aristotle argues that for poetic narrative the relationship is one of mimesis: Events in the story are an imitation of events in the world. In this view, the coherence of a given plot is understood to derive from the inherent coherence of the events being imitated. Many theories of narrative similarly recognize this relationship as one of parallelism or iconicity (e.g., Enkvist 1981; McDowell 1982; Scholes 1981). Yet an iconic relationship between events and a narrative representation of those events does not necessarily imply that it is the events that inform the story with coherence. Hayden White, for instance, asks: "Does the world really present itself to perception in the form of well-made stories, with central subjects, proper beginnings, middles, and ends, and a coherence that permits us to see 'the end' in every beginning?" (1987, 24). From this perspective, coherence is more a property of the formal features of storytelling than it is of events in the world. Consequently, some scholars emphasize the creative role of the narrator in selecting, interpreting, organizing, and presenting events in the world so that they form coherent and meaningful wholes that can be followed and comprehended by listeners (e.g., see Bauman 1986; Mink 1978; White 1987).

Yet, coherence does not derive from universal qualities or truths. Specific interpretations, formal patterns, and presentational styles evoke a sense of coherence and meaning precisely because they are warranted by underlying facets of worldview (Braid 1996b, 12–18). In telling personal experience narratives, for example, narrators must select and shape the "flux of experience" into coherent and followable stories. While many divergent presentations of experience might be possible, narrators will create stories that conform with the beliefs, patterns, and expectations that constitute their own worldview. Consequently, when tellers are able to construct a coherent and cohesive story out of an experience, they may feel they have understood the experience and discovered its meaning.[4] For this reason, the creative process of narrating experience functions as a way of comprehending or knowing the world by harmonizing events with respect to worldview.

Coherent storytelling performances also work as a way of knowing because they provide a medium for communicating experiences, ideas, values, and beliefs to others. Performers can use stories to replay past events or fictional events in such a way that they are foregrounded and open for re-experiencing, evaluation, and analysis in the performance event. Performers may also use stories to encode significant meaning. As I argued in chapter 2, however, listeners do not passively absorb storytelling performances. Listeners endeavor to follow and understand the unfolding story and therefore re-experience the event being narrated. The interpretation of the narrated event is therefore not solely in the hands of the performer. Although listeners' interpretations will be guided by the formal features of the performance text and the performed coherence, interpretation will take place with respect to the listener's own worldview, life experience, and apprehension of the dynamics of the performance interaction. The coherence listeners discover in following will therefore be their own. Different listeners may perceive coherence differently. A listener's experience of following, therefore, must be understood as a way of knowing that is strongly influenced by the performed coherence but is not fully determined by it.

Thus far, I have been discussing how coherent stories work as a way of knowing and communicating about the world. But what happens if a story lacks coherence? What about Traveller dream stories, which deliberately inhibit the normal process of prediction and following that takes place in listening to a story? As I noted earlier, these performances play with the temporal referencing and coherence-making functions of story, thereby creating ambiguity. On a purely abstract level, this play can be seen as evidence of Traveller narrative competency. But I believe this play has much deeper significance.

As I have argued throughout this book, Traveller stories are deeply interconnected with Traveller lives, providing a potent medium for representing and understanding their world. But remember that storytelling performance is a creative act. Storytellers are not limited to iconically re-presenting events and experiences. Storytellers play an active role in constructing the temporal references, formal patternings, and coherencies that are central to their ability to suggest meaning for the listener (Braid 1996b, 16–18). Fictional stories, in particular, allow storytellers broad license to create events without the need to conform to experience or even to the possible. Storytellers may also transform events to fit their own purposes. As Richard Bauman has noted, not only does narrative have the potential to make "the flux of experience" comprehensible, "it may also be an instrument for obscuring, hedging, confusing, exploring, or questioning what went on, that is, for keeping the coherence or comprehensibility of narrated events open to question" (1986, 5–6). Performances may therefore lead to distortions and even expressive lies that play with or transcend the boundaries of believability.

I propose that the deliberate lack of resolvability that is characteristic of dream stories functions as a metanarrative commentary on the intrinsic creativity of the storytelling process and therefore on the validity of narrative knowing. Inherent in the ability to perform and understand dream stories is the recognition that the coherence of stories does not derive from some objective quality of the real world, but that this coherence is at least partly constructed in the act of performance. Dream stories may therefore serve as a reminder that stories of "what happened"—including experiential stories and the narrative quality of experience itself—rest on an equally nonobjective coherence making and not objective truth.

Yet the message communicated by dream stories is not that stories are fabrications and therefore devoid of significant meaning. Rather, dream stories caution that because stories are a creative medium, this creativity must be taken into account in interpreting storytelling performances and in understanding how and what stories mean. By presenting unresolvable or incoherent stories that still meaningfully communicate about the world, dream stories intimate that all stories—no matter what creative transformations or artistic devices are employed—may similarly embody meaningful communications about the world. By highlighting the kinds of transformations, literary devices, formal patternings, goals, and genres that inform narrative knowing, dream stories enhance interpretive skills and thereby enrich the potential and effectiveness of story as a mode of communication. In this sense, dream stories remind listeners that life does not happen like stories, but they do it in a way that suggests that stories can be used to make sense out of life.

Coherence and Worldview

Because dream stories highlight the role of creativity in storytelling performances, they implicitly focus attention on the relationship between coherence and worldview that lies at the heart of narrative knowing. In the previous section I argued that narrative knowing involves a process of coherence-making that is warranted by worldview. I further argued that success in constructing coherent interpretations of experiences, including the experience of following a storytelling performance, is taken as a sign that the events have been understood and that whatever meaning or message they embody has been comprehended. But, as dream stories caution, not all stories are coherent. In this section I therefore focus on the relationship between legends and dream stories in order to explore what happens when storytelling performances cannot be reconciled with respect to worldview.

In chapter 2, I use the term *worldview* to name the shared belief and ideational systems that are generated through the unfolding of individual experience in relation to community interaction. I further argue that worldviews exist as emergent personal constructs that are not necessarily systematic or coherent but pragmatic—providing an essential framework that orients individuals to their world and to their community. They are therefore personal, shared in the sense that they may be attuned with others, and open to reformulation whenever they are sufficiently challenged by experience in the world.

While many stories an individual hears will yield coherent followings—and therefore may serve to validate existing constructs of worldview—some stories will resist coherent understanding. When a storytelling performance proves not to be followable, that is, when an individual's worldview does not enable a coherent reading of the events, the search for coherence will create interpretive tensions. These tensions can be resolved either if the performance is rejected as nonsense or if changes in worldview are made that will accommodate the apparent coherence of the narrated events. These changes may be subtle or profound. Note that performers may evoke interpretive tensions as part of a deliberate strategy to challenge and negotiate worldview.

How directly a given storytelling performance is perceived to engage the real world, and therefore to challenge worldview, is an issue that is normally framed in terms of genre. Experientially based genres such as legend and personal experience narrative are often believed to be "true" and therefore to have direct relevance to comprehending the world of lived experience; fictional genres are frequently believed to be fantasies that require a "willing suspension of disbelief" and therefore to have no direct relevance to the world of lived experience (Bascom 1984; Ben-Amos 1992). Yet this sharp distinction between experiential and fictional genres is misleading—a point that is clearly illustrated with regard to questions of genre in dream stories.

I have framed dream stories as fictional folktales, yet, depending on the resources invoked by tellers and drawn into interpretation by listeners, dream stories evoke characteristics of a number of different genres. With regard to "The Black Laird and the Cattleman," Betsy's version of the story seems to incorporate elements of both folktale and riddle. When Willie MacPhee tells this story as a first-person narration, the story blurs the boundaries between personal experience narrative and tall tale (cf. Bauman 1986, 11–32). When Duncan Williamson comments that many dream stories "could have happened," he raises questions about the relationship between dream stories and legends (TS92016). This ambiguity of genre should be understood as a creative achievement of performance (Briggs and Bauman 1992). In other words, one of the ways dream story performances deepen the interpretive effort is by multiplying the number of possible interpretive strategies a listener might need to adopt to follow the performance.

This ambiguity of genre also affords insight into the nature of the relationship between coherence and worldview that lies at the heart of narrative knowing. Consider the following story that Duncan Williamson told during an interview on the topic of dream stories.

I'll tell you a wee story, a modern folktale.
Probably you have heard this story.
There may be more versions of this.
But this story is supposed to have happened in Aberdeenshire.

This taxi driver in Aberdeenshire,
when the first taxis came out,
he took a gentleman on a long journey,
    one-way journey,
        way out on the other side of Aberdeen,
            away up to Ellon.
And he dropped the gentleman off.
And it was a terrible rainy night.

And he paid him, and,
"Thank you very much," he said, "my son," he said.
"Thank you very much," he said.
"I'm glad you took me home," he said,
"because it was a very terrible night
and the taxis was very scarce."
Which it was (with?) the first old cabbies.

But on the way back from Ellon,
he saw a young woman.
And she waved him down.
And he stopped.
And she said, "I'm sorry sir," she said.
    "It is a terrible night.
        I'm very soaking wet.
            I don't have any money."
"Well," he said, "I've been paid, my dear, for coming this way,
    so I have got an empty car.
        I'll take you back."
He said, "Where have you been?"
"Oh," she says, "I'm very cold, and I'm wet."
"Well," he says,
"Come on, come on in.
Sit down beside me."

So she sat down beside him.
He said—.
She started to shiver.
And he could see that she was very pale.
So he took his jacket off.

"Put that round you, dear," he says.
"That will probably bring some heat in your body."
You know?

And he drove her into Aberdeen.
And he says, "Where do you stay?"
She says, "I stay down in Seaton."
So he took her to—
She says, "That's my mother's house over there."
"Well," he said, "I don't want to trouble your mother."
Because it was late at nighttime.
"I don't want to trouble your mother tonight."
She says, "I'll be all right."
And she said, eh, "Thank you very much, sir."
And she run off.

And he saw the light at the door.
   He saw the door opening.
      and he saw her going in,
         and he saw the door closing.

And then he drove—
And then he remembered.
He forgot to get back his jacket from her.
He forgot to get his jacket back.
"Ah, never mind," he said.
"I'll pick it up some other time.
   I'll pick it up later.
      I'll pick it up tomorrow."
Took the address of the house and number.

And the next day it was a beautiful sunny morning and the rain was gone.
And he actually took a passenger to Seaton.
And he thought while he was there, he would go and pick up his jacket.
Because it was a very expensive jacket, and it cost a lot.
It was one of these tweed jackets.
It cost a lot of money,
Harris Tweed jacket.

And he went to the door and knocked. [DW knocks on the table]
A woman came out.
He says, "I'm sorry, miss," he says, "to trouble you this morning.
But," he said, "Eh,
I took your daughter home last night."
She says, "You did?"

"Took your daughter home last night," he says.
And he said, "I picked her up near Ellon.
And," he said, eh, "I was—.
She was wet and cold.
And," he says, "I gave her my jacket to keep her warm.
And I dropped her off because I was taking a gentleman to Ellon."
Which is about twenty miles away.
"And," he said, "I took her back and I dropped her off here."

And the woman began to cry, hey?
She had tears running down her cheeks.
She began to cry.
The tears was running down her cheeks.
She said, "It's so sad," she said, "so sad."
He says, "What's so sad about it?"
"Just let me talk to her and get my jacket back.
She'll tell you the truth."
She said, "I think you'd better come in."

She brought him in the little house.
And she (?)
"Would you like a cup of tea?"
So she gave him a cup of tea.
And he was wondering what it was all about.
And the tears was still running.
And she was drying her eyes with her apron. You know?

He says, eh, "Can you tell your daughter, and I'll get my jacket back."
She says, "I'm terrible sorry, sir," she says.
She says, "My daughter was killed in Ellon," she says,
   "five years ago,
     with a car."
He says, "You're having me on."
"No," she said, "sir.
I'm telling you the truth.
My daughter was killed with a car in Ellon five years ago."
"But," he says, "it's impossible.
I picked her up in Ellon."

And he told the bad bend where he picked her up.
She said, "That's right.
That's where she was killed five years ago."
She said, "She went to meet her boyfriend,
and she was ran over with a car and killed.

Creativity, Worldview, and Narrative Knowing   277

And she's buried in the little church in Seaton.
And if you don't believe me," she says,
"come.
I'm going, I'm just going to visit."
And the woman had a bunch of flowers sitting on the table.
"I'm just off to visit her."

And the two of them walked to the churchyard in Ellon, in Seaton. Sorry.
And she went to the grave.
And the woman went down on her knees
and she was crying, the tears running down her cheeks.
And she placed the flowers on the grave.
And folded up on the top of the grave was his jacket.

DB That's wild.
DW That's true.
Folded nice and tidy on the top of the grave
was his jacket that he gave her in the (?) car.
DB How do you know that story?
I mean how do you know the story?
DW I was told that story by a chap
who was supposed to have known the guy,
who was the taxi driver in Aberdeen,
when I worked in Aberdeen.
DB Oh, yeah.
DW And he swore that was a true story.
Now that is a ghost story.
Now we cannae say that guy was telling a lie, could we?
DB No.
DW Because we don't know.
He never made it up.
And he took his jacket back and it was dry as could be.
And he put it on.
And he thanked the woman for the tea,
and he walked back.
And to the day he went to his grave,
he never, never, never, knew,
did that actually happen or did it not. (TS92021)

Duncan frames this story as a "modern folktale," and later as a "ghost story," but folklorists will recognize this as a well-told version of the "Vanishing Hitchhiker" legend (Brunvand 1981, 24–46). The story also exhibits many characteristics of the dream stories I have discussed earlier—and

I believe this is Duncan's point in telling the story during our interview. The story cannot be resolved into a coherent picture of "what happened" in the narrated event. How could the cab driver give a ride to a woman who had been dead for five years? How could he find the house where the woman lived if she had not directed him to it? How could his coat appear on the gravestone unless he had loaned it to the woman? How is it possible that his coat was dry when it was raining the night he lost it? This story cannot be resolved into a clear account of events, *unless* ghosts are real and can interact in the world of the living. With a legend performance this is exactly the point (Dégh 1991, 30; Oring 1986, 126). Legends challenge listeners in their effort to find coherence, and force them to consider the possibility that their worldviews must be modified in order to accommodate the narrated events. In other words, the believability of the narrated events is at issue. Is it possible that x happened? If x has happened, what do I need to believe about the way the world works to understand how and why it has happened?

Since dream stories are not explicitly framed as true events, they may not appear to challenge listeners' worldviews. Yet dream stories frequently embody many of the characteristics typically associated with legends. Dream story performances ask listeners to ponder issues of belief and believability. With respect to the "Black Laird and the Cattleman," for example, what is more believable: a vivid dream, the magic power of the laird, the propensity of farm hands to lie, or the possibility of strange happenings in the world? Additionally, dream stories, like legends, can be coherently resolved if listeners accept certain beliefs about how the world works. If the black laird does have the power to collapse several years' experience into the space of twenty minutes, or if the cattleman had a particularly vivid hallucination, then a coherent following of the narrated event is possible.

My point, however, is not that dream stories and legends are identical, but that there are significant parallels in terms of how these genres work as ways of knowing. These parallels arise, in part, because the same process of following underlies the interpretive experience for both genres. This process necessarily engages issues of belief, believability, and worldview—even with fictional stories. In following a folktale, for instance, listeners must discover which properties of the fictional world will, when accepted, enable the narrated event to be coherently resolved. These contingently accepted properties or beliefs may derive from genre conventions or from careful interpretation of the tale itself. But when stories demand that listeners entertain strange or divergent beliefs in order to follow the performance, these beliefs do not directly motivate a reformulation of worldview. Rather, by prompting listeners to contingently accept strange or divergent beliefs, fictional stories ask listeners to contemplate and experience alternate coherencies that may differ from their lived world in subtle—or radical—ways.

The influence of this process on worldview is indirect. When listeners contingently accept alternate coherencies, the possibility is raised that they will apply the beliefs, ideas, relationships, and interpretive strategies embodied in these coherencies to events in the lived world. Where these applications prove useful or revealing in understanding experience, they may be integrated into worldview. In other words, where legends communicate about what is, folktales communicate about the possible, about what might be.

Despite the indirectness of the influence on worldview, this imaginative play with possibility is serious business. Fictional stories may present veiled critiques of events or metaphorical analogies that have profound influence on how listeners interpret experience (see chapters 2 and 4). Fictional stories may communicate significant practical knowledge. Most importantly, this play provides a way of exploring alternate worlds and meanings without invoking resistance that might accompany direct challenges to accepted conceptions of worldview. In this way, play with possibility embodies a potent adaptive strategy that facilitates survival (Bateson 1972; Csikszentmihalyi 1981).

Because dream stories bend conventions and ways of understanding in novel and memorable ways, they are a particularly effective genre for playing with possibility. But performances of dream stories hint at something more. By asking listeners to explore a number of possible assumptions that might plausibly lead to a coherent resolution of the narrated event and by inhibiting a fully coherent resolution of these events, dream story performances force listeners to entertain a range of alternate coherencies that appear to have equal validity. Since each of the potential coherencies may invoke a different set of beliefs, dream stories embody the suggestion that multiple coherencies and therefore multiple worldviews may equally lead to coherent understandings of the world.

While this insight may seem to undermine the pragmatic value of maintaining a shared worldview as a foundation for daily life, it does help Travellers survive in their world. Comprehending the value of this insight requires recalling that Travellers do not exist independently of non-Travellers but coexist with them. It is therefore crucial that Travellers not only understand that non-Travellers are different but also understand how they are different, that they are aware of how non-Travellers think and make sense of their world. For example, when deals are made with non-Travellers, it is essential that both participants feel that they are getting a good deal. Since the beliefs and values that inform perceptions of "good dealness" are different for Travellers and non-Travellers, knowledge of how non-Travellers comprehend economics gives Travellers an edge.

Similarly, awareness of non-Traveller worldview is essential for survival in a world where non-Travellers set the rules and frequently discriminate against Travellers. Understanding non-Traveller worldview enables Travellers to respond and act in productive ways. This awareness is especially important in comprehending discourse that takes place between Travellers and non-Travellers. Consider, for instance, stories that try to make sense of the ongoing conflicts over Traveller camping (see Gentleman and Swift 1971, 86–89; Gentleman 1993). Newspaper accounts, requests for arrest warrants, and neighborhood gossip may string together legal precedents and "common sense" into coherent stories that condemn Traveller camping practices (in specific instances or in general). Travellers need to be able to follow these accounts in order to understand the underlying beliefs and assumptions that give them their apparent validity. Once they understand the implicit worldview behind these perceptions, Travellers can and do respond in effective ways that make use of settled beliefs to challenge the validity of these narrative interpretations. These responses may take the form of physical acts such as producing contradictory evidence or challenging the legal authority that warrants the conclusions and actions motivated by the underlying beliefs (for example, see Betty's story about the trailer in chapter 4). These responses may also take symbolic form. For example, understanding the underlying beliefs and values of non-Traveller worldview enables Travellers to construct stories that make sense to non-Travellers yet which embody a persuasive critique of the history of interaction between Travellers and non-Travellers (see chapter 4). Sympathetic media attention (though rare), scholarly interest, and the performance stage allow Travellers the opportunity to present these alternate interpretations to the non-Traveller audience and thereby challenge outsider conceptions of who the Travellers are.

The creative play present in dream stories reflects on the properties of Traveller storytelling in general. Travellers use stories as a potent medium for creating, maintaining, and playing with the conceptions of identity, belief, and worldview that inform their perceptions of the world and their lives. Because storytelling performances afford listeners an engaging experience of similarity and difference, they can also foster understanding across cultural boundaries. This makes storytelling an attractive medium for studying differences in worldview. Yet, as dream stories caution, the relationship between story and worldview is a complicated one. Any reading of a worldview or belief in a given performance must take into account the creativity and flexibility of performers in creating narrative worlds that argue for coherency.

Conclusion

Lives and Stories—Stories and Lives

This book is about the mutual influence between stories and lives. One story I tell here is my own. This story relates how my discovery of the world of oral storytelling and my meeting with Duncan Williamson and other Traveller storytellers transformed my life from that of a physicist with a scientific worldview to that of a scholar studying the world of human experience. This is a story of a journey still in progress.

Another story I tell is about the Travelling People and the interplay between their storytelling traditions and their lives. In the previous chapters I present transcriptions of actual performances in order to give a glimpse of Traveller lives and stories. My discussions of these stories touch on a number of important aspects of the relationship between Traveller stories and Traveller lives. In this regard, I examine how Traveller storytelling works as a medium for shaping experience and worldview, demonstrate the role of Traveller stories in creating and preserving perceptions of community, argue that Travellers use stories to negotiate identity with outsiders, and explore the function of Traveller storytelling as a medium in which reality itself can be explored and constructed.

These are not the only links between Traveller lives and Traveller stories. In some performances I transcribe in this book, for example, there are clues as to the meaningful connections Travellers make between stories and place. Note, for instance, how some performers take great care to identify the place where events occurred as an essential element of context for the story. In other cases stories are used to create a meaningful landscape that traditionalizes the context within which Travellers live their lives. Betty Townsley, for example, commented to me that her husband tells a lot of stories about place to their children: "When we are moving on the road and there's camping places, Heather's daddy will point them out the camping places. And maybe tell what happened there, or maybe some event that brought back memory to that . . . little bit" (TS92025). Much more elusive is my sense that Travellers experience their movement through the landscape in narrative terms, an unfolding of place through time. These aspects of the relationship between story and place deserve further study.

Similarly, what is going on when tellers choose not to tell a story they know? In this regard, Betsy Whyte's refusal to tell some of her stories to collectors is intriguing. These were stories that had particular meaning for her—that she "felt the deepest" (TS88002). Of this decision, she commented, "It wouldnae do any harm to the stories. But I think it would—they would lose their meaning. Because now the way they're being told, they're, they have no meaning. They're just being told as stories" (TS88002). In choosing not to perform these stories, Betsy alludes to a private dimension of the connection between her stories and her life. This feeling of Betsy and other Travellers deserves more exploration as well.

Incompleteness, however, is an inevitable part of any attempt to illuminate the essence of a tradition within the pages of a single book. I must therefore be satisfied to present a brief glimpse of Traveller storytelling that leaves a great deal more unsaid than is said. Yet, I trust that the discussions I do present demonstrate ways in which Traveller lives are shaped through stories and, conversely, how the lives of those who tell stories can exert a formative influence on the stories they tell.

Although some may argue that academics are ruined to normal human experience because of their desire to analyze and understand human behavior in comparative terms, I am convinced that this analytic process yields a deeper appreciation of our common humanity. Consequently, there is a third story about the role of storytelling in human communication implicit in these pages. I believe that my ethnographic exploration of the relationship between lives and stories among the Travelling People of Scotland can offer insight into how stories and storytelling work in other communities and lives, including our own, as well. I therefore sketch some tentative conclusions about how storytelling works as a medium for communicating about, comprehending, shaping, and transforming the world of lived experience, both within and between cultural groups.

First, I conclude that storytelling is a potent means of communication because storytelling performances engage listeners. A narrator's creativity and his or her artistic patterning of the story are important in motivating this engagement. Listeners' desire to follow might be motivated by a sense of identification with effectively constituted characters or events in a story (Gallie 1964, 41–48), sound symbolism (Nuckolls 1992, 52–55), symbolic strategies that collapse the boundary between performance event and narrated event (McDowell 1982, 133–35), or significant formal patternings that evoke an expectation of fulfillment (Burke 1953; see also McDowell 1992). Dream stories raise the possibility that incoherency is a powerful way of engaging listeners by creating puzzles to be solved. But whatever the underlying motivation, the deeper the sense of engagement a performer manages to elicit, the more effectively the storytelling performance can work in the exchange between teller and listener—evoking meaning, teaching, negotiating worldview, fostering intercultural understanding, and affecting listeners.

Second, storytelling is an effective medium for comprehending the world of lived experience because the interpretive process it elicits is experientially based. In following, listeners endeavor to make sense out of a performance and to understand the coherence of the narrated event. While listeners may entertain coherencies suggested in performance, they actively envision and construct these coherencies with respect to their own knowledge, experience, and worldview. In this sense, following can give rise to experiential resources that can be thought with and thought through in ongoing interpretations of the world (Braid 1996b, 20). If these experiences are incorporated into personal constructs of worldview and identity, they may acquire significant influence over interpretation and behavior.

Finally, storytelling is a powerful vehicle for shaping and transforming lived experience because creativity permeates the dynamic exchange that takes place between performer and audience. This creativity not only enables performers to adapt stories in order to accomplish valuable functions within the performance event but also gives performers freedom to play with possibility and explore the dialectic between experience and worldview. Stories can therefore be used to suggest alternate beliefs, ideas, relationships, and interpretive strategies. It is because of this creative freedom that storytelling performances provide a medium within which worldviews can be effectively created, attuned, affirmed, challenged, or transformed. This creative freedom also means that storytelling performances can be used to explore imaginative worlds in a way that may have important consequences for the survival of individuals and communities.

Despite my desire for broad conclusions about the role of storytelling in human life, I am well aware that human interactions are exceedingly complex. Given this complexity, it is far too easy to mistake the trees for the forest, to become focused on one cultural practice to the exclusion of all else. By focusing so completely on the connection between Traveller stories and Traveller lives, I do not intend to give the impression that Traveller interactions are saturated with would-be performers vying for the stage in an ongoing critical interpretation of reality. Travellers live their lives in a world that requires a great deal of time and effort to be expended just to earn a living and deal with the necessities of survival. Stories are a sometimes central, sometimes peripheral, part of this process. Yet there is more to life than survival. For Travellers, witty and entertaining engagement with others is an essential part of their lives. Stories often play a central role here. While many Travellers would not consider themselves to be storytellers, Traveller interactions are nonetheless permeated with personal experience stories and narrative cracks. For some, folktales are an important part of this process.

Stories may be so much a part of normal interaction for Travellers that they are not consciously singled out as performances that serve unique and profound functions within a given exchange. Consequently, some Travellers questioned my research premise about the meaningful and pervasive use of storytelling among the Travellers. Where I search for meaning behind every story, Tracy Donaldson, in her 20s at the time, wisely cautions: "Probably back further it would have meant more. Today, if somebody tells a story, it is just another story really, isn't it? That's the way, well, younger generations think" (TS93025). I suspect many in the older generations might say something similar.

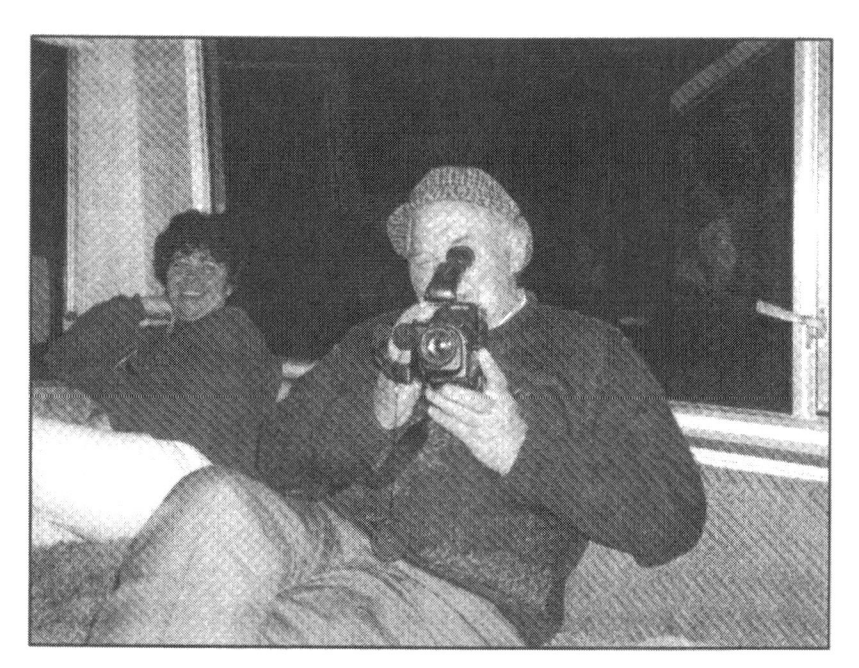

Nancy MacDonald and Eckie Sutherland playing "the ethnographer," 1998

The questions I posed during research asked Travellers to reflect on story meaning and storytelling practice at a level of analysis not normally a part of the exchange of stories in their interactions. It might be expected that Traveller knowledge of stories and storytelling is a pragmatic knowledge that is focused on doing stories, not on arguing about how stories work as a medium of reflexive thought. Yet my questions received answers that reveal careful thought and understanding of the place of stories in Traveller lives. What this means is that Travellers are capable of thinking about stories in analytical ways although they may not choose to do so on a day-to-day basis. By way of analogy, human beings are capable of thinking about breathing in analytical ways although they may not choose to do so on a daily basis. The good storytellers, in particular, know what they are doing and why they are doing it. They recognize the nuances of the medium and can use it to good effect.

In addition, it is certainly not the case that stories are the only medium Travellers use in reflecting on and shaping their lives. Traveller songs and ballads, for example, share some similar functions with stories, although they are not always strictly narrative in character.[1] Like stories, songs provide a medium of reflection and commentary on issues of identity and worldview. These songs range from original compositions that comment on facets of Traveller life or current events to internationally known Child Ballads. I have used a few songs in previous chapters to illustrate my points, but in this book I have not addressed key questions about why Travellers choose to use songs as a medium for expressing lived experience. Why sing some stories? What do the songs add to the stories? What do the stories add to the songs? A partial answer to these questions might focus on the consequences of the increased formal patterning that takes place in conjoining story and melodic pattern. On the one hand, this patterning opens performances to the possibility of community involvement through "singing along." On the other hand, this patterning opens up new degrees of expressive freedom, and allows interpretation, aural imagery, and emotion to be blended with the narrative line of the song. These additional degrees of expressive freedom might also be used as channels for hinting at implicit meanings—for example, through subtle deviations from expected patterns.

Consider the following song composed by Jimmy Williamson in 1992. The song looks back over Traveller life and traditions. But as Jimmy said about the mood of the song, he was not "regretting the passing of the old times," he was "just making a reflection, or a statement . . . It's past, we can remember it, but it's maybe as well to be past" (TS94001).[2]

Slow Going Easy

> Gone are the days of slow going easy.
> Life is much faster now, we understand.
> But we don't want to catch up, live the life of the gorgio,*
> just be free living, free moving Travelling men.
>
> Our ways have changed since horse was the master,
> and we didn't worship that god we call oil.
> I know it's improved things, but it goes a lot faster.
> We don't want to earn wages with good honest toil.

---

*gorgio = Romani term for non-Gypsy or non-Traveller

Slow Going Easy

Gone are the days of slow going easy.
Life is much faster now, we understand.
We don't want to catch up, live the life of the gorgio,
just be free living, free moving Travelling men.

Campfires are the places where stories remember,
are told to the listener, the old and the young.
Our deeds and our glories will ne'er be forgotten
when songs are still lilted in our mother tongue.

Conclusion 289

> *Gone are the days of slow going easy.*
> *Life is much faster now, we understand.*
> *We don't want to catch up, live the life of the gorgio,*
> *just be free living, free moving Travelling men.*
>
> *But the smoke seldom rises over new camping places,*
> *stories only remembered in some greying head.*
> *Who will remember when the old have forgotten?*
> *When no one remembers, tradition is dead.*
>
> *Gone are the days of slow going easy.*
> *Life is much faster now, we understand.*
> *We don't want to catch up, live the life of the gorgio,*
> *just be free living, free moving Travelling men.*
> *Yes be free living, free moving Travelling men. (TS94001)*

Jimmy's song is filled with nostalgia for the old ways of Traveller life, for campfires and horses and freedom. Although it embodies understanding of change, the song expresses a deep sense of loss at what is gone or disappearing. Yet this commentary about the "good old days" should not be interpreted as an unreflective preoccupation with the past. During the same interview, Jimmy suggested that the nostalgia Travellers often express for the past does not imply that they would give up everything and return to that life with its grim realities. To illustrate his point, he sang me a song he had written a few weeks earlier while camped with others "on the road."

JW [Travellers] enjoy the privilege of being able to jump in the motor
    and drive to wherever they want to.
    But then there are other times when they sit and they say,
    "Oh, those were the good old days." You know?
DB Yeah.
JW But then I've got a—
    I wrote another song . . . called "Those Were the Good Old Days."
    But it's a kind of sarcastic look at the good old days.
    Do you know what I mean?
DB Do you want to sing it?
JW I'm saying "the good old days,"
    but it's a kind of sarcasm in it, you know?
DB Yeah, yeah.
JW But, what were the good old days?

The Good Old Days

We were rich if we'd a horse and cairt to help us wi' our load,
to pile our bits and pieces on as we walked the weary road.
We never had many claes that fit and nae shoes upon our feet.
And it wasnae very often that we had enough to eat.

Oh, I remember,
yes, I remember,
oh, I remember,
those were the good old days.

Mother'd go fae door to door and earn whate'er she could.
But it wasna very easy for to feed a hungry brood.
Faither'd always dae his share but looking back it seems
the life that we are living now could be only lived in dreams.

Oh, I remember,
yes, I remember,
yes, I remember,
those were the good old days.

We never had much worldly goods, we could only carry few,
a blanket for to mak our bed, a pot, a cup or two,
a kettle for to mak our tea, a cover for our tent.
And often with this on our backs, on the road we went.

Oh, I remember,
yes, I remember,
oh, I remember,
those were the good old days.

We were rich if we'd a horse and cart to help us wi' our load,
to pile our bits and pieces on as we walked the weary road.
We never had many claes that fit and nae shoes upon our feet.
And it wasnae very often that we had enough to eat.

Oh, I remember,
yes, I remember,
oh, I remember,
those were the good old days. (TS94001)

In addition to serving as an illustration of Traveller reflexivity in a medium beyond storytelling, these songs illustrate a final unresolved issue in this study. Travellers are still telling stories, composing songs, and living in a world that continues to change despite the permanence of the words I print on this page. Some of those I have gotten to know are growing older, and I fear that I may lose the joy of their company and their stories. Others are changing their relationships to their cultural practice.[3] This study must therefore be understood to be a work in progress. There is no doubt in my mind that Traveller storytelling will continue to change in response to the changing world and changing opportunities. What I am sure of is that Travellers will continue to tell stories. As Tracy Donaldson commented: "Storytelling will never die out" (TS93026).

Notes

Introduction

1. Ken Feit was a storyteller from the Chicago area. He left graduate school at UC Berkeley to join the Jesuit order, but eventually discovered his true vocation: what he called being an "itinerant fool." Under this title, he traveled around the world, telling stories, doing mime, and teaching workshops. He never claimed any specific cultural or religious heritage; instead, he drew his material from a wide range of cultural and religious traditions. He was tragically killed in a car accident at age 41 in 1981. A sense of his unique philosophy can be found in "A Letter to My Friends on the Occasion of My Fortieth Birthday" and "Reflections of a Foolish Storyteller," both published in *Theaterwork Magazine*, in July/August 1982. See also his book *Soundways* (1971).

2. Hamish Henderson is widely known as a poet and songwriter in addition to his role as a scholar. For an excellent introduction to his life's work, see his collection of essays titled, *Alias MacAlias: Writings on Songs, Folk and Literature* (1992).

3. Linda Williamson's doctoral thesis, "Narrative Singing among the Scots Travellers: A Study of Strophic Variation in Ballad Performance" (1985), is an insightful exploration of the creativity of Traveller singers. Unfortunately, it remains unpublished and can be accessed only in the library of the School of Scottish Studies, at the University of Edinburgh.

4. "Lady Margaret" is a version of Child 39—frequently titled "Tam Lin" after the name of the human/fairy man here identified as Lord William. Duncan says that Travellers call the ballad "Lady Margaret" because they feel it focuses most centrally on the actions and identity of the woman in the narrative—not the actions of the human/fairy man. For more about the long history of this ballad, see Child 1965, 1:335–58. A detailed transcription of one of Duncan's performances of this ballad can be found in *A Thorn in the King's Foot* (D. Williamson 1987a, 258–64). Recordings of two alternate versions of this ballad sung by Travellers can be found on *The Muckle Sangs* (School of Scottish Studies 1992).

5. An analysis of the "Laird and the Crane," for example, might begin with a consideration of the value placed on wit within Traveller communities. An analysis of "Lady Margaret" might note the strength and fearlessness of the heroine in standing up to the fairy queen and relate this to Traveller beliefs about gender or self-sufficiency.

6. Pearl fishing refers to a largely Traveller occupation of fishing for pearls that grow in the freshwater mussels found in Scottish rivers. For a discussion of pearl fishing in Scotland, see MacLean 1982 and Neat 1996.

7. I am not the first to ask Duncan questions about Traveller culture. He has been asked similar questions by other researchers who have been interested in diverse aspects of Traveller life. This experience has a complex influence on the content of his answers. On the one hand, it has allowed him time to contemplate accurate and complete answers to questions he has been asked before. On the other hand, ethnographic fieldwork is a dialog that influences both ethnographer and informant in subtle ways. Dennis Tedlock describes this process as a search for interobjective understanding (1983, 321–38). This past experience has given Duncan a chance to learn and incorporate scholarly conceptions of the Travellers into the answers he gave to me. Evidence of his use of analytic terms about culture and storytelling, for example, will come out in the following chapters. Yet I do not believe that this past experience has in some way "tainted" Duncan as a valuable source on Traveller culture and storytelling traditions. If anything, it has enhanced his skill as a "native ethnographer." By this I mean that his knowledge of the culture of academics has made it easier for him to translate his understanding of the Travellers in a way that makes sense to academics. Simultaneously, Duncan's experience gives him the ability to understand the blindness or theoretical inadequacies that often accompany scholarly inquiry. A number of publications explore Duncan's life and storytelling skills. For a general overview of his life, see the essays on Duncan in Bruford 1980. Duncan's role as a tradition bearer is explored in Niles 1995 and 1999. A portrait of his early life is available in his autobiography *The Horsieman* (D. Williamson 1994).

8. The making of horn spoons is a traditional Traveller craft. Horn was boiled and then shaped into spoons in wooden presses. These spoons were then sold door to door.

9. Careful research has shown that genetic inheritance does not somehow predetermine culture (see Boas 1988; Stocking 1982).

10. For those who would like to explore the culture and history of Travellers in more detail than I present here, I suggest a number of sources. For an exploration of the early history of Scottish Gypsies, see MacRitchie 1894. Farnham Rehfisch provides a useful summary of Traveller culture and worldview in "Scottish Travellers or Tinkers" (1975, 271–83). Similarly, the government report *Scotland's Travelling People* (Gentleman and Swift 1971) works from data obtained as part of the 1969 Traveller census and presents a detailed survey of many facets of Traveller life. This research was updated in Gentleman's 1993 publication, *Counting Travellers in Scotland*. Other works adopt a primarily ethnographic approach to describe aspects of Traveller life and beliefs (Rehfisch 1958, 1961; Vallee 1955). Several publications provide insight into their daily life by focusing on the words of individual Travellers (MacColl and Seeger 1986; Neat 1996; Niles 1999; Porter and Gower 1995; L. Williamson 1981) or by presenting extended biographical or autobiographical accounts (Leitch 1988; Whyte 2001, 1990; D. Williamson

1994). A number of works specifically address Traveller narrative traditions. See, for example, Alan Bruford's overview article on Traveller storytelling (1979), Sheila Douglas's dissertation (1985) on Traveller storytelling in Perthshire, Barbara McDermitt's doctoral thesis (1986) comparing Aberdeenshire Traveller Stanley Robertson with South Carolina storyteller Ray Hicks, or my own publications on various aspects of Traveller storytelling (1993, 1997, 1998a, 1999). For insight into the broader context of Gypsy and Traveller life in the British Isles, see Judith Okely's study of English Gypsies (1983) or work by George Gmelch or Sharon Gmelch (for example, G. Gmelch 1985 or S. Gmelch 1986). An excellent overview of Gypsy and Traveller groups throughout Europe can be found in Jean-Pierre Liégeois's book *Gypsies and Travellers* (1987). Current social and political issues facing Gypsies and Travellers are nicely covered in a series of articles published in two books: *Gypsy Politics and Traveller Identity* (Acton 1997) and *Romani Culture and Gypsy Identity* (Acton and Mundy 1997). References to scholarship on Traveller ballads and songs can be found in note 53.

11. Since this term appears only in Traveller cant and is therefore only used orally, it has no standard spelling. When I asked Travellers how to spell this word, I was told variously "Nachins," "Knackins," or "Nawkins." The term is pronounced "KNOCK-ins."

12. These numbers do not include "New Age Travellers"—a group described in the notes to the 1992 census thus: "They [New Age Travellers] are not a group based on descent in the same way as Travellers. They tend to be younger and generally better educated than indigenous Travellers but have chosen to 'drop out' of conventional society. They do not normally associate with the regular Traveller community, nor are they generally accepted by them" (Gentleman 1993, appendix II).

13. For an overview of the general pattern of discrimination suffered by Gypsies and Travellers throughout Europe, see Liégeois 1987.

14. The exact origin of the term *Egyptian* is somewhat obscure, but it may have originated in a mistaken assumption that the origin of the Gypsy migrations was Egypt (see Fraser 1992, 47–48). The term *Egyptian* first appears in Scotland in 1505 in reference to the migrations of Gypsies, but no clear distinction is made between tinkers and Gypsies (Departmental Committee on Tinkers in Scotland 1918, 5). This term should therefore be interpreted as an inclusive term that is synonymous with *tinker, Traveller, or Gypsy* (see also Gentleman and Swift 1971).

15. This is a policy that was set forth in the *Report of the Departmental Committee on the Tinkers in Scotland 1918*. For an overview of this report, see Gentleman and Swift 1971, 11–12.

16. In the present work, I intentionally avoid addressing questions about the origins of the Scottish Travellers. Theories about their origins abound, but clear answers do not. Some scholars argue that the Scottish Travellers are a remnant of an aboriginal nomadic Scottish population (e.g., Neat 1979; Henderson 1992, 229). Others suggest that Travellers are composed of settled folk who lost their homes during social upheavals such as the Clearances (Departmental Committee

on Tinkers in Scotland 1918, 6; Henderson 1992, 229). Another theory proposes that Travellers appeared in Scotland as the result of the migrations of Romani Gypsies that first reached Western Europe during the 15th and 16th centuries (Departmental Committee on Tinkers in Scotland 1918, 5–6). Perhaps the most reasonable suggestion is that the current-day Travellers, like national Gypsy and Traveller populations in other European countries, are the result of some amalgamation of local groups and the Gypsy migrations (e.g., Fraser 1992, 113; Acton 1993, 1).

17. "The Travelling Stewarts" is a reference to one of the families of Travelling People in Scotland. Although I cannot be sure as to the specific individuals Hamish was visiting, many of the Stewarts are well known for their singing and storytelling abilities. An account of one branch of the Stewart family can be found in MacColl and Seeger 1986. Other Stewarts are featured in Roger Leitch's work *The Book of Sandy Stewart* (1988) and Timothy Neat's book *The Summer Walkers* (1996).

18. I am leaving out one episode of my fieldwork story. About a week after leaving Duncan, I visited Traveller Stanley Robertson in Aberdeen. Although I stayed with Stanley for less than a week, he made me welcome and told me many wonderful stories, played his bagpipes, and sang me songs. Stanley is an excellent storyteller and has deep insight into Traveller storytelling traditions. I leave him out at this point only because his experience as a Traveller is somewhat different than that of the family group on which I place my primary focus in this book. I will include Stanley's comments where they help illuminate the discussions that follow. I hope to devote an upcoming publication to an exploration of Stanley's storytelling and singing.

19. Since a great deal has been written on the process of field research in folklore, I do not address this issue here. For a general background in the methods and practices of this work, see Goldstein 1964, Jackson 1987, Ives 1974, and Tedlock 1983.

20. For a brief biographical note and several examples of Jimmy Williamson's singing and storytelling, see Burton 2000.

Chapter 1

1. This usage parallels the comments made by Henry Glassie about the use of crack in Northern Ireland (cf. Glassie 1982, 36). *The Concise Scots Dictionary* lists several definitions for the verb *crack*. Most relevant to this discussion are the usages as a verb: "boast, brag" and "talk, converse, gossip," and the usages as a noun: "loud boasts or brags," "a talk, gossip, conversation," and "a story, tale" (120).

2. The comments I present here are a suggestive but overly brief introduction to the influence of gender on Traveller storytelling traditions. A full exploration of this issue will depend on careful research.

3. Sylvia Dunn made this comment during a meeting of the Economic and

Social Research Council's seminar on Romani Studies held at Greenwich University in London on July 7, 1994.

4. Government Traveller sites in Scotland are patterned after Gypsy sites mandated in England by the Caravan Sites Act 1968. The second report of the Secretary of State's Advisory Committee on Scotland's Travelling People (1978) included the recommendation that Scottish local authorities should "establish over the next three years a network of properly constituted sites for travelling people" (14). Although these sites provide legal places for Travellers to camp, they are problematic from a Traveller perspective for a number of reasons. They are frequently built on waste ground near environmental hazards such as motorways, power lines, or garbage dumps (Save the Children 1996b). Travellers also complain that the division of sites into separate pitches by steel railings fosters a sense of individual ownership and thereby isolates Travellers from each other (TS93026).

5. For more about personal experience narratives, see Stahl 1983 and Langellier 1989.

6. A spirit or supernatural figure who comes to test people. See D. Williamson 1985, 13–15.

Chapter 2

1. Another term that could be used here is "ideology"—in the sense of ideology as a constitutive system of ideas (see Geertz 1973, 193–229). Jane Hill and Bruce Mannheim, however, suggest that ideology is often used to reflect the "fragmented and contingent nature of human worlds as opposed to their 'wholeness' and persistence" (1992, 381–2). While I do not feel that worldviews are fully whole and persistent, I want avoid the negative connotations of the term ideology. For an examination of the issues raised in using the term worldview see Schrempp 1996. For comments on the centrality of worldview to folkloristics see Dégh 1994.

2. For overviews of performance approaches to folklore, see Bauman 1977, 1992; Bauman and Braid 1998; Bauman and Briggs 1990; and Fine 1984.

3. For a detailed discussion of the concept of metanarrative commentary, see Babcock 1977.

4. My focus on the listener has been influenced by Alan Dundes's call for "oral literary criticism" (1975) and by Sandra Dolby Stahl's recent work on interpreting personal narratives (1989). The argument I present here can be read as an "aural-response criticism"—in reference to the reader-response criticism developed by literary theorists (for an overview of this theory, see Tompkins 1980, Freund 1987, and Beach 1993; on the relevance of reader-response theory to folkloristics, see Brown 1984). There are some parallels between my suggestions and the models of reader-response critics. My use of insights from phenomenology and Gestalt psychology calls to mind the work of Wolfgang Iser (1978, 1989). My focus on the temporal foundation of the listener's experience has analogues in the work of Stanley Fish (1980).

5. The relationship between sequence in the world and sequence in story has often been termed one of iconicity (Bauman 1986, 5). Yet the relationship need not be as simple as the term *iconicity* suggests. Varying degrees of artistry may transform the sequence creating a recoverable but complex relationship between the events and their portrayal in story (e.g., McDowell 1982, 124).

6. In a similar vein, Jan Mukarovsky suggests that literature exhibits wholeness in terms of what he terms "contexture"—"a sequence of semantic units . . . in which meaning accumulates successively. . . . Only when the contexture has been completed, do the whole and each of the individual partial meanings acquire a definite relation to reality" (1978, 73–74).

7. Reader-response critic Stanley Fish makes a similar point in suggesting that a focus on the temporal unfolding of the reader's experience is essential to understanding the meaning of a literary work. In his analysis he asks, "What does a sentence do?" A sentence is suggested to be "an event" and what "happens" to readers—their temporally situated experience—is suggested to be the meaning of the utterance (1980, 72).

8. In their paper on poetics and language, Richard Bauman and Charles Briggs suggest a theoretical framework for investigating how discourse can be rendered separable from one situational context and then recontextualized through performance in another context (1990, 72–78; see also Braid 1998b). By examining the emergent properties of Duncan's 1988 performance of "The Traveller and the Hare" in relation to the performances of this story I recorded in 1987, my analysis explores some features of the process of recontextualization.

Chapter 3

1. A recording of Jimmy Williamson singing this song can be found on his CD *Jimmy Williamson: Born Tae the Road* (1999).

2. A recording of this song is available on J. Williamson 1999.

3. In this sense the meaning that is evoked includes and transcends the meaning of phatic relationship between teller and audience (see Malinowski 1953, 313–16; Jakobson 1960, 355–56).

4. Linda Headlee later married Duncan and changed her name to Linda Williamson.

5. For an English translation of this variant, see Lang [1889]1965, 64–71.

Chapter 4

1. This committee was formed by the U.K. Secretary of State for Scotland in June 1971 "to keep the whole situation relating to 'Scotland's Travelling People' under review over a three year period, in particular to provide a bridge between the travellers and the settled community with a view to achieving greater tolerance and understanding of each other's point of view, and in general to act as a focal point for the further consideration of the welfare of travellers" (quoted in

Secretary of State's Advisory Committee 1974, 1). The committee has been reappointed every three years since this time and has issued a series of reports on the state of Travellers in Scotland.

2. Note that for clarity I have reserved quotes in my transcription for the dialog in the narrated event and not Duncan's reporting of Maggie's words.

3. Presumably, under Scottish law the laird owns not only owns the land surrounding the river or loch but also the fishing rights to the water on his property.

4. The non-harassment policy was set forth by the Scottish Development Department in recognition of the fact that it is a waste of local resources to harass Travellers for unauthorized camping when the local authority has not provided enough legal sites for camping. A Scottish Development Department Circular setting forth this policy suggests that moving Travellers from an unauthorized site should not take place unless local authorities "have a pressing need to do so" and "they have identified a satisfactory alternative stopping place to which they can direct Travellers (Scottish Development Department 24/1982; see also Secretary of State's Advisory Committee 1982, 18–19).

5. For a full transcription of this story, see Braid 1996a, 287–93 Another performance of this story is presented in Bruford 1980, 160–64.

6. For a variant of this story, see *Aesop's Fables* (1947, 22–24).

7. John McDowell argues that these moments of reported speech function as cases of "marked *ostension*," which give the illusion of collapsing the boundaries between the time of performance event and the time of the narrated event, thereby allowing the listener a more direct experience of the narrated events (1982, 128–29).

8. Interestingly, in his work *Discourse on the Origin of Inequality*, Jean-Jacques Rousseau argues that civilized man may willingly accept such control in exchange for security (1987, 72).

Chapter 5

1. This kind of story is not unique to the Travellers. Similar kinds of stories can be found in many, perhaps all, cultures. In terms of general classification, these stories fall under motifs F1068 "realistic dream" and F1068.1 "tokens from a dream" (Thompson 1932–1937).

2. I thank Peter Cooke for not only giving me permission to use this performance but also for providing me with his transcription of the performance. Although I have mostly preserved the spellings used in the original transcription, I have significantly modified its presentational form.

3. This story is a version of Aarne and Thompson type 753, "Christ and the Smith." Another performance of this story is transcribed in D. Williamson 1987a, 78–85; cf. Douglas 1987, 138–40 and Groome 1963, 247–50. For similarly structured dream stories, see S. Robertson 1989, 63–67, and D. Williamson 1991, 73–80.

4. From a phenomenological perspective, human consciousness itself may

have a fundamentally narrative character. This idea is explored in detail in Carr 1986. Building on Carr's ideas, John M. Allison develops the suggestion that human beings are constantly creating and living stories as a part of their ongoing temporal engagement in the world (1994).

Conclusion

1. A great deal has been written about Traveller ballad and song traditions. Some publications are predominantly collections of songs and ballads (Douglas 1992; Hall 1975; Henderson and Collinson 1965; MacColl and Seeger 1977, 1986) or focus on presenting relationships between Traveller singers and their repertoires (Gower 1968; Gower and Porter 1970; Munro 1970; Porter 1978). Other publications focus on Traveller singers and singing traditions as a context for theoretical insights. In this regard, see James Porter's articles on Jeannie Robertson (1976) and Belle Stewart (1985), James Porter and Hershel Gower's recent book on Jeannie Robertson (1995), the sections of John Niles's work *Homo Narrans* that focus on Traveller ballads (1999), and Linda Williamson's dissertation on narrative song among the Travellers (1985). For works that specifically address the interplay between Traveller singers and the folk revival in Scotland, see Gower 1983 and Munro 1984. A number of commercial recordings feature Traveller singers or include items recorded from Travellers. See, for example, Higgins 1987, J. Robertson 1984, School of Scottish Studies 1992, Stewart 1992, Turriff 1996, and J. Williamson 1999).

2. A recording of Jimmy Williamson singing this song can be found on his CD *Jimmy Williamson: Born Tae the Road* (1999).

3. Over the years we have known him, for example, Jimmy Williamson only told his stories and sung his songs to those in his extended family. Recently he has started telling stories in public events. This is a far cry from his shy refusal to tell us stories during our initial meetings. It took six months, in fact, before Jimmy felt comfortable enough to tell us a story. He has now recorded a CD of his own songs, *Jimmy Williamson: Born Tae the Road* (1999). Other Travellers, such as Duncan Williamson, Stanley Robertson, Elizabeth Stewart, and Sheila Stewart, have built reputations that transcend Scotland and bring them invitations for performances in the United States and other nations around the world.

Works Cited

Aarne, Antti, and Stith Thompson. 1961. *The Types of the Folktale: A Classification and Bibliography*. Translated and enlarged by Stith Thompson. Folklore Fellows Communications no. 184. Helsinki, Finland: Suomalainen Tiedeakatemia.

Acton, Thomas. 1993. Draft Report to UNISAT/Etudes Tsiganes Research Project on "Gypsies and Travellers: What Future in the Europe of 1993?" Duplicated.

———. 1997. *Gypsy Politics and Traveller Identity*. Hatfield, England: University of Hertfordshire Press.

Acton, Thomas, and Gary Mundy. 1997. *Romani Culture and Gypsy Identity*. Hatfield, England: University of Hertfordshire Press.

Acton, Thomas, Susan Caffrey, and Gary Mundy. 1997. The Theory of Gypsy Law. In *Gypsy Politics and Traveller Identity*, edited by Thomas Acton, 142–52. Hatfield, England: University of Hertfordshire Press.

Aesop. 1947. *Aesop's Fables*. Kingsport, Tenn.: Grossett & Dunlap.

Allison, John M. 1994. Narrative and Time: A Phenomenological Reconsideration. *Text and Performance Quarterly* 14:108–25.

Babcock, Barbara A. 1977. The Story in the Story: Metanarration in Folk Narrative. In *Verbal Art as Performance*, edited by Bauman Richard, 61–79. Rowley, Mass.: Newbury House.

Bascom, William. 1984. The Forms of Folklore: Prose Narratives. In *Sacred Narrative*, edited by Alan Dundes, 5–29. Berkeley: University of California Press.

Basso, Keith H. 1979. *Portraits of the Whiteman: Linguistic Play and Cultural Symbols among the Western Apache*. Cambridge: Cambridge University Press.

Bateson, Gregory. 1972. A Theory of Play and Fantasy. In *Steps to an Ecology of Mind*, 177–93. New York: Ballantine Books.

Bauman, Richard. 1972. Differential Identity and the Social Base of Folklore. In *Toward New Perspectives in Folklore*, edited by Américo Paredes and Richard Bauman, 31–41. Austin: University of Texas Press.

———. 1977. *Verbal Art as Performance*. Rowley, Mass.: Newbury House.

———. 1986. *Story, Performance, and Event*. New York: Cambridge University Press.

———. 1989. American Folklore Studies and Social Transformation: A Performance Centered Perspective. *Text and Performance Quarterly* 9:175–84.

———. 1992. Performance. In *Folklore, Cultural Performances, and Popular Entertainments: A Communications Centered Handbook*, 41–49. Oxford: Oxford University Press.
Bauman, Richard, and Donald Braid. 1998. The Ethnography of Performance in the Study of Oral Traditions. In *Teaching Oral Traditions*, edited by John Miles Foley, 106–22. New York: Modern Language Association.
Bauman, Richard, and Charles L. Briggs. 1990. Poetics and Performance as Critical Perspectives on Language and Social Life. *Annual Review of Anthropology* 19:59–88.
Beach, Richard. 1993. *A Teacher's Introduction to Reader-Response Theories*. Urbana, Ill.: National Council of Teachers of English.
Ben-Amos, Dan. 1992. Folktale. In *Folklore, Cultural Performances, and Popular Entertainments*, edited by Richard Bauman, 101–18. New York: Oxford University Press.
Binns, Dennis. 1984. *Children's Literature and the Role of the Gypsy*. Manchester, England: Manchester Travellers' School.
Boas, Franz. 1988. *Race, Language, and Culture*. Chicago: University of Chicago Press, 1940. Reprint, Chicago: University of Chicago Press.
Braid, Donald. 1993. The Traveller and the Hare: Meaning, Function, and Form in the Recontextualization of Narrative. *Folklore Forum* 26:3–29.
———. 1996a. The Negotiation of Meaning and Identity in the Narratives of the Travelling People of Scotland. Ph.D. diss., Indiana University.
———. 1996b. Personal Narrative and Experiential Meaning. *Journal of American Folklore* 109:5–30.
———. 1997. The Construction of Identity through Narrative: Folklore and the Travelling People of Scotland. In *Romani Culture and Gypsy Identity*, edited by Thomas Acton and Gary Mundy, 38–66. Hatfield, England: University of Hertfordshire Press.
———. 1998a. "Did It Happen or Did It Not?" Dream Stories, Worldview, and Narrative Knowing. *Text and Performance Quarterly* 18:319–43.
———. 1998b. Recontextualization. In *Encyclopedia of Folklore and Literature*, edited by Mary Ellen Brown and Bruce A. Rosenberg, 541–43. Santa Barbara, Calif.: ABC-Clio.
———. 1999. "Our Stories Are Not Just for Entertainment": Lives and Stories among the Travelling People of Scotland. In *Traditional Storytelling Today: An International Encyclopedia*, edited by Margaret Read MacDonald, 301–309. London: Fitzroy-Dearborn.
Briggs, Charles L., and Richard Bauman. 1992. Genre, Intertextuality, and Social Power. *Journal of Linguistic Anthropology* 2:131–72.
Brown, Mary Ellen. 1984. Pot of Gold: Rainbow's End. *ARV: Scandinavian Yearbook of Folklore* 40:89–94. Stockholm, Sweden: Almquist and Wiksell.
Bruford, Alan, ed. 1979. Storytellers and Storytelling. *Tocher* 31:35–66. Edinburgh: School of Scottish Studies, University of Edinburgh.
———. 1980. Duncan Williamson. *Tocher* 33:141–87. Edinburgh: School of Scottish Studies, University of Edinburgh.

Brunvand, Jan Harold. 1981. *The Vanishing Hitchhiker: American Urban Legends and Their Meaning*. New York: W W Norton.

Burke, Kenneth. 1941. Literature as Equipment for Living. In *Philosophy of Literary Form*, 293–304. Berkeley: University of California Press.

———. 1953. Lexicon Rhetoricae. In *Counter-Statement*, 123–83. Los Altos, Calif.: Hermes Publications.

———. 1969. *A rhetoric of Motives*. Berkeley: University of California Press.

Burton, Thomas. 2000. Jimmy Williamson. *Tocher* 56: 371–87. Edinburgh: School of Scottish Studies, University of Edinburgh.

Campbell, J. F. [1860] 1983. *Popular Tales of the West Highlands*. 4 vols. Reprint, Hounslow, Middlesex, England: Wildwood House.

Carr, David. 1986. *Time, Narrative, and History*. Bloomington: Indiana University Press.

Cazden, Courtney, and Dell Hymes. 1978. Narrative Thinking and Story-Telling Rights: A Folklorist's Clue to a Critique of Education. *Keystone Folklore* 22:21–36. West Chester, Pa.: Pennsylvania Folklore Society and West Chester State College.

Child, Francis J. [1882–1898] 1965. *The English and Scottish Popular Ballads*. Reprint. 5 vols. New York: Dover.

Chisholm, John, ed. 1897. *Green's Encyclopaedia of the Law in Scotland. Vol. 4*. Edinburgh: William Green and Sons.

Csikszentmihalyi, Mihaly. 1981. Some Paradoxes in the Definition of Play. In *Play as Context*, edited by Alyce Taylor Cheska, 14–26. West Point, N.Y.: Leisure Press.

Dégh, Linda. 1972. Folk Narrative. In *Folklore and Folklife: An Introduction*, edited by Richard M. Dorson, 53–83. Chicago: University of Chicago Press.

———. 1991. What Is the Legend After All? *Contemporary Legend* 1:11–38.

———. 1994. The Approach to Worldview in Folk Narrative Study. *Western Folklore* 53:243–52.

Department of the Environment (U.K.). 1992. *Gypsy Sites Policy, and Illegal Camping: Reform of the Caravan Sites Act 1968*. Consultation Document.

Departmental Committee on Tinkers in Scotland (Scotland). 1918. *Report of the Departmental Committee on Tinkers in Scotland*. Edinburgh: Her Majesty's Stationery Office.

Douglas, Sheila. 1985. *The King o' the Black Art: A Study of the Tales of a Group of Perthshire Travellers in Their Social Context*. Ph.D. diss., University of Sterling, Scotland.

———. 1987. *The King o' the Black Art: And Other Folk Tales*. Aberdeen: Aberdeen University Press.

———. 1992. *The Sang's the Thing: Voices from Lowland Scotland*. Edinburgh: Polygon.

Dundes, Alan. 1969. Thinking Ahead: A Folkloristic Reflection of the Future Orientation in American Worldview. *Anthropological Quarterly* 42:53–72.

———. 1975. Metafolklore and Oral Literary Criticism. In *Analytical Essays in Folklore*. The Hague: Mouton.

———. 1983. Defining Identity through Folklore. In *Identity: Personal and Socio-Cultural: A Symposium, Uppsala 1983*, edited by Anita Jacobson-Widding, 235–61. Atlantic Highlands, N.J.: Humanities Press.

Enkvist, Nils Erik. 1981. Experiential Iconism in Text Strategy. *Text* 1:77–111.

Erikson, Erik H. 1968. *Identity: Youth and Crisis*. New York: W W Norton.

Fabian, Johannes. 1983. *Time and the Other: How Anthropology Makes Its Object*. New York: Columbia University Press.

Feit, Ken. 1971. *Soundways*. Chicago: Loyola University Press.

———. 1982a. A Letter to My Friends on the Occasion of My Fortieth Birthday. *Theaterwork Magazine* 2 (July/August):25–31.

———. 1982b. Reflections of a Foolish Storyteller. *Theaterwork Magazine* 2 (July/August):32–37.

Fine, Elizabeth. 1984. *The Folklore Text: From Performance to Print*. Bloomington: Indiana University Press.

Fish, Stanley E. 1980. Literature in the Reader: Affective Stylistics. In *Reader-Response Criticism: From Formalism to Post-Structuralism*, edited by Jane P. Tompkins, 70–100. Baltimore, Md.: Johns Hopkins University Press.

Fraser, Angus. 1992. *The Gypsies*. Oxford: Blackwell.

Freund, Elizabeth. 1987. *The Return of the Reader: Reader Response Criticism*. London: Methuen.

Gallie, W. B. 1964. *Philosophy and the Historical Understanding*. New York: Schocken Books.

Geertz, Clifford. 1973. *The Interpretation of Cultures*. New York: Basic Books.

Gentleman, Hugh. 1993. *Counting Travellers in Scotland: The 1992 Picture: Estimates of the number, Distribution and Characteristics of Travelling People in Scotland in 1992 Based on a Count undertaken for the Scottish Office*. Edinburgh: The Scottish Office Central Research Unit.

Gentleman, Hugh, and Susan Swift. 1971. *Scotland's Travelling People: Problems and Solutions*. Edinburgh: Her Majesty's Stationery Office.

Glassie, Henry. 1982. *Passing the Time in Ballymenone: Culture and History of an Ulster Community*. Philadelphia: University of Pennsylvania Press.

Gmelch, George. 1985. *The Irish Tinkers: The Urbanization of an Itinerant People*. Prospect Heights, Ill.: Waveland Press.

Gmelch, Sharon. 1986. Groups That Don't Want In: Gypsies and Other Artisan, Trader and Entertainer Minorities. *Annual Review of Anthropology* 15: 307–30.

Goffman, Erving. 1967. On Face-Work. In *Interaction Ritual: Essays in Face to Face Behavior*, 5–45. Chicago: Adeline Publishing Co.

———. 1974. *Frame Analysis*. New York: Harper Colophon.

———. 1983. The Interaction Order. *American Sociological Review* 48:1–17.

Goldstein, Kenneth S. 1964. *A Guide for Field Workers in Folklore*. Hatboro, Pa.: Folklore Associates.

Gower, Herschel. 1968. Jeannie Robertson: Portrait of a Traditional Singer. *Scottish Studies* 12:113–26.

———. 1983. Analyzing the Revival: The Influence of Jeannie Robertson. In *The

Ballad Image: Essays Presented to Bertrand Harris Bronson, edited by James Porter, 131–47. Los Angeles: Center for the Study of Comparative Folklore & Mythology, University of California.

Gower, Herschel, and James Porter. 1970. Jeannie Robertson: The Child Ballads. *Scottish Studies* 14:35–58.

Grant, William, and David D. Murison, eds. 1974. *Scottish National Dictionary*. 10 vols. Edinburgh: Scottish National Dictionary Association.

Groome, Francis Hindes. [1899] 1963. *Gypsy Folk Tales*. Hatboro, Pa.: Folklore Associates.

Gumperz, John J. 1982. *Discourse Strategies*. Cambridge: Cambridge University Press.

Hall, Peter A. 1975. Scottish Tinker Songs. *Folkmusic Journal* 3:41–62.

Henderson, Hamish. 1970. Tinkers. In *Man, Myth and Magic*, vol. 21 of *An Illustrated Encyclopedia of the Supernatural*, edited by Richard Cavendish, 2853–55. 24 vols. New York: Marshall Cavendish Corporation.

———. 1992. *Alias MacAlias: Writings on Songs, Folk and Literature*. Edinburgh: Polygon.

Henderson, Hamish, and Francis Collinson. 1965. New Child Variants from Oral Tradition. *Scottish Studies* 9 (1):1–33.

Higgins, Lizzie. 1987. *Princess of the Thistle*. Springthyme Records audiocassette SPRC 1021.

Hill, Jane H., and Bruce Mannheim. 1992. Language and Worldview. *Annual Review of Anthropology* 21:381–406.

Hymes, Dell. 1975a. Folklore's Nature and the Sun's Myth. *Journal of American Folklore* 88:345–69.

———. 1975b. Breakthrough into Performance. In *Folklore Performance and Communication*, edited by Dan Ben-Amos and Kenneth Goldstein, 11–74. The Hague: Mouton.

———. 1981. Discovering Oral Performance and Measured Verse in American Indian Narrative. In *In Vain I Tried to Tell You*, 309–41. Philadelphia: University of Pennsylvania Press.

Hymes, Virginia. 1987. Warm Springs Sahaptin Narrative Analysis. In *Native American Discourse: Poetics and Rhetoric*, edited by Joel Sherzer and Anthony C. Woodbury, 62–102. Cambridge: Cambridge University Press.

Iser, Wolfgang. 1978. *The Act of Reading: A Theory of Aesthetic Response*. Baltimore, Md.: Johns Hopkins University Press.

———. 1989. *Prospecting: From Reader Response to Literary Anthropology*. Baltimore, Md.: Johns Hopkins University Press.

Ives, Edward D. 1974. *The Tape-Recorded Interview: A Manual for Field Workers in Folklore and Oral History*. Knoxville: University of Tennessee Press.

Jackson, Bruce. 1987. *Fieldwork*. Urbana: University of Illinois Press.

Jakobson, Roman. 1960. Closing Statement: Linguistics and Poetics. In *Style in Language*, edited by Thomas Sebeok, 350–77. Cambridge, Mass.: MIT Press.

Jansen, William Hugh. 1965. The Esoteric-Exoteric Factor in Folklore. In *The*

Study of Folklore, edited by Alan Dundes, 43–51. Englewood Cliffs, N.J.: Prentice-Hall.

Kenrick, Donald. 1984. The Portrayal of the Gypsy in English Schoolbooks. *Zeitschrift des Georg-Eckert Instituts* (Germany) 6:38–47.

Labov, William. 1972. The Transformation of Experience in Narrative Syntax. In *Language in the Inner City: Studies in the Black English Vernacular*, 354–96. Philadelphia: University of Pennsylvania Press.

Labov, William, and Joshua Waletzky. 1967. Narrative Analysis: Oral Versions of Personal Experience. In *Essays in the Verbal and Visual Arts*, edited by June Helm, 12–44. Seattle: University of Washington Press.

Lamont-Brown, Raymond. 1994. Scotland's Colorful Tinkers. *The Highlander* 32:40–42.

Lang, Andrew, ed. [1889] 1965. *The Blue Fairy Book*. Reprint, New York: Dover.

Langellier, Kristin M. 1989. Personal Narratives: Perspectives on Theory and Research. *Text and Performance Quarterly* 9:243–76.

Leitch, Roger. 1988. *The Book of Sandy Stewart*. Edinburgh. Scottish Academic Press.

Liégeois, Jean-Pierre. 1987. *Gypsies and Travellers*. Strasbourg: Council of Europe.

MacColl, Ewan, and Peggy Seeger. 1977. *Travellers' Songs from England and Scotland*. Knoxville: University of Tennessee Press.

———. 1986. *Till Doomsday in the Afternoon: The Folklore of a Family of Scots Travellers, the Stewarts of Blairgowrie*. Manchester: Manchester University Press.

MacLean, Ishbel. 1982. The Pearl Fishers. In *Odyssey: The Second Collection*, edited by Billy Kay, 56–63. Edinburgh: Polygon Books.

MacRitchie, David. 1894. *Scottish Gypsies under the Stewarts*. Edinburgh: David Douglas.

Malinowski, Bronislaw. 1953. The Problem of Meaning in Primitive Languages. In *The Meaning of Meaning*, edited by C. K. Ogden and A. I. Richards, 296–336. New York: Harcourt Brace.

Mathisen, Stein R. 1993. Folklore and Cultural Identity. In *Nordic Frontiers: Recent Issues in the Study of Modern Traditional Culture in the Nordic Countries*, edited by Pertti J. Anttonen and Reimund Kvideland, 35–47. Turku, Finland: Nordic Institute of Folklore.

McCormick, Andrew. [1907] 1973. *The Tinkler-Gypsies*. Reprint, Darby, Pa.: Norwood.

———. 1908. Nan Gordon. *Journal of the Gypsy Lore Society*, n.s., 1(3):211–18.

McDermitt, Barbara. 1986. A Comparison of a Scottish and American Storyteller and Their Märchen Repertoires. Ph.D. diss., Edinburgh University.

McDowell, John H. 1982. Beyond Iconicity: Ostension in Kamsá Mythic Narrative. *Journal of the Folklore Institute* 19:119–39.

———. 1992. Folklore as Commemorative Discourse. *Journal of American Folklore* 105:403–423.

Mink, Louis O. 1978. Narrative Form as a Cognitive Instrument. In *The Writing of History,* edited by Robert H. Canary and Henry Kozicki, 129–49. Madison: University of Wisconsin Press.

Mukarovsky, Jan. 1978. The Concept of the Whole in the Theory of Art. In *Structure, Sign, and Function.* Edited and translated by John Burbank and Peter Steiner, 70–81. New Haven, Conn.: Yale University Press.

Munnings, Sir Alfred. 1984. *Defining a Gypsy.* Department of the Environment (England). Gypsy Sites Branch.

Munro, Ailie. 1970. Lizzie Higgins, and the Oral Transmission of Ten Child Ballads. *Scottish Studies* 14:155–88.

———. 1984. The Travelling People. In *The Folk Music Revival in Scotland,* 205–32. London: Kahn and Averill.

NAPPS (National Association for the Preservation and Perpetuation of Storytelling). 1991. *Best Loved Stories Told at the National Storytelling Festival.* Jonesborough, Tenn.: National Storytelling Press.

Neat, Timothy. 1979. The Summer Walkers. *Seer* 42:40–48. Dundee: Duncan of Jordanstone College of Art.

———. 1996. *The Summer Walkers.* Edinburgh: Canongate Books.

Niles, John D. 1995. The Role of the Strong Tradition-Bearer in the Making of an Oral Culture. In *Ballads and Boundaries: Narrative Singing in an Intercultural Context,* edited by James Porter, 231–40. Los Angeles: Department of Ethnomusicology and Systematic Musicology, University of California.

———. 1999. *Homo Narrans: The Poetics and Anthropology of Oral Literature.* Philadelphia: University of Pennsylvania Press.

Nuckolls, Janis B. 1992. Sound Symbolic Involvement. *Journal of Linguistic Anthropology* 2:51–80.

Okely, Judith. 1983. *The Traveller Gypsies.* Cambridge: Cambridge University Press.

Oring, Elliott. 1986. Folk Narratives. In *Folk Groups and Folklore Genres: An Introduction,* 121–45. Logan: Utah State University Press.

———. 1994. The Arts, Artifacts, and Artifices of Identity. *Journal of American Folklore* 107:211–33.

Pace, David. 1982. Beyond Morphology: Lévi-Strauss and the Analysis of Folktales. In *Cinderella: A Folklore Casebook,* edited by Alan Dundes. New York: Garland.

Polanyi, Livia. 1985. Conversational Storytelling. In *Discourse and Dialogue,* edited by Teun A. Van Dijk, 183–201, vol. 3 of *Handbook of Discourse Analysis.* London: Academic Press.

Porter, James. 1976. Jeannie Robertson's "My Son David," a Conceptual Performance Model. *Journal of American Folklore* 89:7–26.

———. 1978. The Turriff Family of Fetterangus: Society, Learning, Creation and Recreation of Traditional Song. *Folk Life* 16:5–25. Cardiff, Wales: Society for Folk Life Studies.

———. 1985. Parody and Satire as mediators of Change in the Traditional Songs of Belle Stewart. In *Narrative Folksong: New Directions,* edited by Carol L. Edwards and Kathleen E. B. Manley, 303–38. Boulder, Colo.: Westview.

Porter, James, and Herschel Gower. 1995. *Jeannie Robertson: Emergent Singer, Transformative Voice*. Knoxville: University of Tennessee Press.

Preston, Dennis. 1982. "Ritin' Fowklower Daun' Rong": Folklorists' Failures in Phonology. *Journal of American Folklore* 95:304–26.

Rehfisch, Farnham. 1958. The Tinkers of Aberdeenshire and Perthshire. Master's thesis, Edinburgh University.

———. 1961. Marriage and the Elementary Family among the Scottish Tinkers. *Scottish Studies* 5:121–47.

———, ed. 1975. *Gypsies, Tinkers and Other Travellers*. London: Academic.

Reid, Willie. 1997. Scottish Gypsies/Travellers and the Folklorists. In *Romani Culture and Gypsy Identity*, edited by Thomas Acton and Gary Mundy, 29–37. Hatfield, England: University of Hertfordshire Press.

Robertson, Jeannie. 1984. *Up the Dee and Doon the Don*. Lismor Recordings audiocassette LIFC 7001.

Robertson, Stanley. 1988. *Exodus to Alford*. Nairn, Scotland: Balnain Books.

———. 1989. *Nyakim's Windows*. Nairn, Scotland: Balnain Books.

Robinson, Mairi. 1985. *Concise Scots Dictionary*. Aberdeen: Aberdeen University Press.

Rousseau, Jean-Jacques. 1987. *Basic Political Writings*. Translated by Donald A. Cress. Indianapolis, Ind.: Hacket.

Save the Children. 1995. *Travellers in Scotland*. Dunfermline: Scottish Division Traveller Section.

———. 1996a. *A Traveller Count—Scotland 1994–95*. Dunfermline: Traveller Section.

———. 1996b. *The Right to Roam: Travellers in Scotland 1995/96*. Dunfermline: Traveller Section.

SAYY.##. These numbers refer to recordings lodged in the Folklore Archives at the School of Scottish Studies, University of Edinburgh. YY refers to the year of recording, and ## indicates the sequentially numbered tape within each year.

Scholes, Robert. 1981. Language, Narrative, and Anti-Narrative. In *On Narrative*, edited by W. J. T. Mitchell, 200–208. Chicago: University of Chicago Press.

School of Scottish Studies. 1992. *The Muckle Sangs: Classic Scots Ballads*. Greentrax Records compact disc CDTRAX 9005.

Schrempp, Gregory. 1996. Dimensions of Worldview: Worldview as an Organizing Concept in Ethnographic and Narrative Research. In *Folk Narrative and World View: Vorträge Des 10. Kongresses der Internationalen Gesellschaft für Volkserzählungsforschung (ISFNR), Innsbruck 1992*, edited by Leander Petzoldt, 21–31. Frankfurt am Main: Peter Lang.

Scottish Development Department. 1982. *Circular No. 24*.

Secretary of State's Advisory Committee. 1974. *Scotland's Travelling People 1971–1974*. Edinburgh: Scottish Office.

Secretary of State's Advisory Committee. 1978. *Scotland's Travelling People 1975–1978. Second Report*. Edinburgh: Scottish Office.

Secretary of State's Advisory Committee. 1982. *Scotland's Travelling People 1979–1982*. Third Report. Her Majesty's Stationery Office.

Seeger, Peggy, and Ewan MacColl. 1982. *Go! Move! Shift!* Scotland: STV Production.

Silverstein, Michael. 1976. Shifters, Linguistic Categories, and Cultural Description. In *Meaning in Anthropology*, edited by Keith H. Basso and Henry A. Selby, 11–55. Albuquerque: University of New Mexico Press.

Stahl, Sandra K. Dolby. 1983. Personal Experience Stories. In *Handbook of American Folklore*, edited by Richard M. Dorson, 268–76. Bloomington: Indiana University Press.

———. 1989. *Literary Folkloristics and the Personal Narrative*. Bloomington: Indiana University Press.

Stewart, Elizabeth. 1992. *'Atween You an' Me*. Hightop Imagery audiocassette HTI 001.

Stocking, George W. 1982. Franz Boas and the Culture Concept. In *Race, Culture, and Evolution: Essays in the History of Anthropology*, 195–233. Chicago: University of Chicago Press.

Tedlock, Dennis. 1972. On the Translation of Style in Oral Narrative. In *Toward New Perspectives in Folklore*, edited by Américo Paredes and Richard Bauman, 114–33. Austin: University of Texas Press.

———. 1983. *The Spoken Word and the Work of Interpretation*. Philadelphia: University of Pennsylvania Press.

Thompson, Stith. 1932–37. *Motif-Index of Folk-Literature: A Classification of Narrative Elements in Folk-Tales, Ballads, Myths, Fables, Medieval Romances, Exempla, Fabliaux, Jest-Books, and Local Legends*. 6 vols. Folklore Fellows Communications nos. 106–109, 116, 117. Helsinki: Suomalainen Tiedeakatemia. Also published simultaneously: Indiana University Studies vols. 19–23. Bloomington: Indiana University Press.

Tompkins, Jane P. 1980. An Introduction to Reader-Response Criticism. In *Reader-Response Criticism: From Formalism to Post-Structuralism*, ix–xxvi. Baltimore, Md.: Johns Hopkins University Press.

Toolan, Michael J. 1988. *Narrative: A Critical Linguistic Introduction*. New York: Routledge.

TSYY###. These numbers refer to my field recordings. YY refers to the year of the recording (19YY) and ### indicates the sequentially numbered tape within each year.

Turriff, Jane. 1996. *Singin' Is My Life*. Springthyme Records compact disc SPRCD 1038.

Vallee, F. G. 1955. The Tinkers of Scotland: Report on a Pilot Study. School of Scottish Studies Library, University of Edinburgh. Typescript.

White, Hayden. 1987. *The Content of the Form: Narrative Discourse and Historical Representation*. Baltimore, Md.: John Hopkins University Press.

Whyte, Betsy. 2001. *The Yellow on the Broom*. Edinburgh W. & R. Chambers Ltd., 1979. Reprint, Edinburgh: Birlinn Ltd.

———. 1990. *Red Rowans and Wild Honey*. Edinburgh: Canongate.
Williamson, Duncan. 1983. *Fireside Tales of the Traveller Children*. Edinburgh: Canongate.
———. 1985. *The Broonie, Silkies and Fairies*. Edinburgh: Canongate.
———. 1987a. *A Thorn in the King's Foot*. Harmondsworth, Middlesex, England: Penguin.
———. 1987b. *Tell Me a Story for Christmas*. Edinburgh: Canongate.
———. 1989. *May the Devil Walk behind Ye: Scottish Traveller Tales*. Edinburgh: Canongate.
———. 1990. *Don't Look Back Jack*. Edinburgh: Canongate.
———. 1991. *The Genie and the Fisherman: And Other Tales from the Travelling People*. Cambridge: Cambridge University Press.
———. 1992. *Tales of the Seal People*. Edinburgh: Canongate.
———. 1994. *The Horsieman: Memories of a Traveller 1928–58*. Edinburgh: Canongate.
Williamson, Jimmy. 1999. *Born tae the Road*. Culcross, Scotland: Tron Workshop compact disc CDTW 017.
Williamson, Linda. 1981. What Storytelling Means to a Traveller. *ARV: Scandinavian Yearbook of Folklore* 37:69–76. Stockholm, Sweden: Almquist & Wiksell.
———. 1985. Narrative Singing among the Scots Travellers: A Study of Strophic Variation in Ballad Performance. Ph.D. diss., University of Edinburgh.

Index

Assimilation, 44
Audience, role of, 91–92, 120–21, 271
Authenticity, 32–34, 50, 294

Ballads, 7–9, 42, 98, 160, 163, 287–88, 293, 300
Belief, 33, 42, 46, 74, 79, 98, 105, 107, 119, 173, 202, 250, 274, 279–82
"Black Laird and the Cattleman, The," 252
"Boy and the Blacksmith, The," 258
Burker stories, 79–83

Campfires, 55, 62, 65–66
Ceilidhs, 60, 125
Change, over time, 33, 53–54, 288, 290, 292
"Cinderella," 174
Coherence, 120, 266, 267–68, 285; and meaning 271–73; and worldview, 250, 270, 273–82
Commemoration of Traveller life, 159, 288
Community, 146–47, 163, 201; definition of, 147
Competence, in performance, 7, 37, 125, 132–34, 266–67, 269, 271–73, 287, 288
Contingency, 120–21, 122–23, 280
Crack, 56, 64–65, 296; definition of, 52–53, 67
Creativity. See Performance
"Crow with the Cheese, The," 149, 172–73

Discrimination, 44, 198–200, 205, 212, 215, 281, 299
Displacement, 164
Dream Stories, 250

Entertainment, 37, 56, 60, 79, 85, 89, 94–95, 268, 286
Ethnocentrism, 41, 43, 105, 199, 219, 221
Ethnographic knowledge, 48–50, 287, 294, 296
Experience, 32, 37, 44, 48; and community, 156–60, 164, 165, 170, 172; and crack, 67–87; exaggeration of (see Lies); and following, 75, 118–24; and stories, 51–52, 65, 71, 204–06, 222, 284–86; and worldview, 105–07, 109, 270–74, 279–82, 286
Experiential meaning, 121–22

Family Stories, 69–71, 165
Feit, Ken, 3, 293
Fiction. See Truth and fiction
Field recordings, numbering system, xi
Fieldwork, process, 47–50
Folk revival, 98, 102, 173
Folktale, 52, 87–98, 172–73, 280; properties of, 119–20
Following, 107, 118–24, 174, 270, 285; definition of, 119–21
Formal patterning, 210, 288
Fox, 172–73, 242–43, 245–46
"Fox and the Dog, The," 239
Freedom, 197, 219, 221, 290

311

Gender, 60–62, 197, 293
Genre, 52, 109, 251, 272, 274, 279–80
Ghost stories, 74–79, 278
"Good Old Days, The," 291
Gypsies, 39, 41, 42, 43, 101, 173, 212, 234, 248, 294–95, 296, 297

Harassment, 44, 205, 212, 216, 299
"Hawker's Lament, The," 217
Headlee, Linda. See Williamson, Linda
Henderson, Hamish, 4, 293
Hilbert, Vi, 3
Horn Spoons, 294

Identity, 105–06, 159, 200; construction of, 141–43; cultural, 19–20, 31–34, 38–46, 200; definition of, 104–08; negotiation of, 172–73, 209–12, 246, 248. See also Negotiating worldview and identity
Interaction order, 247
Interaction stories, 202–03
Interdependence, 45, 281
Interpretation, process of, 121–24, 212, 214–16, 226, 269, 271–74, 279–80, 284, 285
Interpretational frame, 112–13
Intonation, 136–40
Isolation, of Travellers, 44–45

Joking, 169
Justice, 216, 219

"Lady Margaret," 8, 293
"Laird and the Crane, The," 13
Legends, 74–79, 278–80
Lies, 83–87

MacDonald, Nancy, 49, 50, 51–52, 63, 65–66, 68–69, 70–71, 95, 159–60, 287
MacPhee, Edie, 49, 64, 89–90, 91–92, 100, 146, 247–48
MacPhee, Willie and Bella, 50, 56–57, 61, 71, 84, 93, 101, 102, 103, 145, 166–72, 247, 248, 274
Magic, 195
Meaning, 158, 159, 196, 270, 286; connection to performer, 155–63, 165; construction of, 118–24, 268–69, 271; emergence in performance, 108–09; experiential, 121–22
Memory, 70, 71, 147, 170, 223; of performer, 133, 150–58, 160–63; of text, 108, 142, 173–74, 269
Metanarration, 113–14, 134–35, 272
Metaphor, 173, 200, 238, 243, 246, 280
Mujuru, Ephat, 3–4

Narrative knowing, 269–73, 279–82
Negotiating worldview and identity, 106–07, 141–43, 173, 202–03, 214–16, 219, 221–23, 246–47, 248–49, 278–82, 283, 285–86, 287–92
Newsing, 71, 166
News Media, 281–82

Pearl Fishing, 294
Performance, 60; artistry of, 125, 136, 233, 251, 266–67, 272; and community, 155–63, 164, 201; creativity in, 124–41, 143, 174, 222–23, 234, 238, 250, 271–73, 280–82, 285–86; definition of, 108–10; dynamics of, 156; emergence in, 108, 109–10, 116, 125, 135, 141, 201, 285–86; and function, 141, 203; mediated, 248–49; multiple, 141–43; refusal to, 284; role of audience, 110, 133; and traditionalization, 160–63
Personal Experience Narratives, 52, 68–69
Philosophical approach, 48
Play, 83, 143, 280, 282, 285–86
Prosody, 136–40

Reported speech, 204, 209, 226, 232–33, 245
Robertson, Stanley, 62, 96, 234, 296

School of Scottish Studies, 4
"Slow Going Easy," 288
Social interaction, 144–46
Songs, 101, 287–92, 300
Sources, of stories, 98–100, 101
Stereotypes, 40, 211, 212
Story. *See also* Folktale
Storytellers: choices in telling, 92; learning stories, 58, 63, 100; reputations, 58–59, 93–94
Storytelling: changes over time, 62–67; contexts for, 54–67; and culture, 173–74; functions of, 37, 46, 85, 91, 94–98, 285–87; mediated, 247–49; and memory, 71, 160–63; as performance, 75, 108–10, 118; and place, 283–84; relevance to present day, 97–98
Success, 196
Sutherland, Eckie, 49, 50, 53, 59, 65, 66, 70–71, 72–73, 76–79, 83–84, 85, 86–87, 88, 91, 287

Tall Tales. *See* Lies
"Tam Lin," 293
"Tinker and the Skeletons, The," 23
Townsley, Betty, 45, 50, 51, 60–61, 64, 65, 89–90, 96–97, 146, 156–57, 205–06, 212–16, 283–84
Traditionalization, 109, 162, 170
Transcriptions, system of notation, xi–xiii
"Traveller and the Hare, The," 110
Travelling People: camping, 204, 281, 297; culture, 6, 20, 32, 37, 43, 195, 294–95; economics, 33, 39, 226–27, 281; language, xi, 295; names for, 38–39; New Age, 295; origins of, 41–42, 295–96; population, 39–40; response to, 40–44 (*see also* Discrimination)
Truth and fiction, 31, 75, 87, 209, 233–34, 250, 257, 272, 274, 279

Verbal artistry, 109, 133, 136, 272
Visiting, 56, 144–45

Whyte, Betsy, 20–23, 50, 91, 126–27, 156, 244–45, 252–57, 266, 284
Whyte, Bryce, 50, 56, 57, 59, 91, 144–45, 163, 223–26, 252
Williamson, Duncan, 4–38, 44, 46, 49, 55–56, 58–59, 60, 62, 63, 67–68, 79–83, 84, 85, 92–96, 97–98, 99–100, 101–02, 110–18, 122–41, 148–55, 157–58, 160–62, 164–72, 174–95, 207–12, 216–23, 226–33, 234–38, 239–47, 250, 257–66, 267–68, 274, 275–79, 294
Williamson, Jimmy (son), 49, 50, 51, 53, 63–64, 74–75, 84, 85, 88, 148–49, 153–60, 162–63, 204–05, 242, 288–92, 300
Williamson, Jimmy (grandson), 102–03
Williamson, Linda, 5–6, 101, 174, 252, 293
Worldview, 197, 198; and coherence, 173, 273–82; construction of, 106, 124, 141–43; definition of, 104–06, 297; and identity, 104; negotiation of, 246, 282. *See also* Negotiating worldview and identity

"Yellow on the Broom," 20

313

Printed in the United States
128161LV00003B/21/A

Printed in Great Britain
by Amazon